Jimmy Page: Magus, Musician, Man

An Unauthorized Biography

Jimmy Page

MAGUS, MUSICIAN, MAN

An Unauthorized Biography

George Case

An Imprint of Hal Leonard
NEW YORK

Backbeat Books
An Imprint of Hal Leonard Corporation
7777 West Bluemound Road
Milwaukee, WI 53213

Trade Book Division Editorial Offices
19 West 21st Street, New York, NY 10010

Paperback edition published in 2009 by Backbeat Books
Originally published in hardcover in 2007 by Hal Leonard Books

Printed in United States of America

Interior design by Mark Lerner

The Library of Congress has cataloged the Hal Leonard edition as follows:
Case, George, 1967–
   Jimmy Page : magus, musician, man : an unauthorized biography / George Case. -- 1st ed.
      p. cm.
   Includes bibliographical references (p. 269) and index.
   ISBN-13: 978-1-4234-0407-1
   ISBN-10: 1-4234-0407-6
   1. Page, Jimmy. 2. Rock musicians—England—Biography. 3. Led Zeppelin (Musical group) I. Title.
   ML419.P37C37 2007
   782.42166092--dc22
   [B]
                  2007000534

Backbeat ISBN: 978-0-87930-947-3

www.backbeatbooks.com

And hath not he that built the walls of Thebes
With ravishing sound of his melodious harp,
Made music with my Mephistophilis?
Why should I die then, or basely despair?
I am resolved! Faustus shall ne'er repent.

—CHRISTOPHER MARLOWE,
THE TRAGICAL HISTORY OF DOCTOR FAUSTUS

Contents

ACKNOWLEDGMENTS

Thanks to Robert Lecker for giving me the opportunity and John Cerullo, Belinda Yong, and Jenna Young at Hal Leonard for shepherding the project to completion. My colleagues at the Vancouver Public Library were encouraging and supportive, and accommodated my absences for writing and research with good grace; much of my bibliography was found at the VPL, and I encourage readers to remember that public libraries are the original and still best search engines. My old friends from Sault Ste. Marie and Ottawa, Canada, were good jamming buddies, whose vocal, instrumental, and songwriting talents fostered my own ability, and enlightened musical enthusiasts who opened my ears forever; memories of my years with them are scored with the coolest rock 'n' roll sound track never compiled.

My family in Sault Ste. Marie and Burnaby were, as always, generous, patient, and caring. Special thanks to my wife, Tonya, who has heard as much Jimmy Page as she ever wanted (she stood in a very long line to get our Page-Plant tickets in '95) but tolerated hearing several albums' worth besides with unstinting loyalty and her natural good humor. My daughter, Genevieve, thought some of the performances on the *Led Zeppelin* DVD were "pretty loud," but she was intrigued by Jimmy Page's Boleskine sequence from *The Song Remains the Same*, where the old man turns into a baby and then waves his magic rainbow. She is only three years old and it's a real fine way to start.

Prologue:
Dazed and Confused

Behold! these be grave mysteries; for there are also of my friends
who be hermits.

—*THE BOOK OF THE LAW*

Los Angeles, 1973. The Forum. Capacity crowd. The multitudes
are gathered in a ritualistic ceremony of community and celebration, the air filled with the incense of sweet mind-expanding
smoke and the cheering, whistling, exhorting sounds that are
this congregation's speaking in tongues. The youngest believers
have barely entered their teens and the oldest are barely out of
them. A vast thrum of wattage, so continuous as to be part of the
atmosphere itself, runs under and through the audience, who
now await the next hymn; it is music they all know yet need to
hear again and again, for it is this paean that has sustained them
in their banal materialist adolescence in contemporary suburban California; it is a song of hope and they have come together
in this house of the holy to hear it played by its authors. The
lights are dimmed except for a single ray that now illuminates
the foremost author of them all.

He is a ghostly presence on stage, slender and voiceless. His clothes
are black, embroidered with inscrutable patterns of astrology and
faiths unknown, and his open shirt is a sign of hot, hard labor. His

curled long hair is dark and descends over his features like a hood, keeping much of his thin face—especially his eyes—in shadow, but his pursed lips reveal concentration and contemplation as he begins his rite. The instrument he wields is a unique two-headed scepter like few have seen before, and though his music is to invoke heaven, its color is a hellish red. His pale hands touch the taut wires and shape the tragic chord of A minor; a delicate arpeggio, at once ethereal and ominous, is sounded. The multitudes are on their feet in an ecstasy of revelation. Small fires are lit. Smoke rises with hands. Enraptured as his listeners, the soloist plays on. Song and sacraments, electric musician and electric magician, all blend together in the sultry, hallowed amphitheater on a warm late-spring evening in the new Babylon.

Bring It on Home
1943-1960

A new Hedonism—that is what our century wants. You might be its visible symbol. With your personality there is nothing you could not do.

—Oscar Wilde,
The Picture of Dorian Gray

The English winter of 1943–1944 was one of the coldest in memory, and the *Luftwaffe* had returned to the embattled island's gloomy night skies. The "Baby Blitz" of those months was a last, futile gesture by the air force of Adolf Hitler's Germany and accomplished little militarily, but it was an unwelcome foreshadowing of later attacks not by swastika-emblazoned planes but by the Nazis' primitive cruise missiles, the V-1 "flying bombs," and their truly futuristic rockets, the wicked V-2s—V for *Vergeltungswaffe*, or vengeance, for Britain was now home base for the awesome Anglo-American bomber fleets delivering World War II into the heart of the German nation around the clock. The Baby Blitz was also a bitter reminder to British civilians of its parent three years past, when the Heinkels and Junkers had inflicted far heavier damage on London and the ancient mill towns of the Midlands, and for older generations it even brought to mind the original air raids of over twenty-five years before, when Albion first came under the shadow of the great and terrible Zeppelin.

It was this pervasive atmosphere of rationing, propaganda, blackouts, and the possibility, too often realized, of sudden violent death that George Orwell recalled in depicting the dystopian Airstrip One of *Nineteen Eighty-Four*. Though the tide of the conflict had turned in the Allies' favor by 1943, British civilians were as war-weary as any frontline soldier. And though they were known to complain that the millions of American servicemen now sharing their land were "overpaid, oversexed, and over here," the GIs had brought an irresistible aura of novelty and freshness with them, manifested in their gangsters' slang and Texas drawls, their nylon stockings, chewing gum, and Coca-Cola, and in their boogie-woogie music derived from that most American of art forms, Negro blues. The combined social impacts of bleak, bombed-out scarcity and the "friendly occupation" of the Yanks would linger in Britain long after the war's end.

National industry had been turned over to war production. In the county of Middlesex, just northwest of the city of London, aircraft manufacturers and contractors had enlisted armies of workers to turn out machines for the Royal Air Force, among them a man named James Patrick Page. Officially described as a wages clerk but later known as an industrial personnel manager—possibly a reclassification or upgrade of a similar position—Jim Page administered payrolls and shift schedules at one of the numerous Middlesex aircraft works: perhaps the extensive De Havilland's at Elstree or Colindale or Cricklewood, or the General Aircraft Company's at Feltham, or the smaller Heston Aircraft Company's at Heston. Page had recently met and married Patricia Elizabeth Gaffikin, who was employed as a doctor's secretary, although her adult son would only say she did "various things."[1] The new Mrs. Page became pregnant in 1943 and carried her child through the last half of the year, as the RAF created the first man-made firestorm at Hamburg, the German army was decimated at Kursk, and as the U.S. and

British high commands made plans for an eventual invasion of occupied Europe, under the code name Operation Overlord.

The couple lived at 26 Bulstrode Road, in Heston, north of Hounslow Heath between Sutton Lane and Lampton Road. Shortly after the New Year, Patricia Elizabeth Page went into labor and, on Sunday, January 9, 1944, delivered her only child, a boy, at the Grove Nursing Home on Grove Road, near where she and her husband lived. The baby was named for his father. On the same day across the ocean, by the slightest of coincidences, a little girl named Joan Chandos Baez was celebrating her third birthday; like the newborn James Patrick Page, she would grow up to become a musician, and before him, she would record her interpretation of an old folk song titled "Babe I'm Gonna Leave You."

Patricia's maiden name of Gaffikin was an uncommon one, probably an Anglicization of the Irish *Geoghegan*, suggesting distant roots in the Emerald Isle. In contrast, Jim's surname is one of the more familiar in England, derived from the occupational title for the household servant or messenger of medieval nobility. Many of the baby's future fellows carried similarly descriptive or professional nouns as second names—Ron *Wood*, Keith *Moon*, Roger *Waters*, Nick *Mason*, Terry "Geezer" *Butler*, Bill *Ward*, John *Deacon*, Ian *Hunter*, Robert *Plant*—but few would have the ancient, arcane allusiveness as the infant Jimmy Page's.

Baptized but not churchgoers, the Pages imparted no serious religious instruction to their son—and no musical instruction, either, although there are accounts that mention his singing in the school choir and investigating the pianos of family friends. "Like most other lads his age, I suppose, he liked to listen to records on the radio," Patricia Page observed with long hindsight. "He seemed mildly interested in music."[2] More significant was what his mother and father did not give him: siblings. According to conventional wisdom only children like Jimmy Page can either suffer from a lack of socialization, growing up to be spoiled, lonely, and withdrawn, or they can enjoy the benefits of being the sole focus of their parents' love and attention, acquiring an early maturity, confidence, and sense of self-worth denied to products of larger families. Jimmy Page seems to have gained more than he lost from an absence of brothers or sisters. His mother looked back: "Jimmy was fun, but quiet fun. He wasn't a 'screamer' sort of boy."[3] "Until around the age of five," Page recalled, "I was totally isolated from kids my own age in our neighborhood. That early isolation probably had a lot to do with the way I turned out. A loner. . . . Isolation doesn't bother me at all. It gives me a sense of security."[4]

While still a toddler, Page and his parents moved south from Heston to Feltham, on the other side of Hounslow Heath. There is also, around this time, an intriguing indication that he spent part of this period on the large, well-appointed Northamptonshire estate of a great-uncle (paternal or maternal is not clear), where he played, fished, collected stamps, and developed his first inklings of an architectural and artistic taste. "I can remember being fascinated by the animals,"[5] he later said. It is known, however, that in the early '50s, the sounds of the new jet aircraft landing and taking off from Heathrow Airport, close by Feltham, motivated the Pages to move again, this time to the quieter environs of Epsom, in Surrey. "When the airport got jets we moved away into the country, it was so noisy," Page remembered. "The jets used to circle the airport and you could hear them going over all the time. Most of my childhood was spent at Epsom where they have horse racing—it's really nice there, lots of countryside."[6] Known for its equestrian derby at Epsom Downs and dominated by the green hills of Epsom Common, the area made a quiet suburban setting where Mr. and Mrs. Page could raise their little boy, settling in on a short residential enclosure at Number 34 Miles Road.

In the '50s and '60s, Surrey was what rock writer Charles Shaar Murray would term "lace curtain land," an expanse of respectably tidy middle- or lower-middle-class homes. "It was still those somber post-war days of rationing in Epsom"[7] was Jimmy

Page's recollection of the epoch. Still recovering from Britain's empire-sacrificing victory in the war and relegated anxiously to a "middle power" status between the two superpowers of the United States and the Soviet Union, the nation's leaders and led alike were coming to grips with reconstruction, waves of immigration from the former colonies, and the nuclear penumbra of the Cold War. Sleepy, proper Surrey was as snugly ensconced in the new realities as any other place in the kingdom. Musicologist Ian MacDonald conveyed the brittle social niceties in which Page and millions of other youngsters were then immersed: "The braying upper-class voices on newsreels, the odor of unearned privilege in parliament and the courts, the tired nostalgia for the war . . ."[8] An intelligent but independent pupil at his nearby Pound Lane primary school ("I had a really fine education from the age of eleven to seventeen on how to be a rebel and I learned all the tricks in the game"),[9] one of Jimmy Page's first explorations of the universe outside his own sedate community took place around 1955. "I read *Magick in Theory and Practice* when I was about eleven but it wasn't for some years 'til I understood what it was about."[10] The author of the puzzling but entrancing book had died nearly forgotten in Hastings, England, almost eight years previously—he was a once-notorious poet and publicity-seeker named Aleister Crowley.

Then there was music. Without any special prodding from his parents, the preteen Page had pretty much absorbed what they and most of their neighbors played around the house—the comforting Home Service and Light Programme strains of the British Broadcasting Corporation's frothy entertainment, swing, and "trad jazz," all of which might today fall under the broad category of pop. But his entry into adolescence in the mid-'50s coincided with a crucial cultural change occurring in Britain and across the ocean in North America, as the novelty of an affluent youth market led to a new commercial viability for the primitive folk songs of poor American blacks and whites. Once dismissed as "race" and "hillbilly" music, the two genres were now blending into each other when played by the adult-alienating likes of Bill Haley and His Comets, whose "Rock Around the Clock" was a huge hit in the United Kingdom in 1955, and Lonnie Donegan, performer of "Rock Island Line," an even more influential smash the following year. Both caught Jimmy Page's ears: "This explosion came through your radio speaker when you were eleven or twelve."[11] Donegan's sound was called "skiffle," a brazenly rudimentary but energetic two- or three-chord derivation of American blues and western ballads whose special appeal to the young was its technical approachability. "Lonnie Donegan was the first person who was really giving it some passion that we related to," Page has said. "Lonnie Donegan was quite important within the early equation of what went on in those days. It was a process of accessing what was going on in skiffle, and then, bit by bit, your tastes changed and matured as you accessed more."[12] But Page would not for long be a mere listener of skiffle, thanks to another source of music that mysteriously materialized in his home.

"The weirdest thing about where I lived in Epsom was that there was a guitar in the house," he recalls. "I don't know whether it was left behind by the people before, or whether it was a friend of the family's—nobody seemed to know why it was there."[13] In another version of the discovery, he tells of the "very old" Spanish-style acoustic instrument "sittin' around the house for years,"[14] though in a third story it is only "sitting around our living room for weeks and weeks."[15] Whenever and however it got there, the guitar went ignored until Page saw another boy at school entertaining a gaggle of students, playing skiffle with a guitar of his own. "I went, 'I've got one of those at home,' and he said, 'Bring it along and I'll tune it for you.'"[16] Following this initial demonstration, and a few flips through Bert Weedon's then-ubiquitous *Play in a Day* instruction text, he took the same path as countless other self-taught six-stringers: "I just went on from there . . . going to guitar shops, hanging around watching what other people were doing."[17]

What really spurred Page to master the guitar, though, was

hearing one of Elvis Presley's archetypal Sun Studios recordings, a twangy number called "Baby Let's Play House," featuring Elvis, bassist Bill Black, and the pioneering Scotty Moore picking on a Gibson Super-400 CES semi-acoustic. "I heard that record and I wanted to be a part of it; I knew something was going on."[18] A Top 10 country hit for the King (its B-side was "I'm Left, You're Right, She's Gone," released in May 1955), the Arthur Gunter–penned boogie boasts some quintessential rockabilly chording from Moore, including a pair of tasty bent-note solos and even, for a few measures, a tight riffing lockup of guitar and bass that draws a *"Yeah!"* from Elvis and which could well be an ancestor of "Communication Breakdown." Jimmy Page's own electric guitar mannerisms would always reflect rockabilly roots in Scotty Moore, as well as in the jangling Fender Telecaster accompaniments of James Burton that graced singles like "Hello Mary Lou" and "Believe What You Say" by Ricky Nelson, and in Cliff Gallup and Johnny Meeks, who backed up Gene Vincent on his most successful songs, e.g., "Be-Bop-A-Lula." Carl Perkins once explained '50s rock 'n' roll music as "a black man's song with a country man's rhythm," and on record and in concert Page often harked back to just such a hybrid: listen to the solo in Led Zeppelin's "Heartbreaker," in "Candy Store Rock," and the live take of "Whole Lotta Love" from *The Song Remains the Same.* It does indeed.

Page's attraction to the blues-flavored playing of Lonnie Donegan, Scottie Moore, and James Burton was fated to expand into a curiosity about the real thing. "There was the blues, there was Leadbelly material in Donegan, but we weren't at all aware of it in those days," he has said. "Then it came to the point where Elvis was coming through and he made no secret of the fact that he was singing stuff by Arthur 'Big Boy' Crudup and Sleepy John Estes."[19] But if the rock songs themselves were largely taboo in Britain in the later '50s ("You've got to understand that in those days 'rock 'n' roll' was a dirty word. . . . You had to stick by the radio and listen to overseas radio to even hear good rock records"),[20] their blues forebears were even more so. Luckily for Page, a friend on Miles Road was a collector: "He had an amazing stash of blues albums, and he was very generous about letting me listen to them. No one was really playing the blues on radio or in clubs yet, so it was still a very underground thing and records were very hard to find."[21]

To British musicians of Page's generation, the blues left an indelible mark. Blues artists were Americans, which linked them with everything fast, slick, and enviable in the New World, but they were also *African* Americans, poor, disenfranchised, and, in some cases, actually illiterate. Their low status in a social hierarchy was recognized and, in a limited way, understood by young guitar strummers in London or Liverpool or Belfast, who were up against an economic and educational caste system of their own, where a wrong accent or a dropped *h* was enough to consign them to a lifetime of servile work and substandard housing. And, of course, the sheer sound of the blues was almost unbearably exotic to thirteen- or fourteen-year-old lads from Surrey: "When I heard those songs for the first time," Page reminisces, "they really did send chills up my spine."[22]

It would take some years before his blues sensibility was fully formed—Muddy Waters, Freddy King, and Howlin' Wolf and his guitarist Hubert Sumlin were still in mid-career when Page became a buff—but exposure to the scratchy, seminal '20s and '30s recordings of Robert Johnson, Bukka White, and Mississippi Fred McDowell was a crucial primer. Most of all, says Page, "I think I gravitated to the blues because I was a guitarist and it was a very guitar-centric music. If you were a guitarist at that time, your appetite was voracious for early rock guitarists, like Chuck Berry and all the blues that was coming out of Chicago."[23] Though certainly more elaborate than the straightforward busking of Lonnie Donegan, the blues also had the value of a theoretical purity in that most pieces were based around a primeval I-IV-V progression (tonic, subdominant, and dominant chords), which meant musicians could usually pick up and improvise over the basic structure of a song without extensive study or re-hearsal. Blues and bluesy rock 'n' roll together made what Page labeled "a good sketchpad for me."[24]

By 1958, Jimmy Page had entered Ewell County Secondary School on Danetree Road and was well gone on playing guitar. Decades later a delightful black-and-white clip from a BBC-TV program of that year surfaced, in which a band of boys—includ-ing a David Hampson and one Jim Page—from Epsom in Surrey perform a cheery sing-along titled something like "Mama Don't Allow No Skiffle Around Here" and follow up with Leadbelly's "Cotton Fields." The grainy footage reveals a smiling Page swing-ing away enthusiastically but competently on a single-cutaway acoustic of unknown make while another lad sings and plays be-side him and a two-piece "rhythm section" backs them up (very faint shapes of things to come). This was a segment from *All Your Own,* a talent show for children and teens hosted by the avun-cular Huw Wheldon, who would genially introduce youngsters' artistic or musical specialties and then query them on future ambitions. After doing their skiffle tune (the Donegan influence had clearly not subsided), Wheldon asks a shy Jim if he plays any styles besides. "Yes," comes the answer, bearing just a trace of defiance, "Spanish guitar." Light and shade in the making. Was there opportunity to play skiffle outside of school? "No," Jimmy Page says, "I could do biological research."[25] His ambition would be fulfilled in hotel rooms around the world.

Other milestones in Page's musical growth are less easily con-firmed. In one report, he went up to Kingston-on-Thames for a brief series of lessons, and later was advised to replace the wound G string of his guitar with a lighter unwound gauge for easier James Burton–like bends; there is also an assertion that his first "name" instrument was a Hofner Senator electric. More definite is Page's acknowledgment, "I have always wanted to be an electric guitarist. I even started a paper round to get my first instrument because I didn't have any money."[26] Once the future dark lord of hard rock had saved his shillings and pence bringing the local news to the neatly swept doorsteps of Epsom, he visited Bell's music store in nearby Surbiton and bought a Grazioso electric solidbody, a Czech-made likeness of the famous American Fender Stratocaster. Sometimes known as a Futurama, the Grazioso had the same sunburst coloring and pseudo-space-age switches as the Strat, and Page plugged it into the back of his parents' radio. "When the sound came through the speakers I couldn't believe it."[27] He then began taking it to school. The teachers took the guitar away from him during class, but he would get it back at the end of every day—which only encouraged him more. "The good thing about the guitar was that they didn't teach it in school. Teaching myself was the first and most important part of my education. I hope they keep it out of schools."[28]

Jimmy Page's classmates had noticed the blossoming and dedicated player in their midst, but one girl in particular made a connection between his apparent obsession and her own younger sibling's. Her name was Annetta Beck, and she told her brother Geoffrey Arnold, or Jeff, about him: "You gotta meet Jimmy, this weird thin guy playing a weird-shaped guitar like yours."[29] Jeff, by his reckoning, "couldn't believe there was another human being in Surrey interested in strange-shaped solid guitars,"[30] and he and Annetta took a bus to Miles Road. He had already assembled his own instrument from scratch after reacting to Cliff Gallup, Buddy Holly, and the "electronic whiz" Les Paul, and it, too, made the journey from Wallington to Epsom. The year was probably 1958, making both Beck and Page just fourteen (Beck was born in June 1944), although Page has also identified Beck as "the guy I had been friends with since the age of eleven,"[31] saying, "I met Beck through a friend of mine who told me he knew this guitarist I had to meet who'd made his own guitar."[32] Elsewhere the date of their encounter is set at 1959 or later, with Beck and Page being introduced by Barry Matthews, a mutual acquaintance.

The meeting, in which ever year it occurred, was significant for both boys. Mr. and Mrs. Page were indulgent enough to let Jimmy have a front room to himself and his music ("There wasn't even room to swing your knob"[33] is Beck's estimation of its space), and the host played and sang Buddy Holly's "Not Fade Away" for his guests. "I never forgot it," Jeff Beck asserts. "I'd never seen anything like it."[34] Page, in turn, was struck by Beck's mastery of James Burton's solo from the Ricky Nelson EP obscurity "My Babe," and the brotherhood between two boys who had no real brothers of their own was cemented. Musical and sound equipment was starting to accumulate in the parlor chez Page as Jimmy's practicing became more serious, and Jeff Beck recalls recording there on an old reel-to-reel unit: "He already had the bass drum sound by putting the mike under a pillow. I went, 'That's no good!' He said, 'Well, hit it and let's have a listen.' *Booofff!* Techno was born!"[35] And in the back of the house, watching telly? "My parents," Page averred, "were very encouraging. They may not have understood a lot of what I was doing, but nevertheless they had enough confidence that *I* knew what I was doing, that I wasn't just a nut or something."[36]

The Pages' confidence, indeed, would extend past fondly brewing tea for their son and his guitar-twanging pals. At one point the hurdling champion of his school, Jimmy Page was turning into a slender and thoughtful young man, with the sensitive, deceptively innocent features of an English James Dean. By his mid-teens he was going out to play in local youth clubs, as remembered by Jeff Beck: "All the girls started talking about you at school and you were the hero just because you had the balls to get up there and play. Even though it was terrible!"[37] Studious enough to pass five O-level exams (sufficient for further schooling or employment, though not alone a prerequisite for university enrolment), his interests leaned toward painting, sculpture, and certainly music, although the one-time aspiring biological researcher got as far as applying for a job as a laboratory assistant. In 1959, at the age of just fifteen, he drifted out of school and made ready to seek his fortune, guitar in hand.

In those fledgling forays into performing—and in just being

out on his own among his own generation—Jimmy Page would have been exposed to some of the broader cultural transformations that were nascent in Britain and throughout the western world as the decade turned. Prime Minister Harold MacMillan had recently told British voters that they'd "never had it so good," and the wealth finally filtering down to the nation's public after years of postwar austerity was bringing fresh freedoms, including the freedoms to cast off longstanding social mores and to critique those that remained. This was the time of angry young men and kitchen sinks on the English stage and in the English cinema, confronting class divides and moral hypocrisies once unmentionable; across the Channel, European existentialists told of fundamental experiential realities to be found underneath layers of social convention and political constraint; across the Atlantic, American Beat writers like Jack Kerouac, William S. Burroughs, and Allen Ginsberg were offering their own transcendent insights into the virtues of cool jazz, free love, Zen Buddhism and other non-Western spiritual traditions, and marijuana. American "Freedom Riders" were demonstrating against the entrenched racism and segregation in the southern states (the sad subtext of so many blues lyrics), while Britons enlisted in the Campaign for Nuclear Disarmament (CND) to protest the growing stockpiles of atomic and hydrogen weaponry stored around the U.K. and ready for use. Surging birthrates in North America and (to a lesser extent) Europe were reaching a peak, producing a demographic "Baby Boom" that would live out its youth from the mid-1960s to the mid-1970s. A collective international momentum was building. Their time was gonna come.

In 1959, few of these trends may have immediately affected Jimmy Page, who has rarely expressed any explicit or contentious social or political judgments and who has seldom lent his name or talent to any really controversial causes. He would have had a more personal interest, though, in the advent of the female contraceptive pill, which ushered in an unprecedented—revolutionary, for a while—wave of sexual convenience and a relaxation of age-old courtship customs, forever altering the obligations and opportunities of male-female relationships. Going into his six-teenth year, such matters were no doubt often in mind, and he has admitted to a sexual initiation around that stage: "It was one particular day in the summer and this girl and I wandered hand in hand through the countryside. It was the first time I felt I was truly in love."[38]

Just as relevant at his age would have been Britain's gradual phasing out of a compulsory two-year term of national service in the military for adult males—after several years during and after the Korean War the requirement was finally abolished on the last day of 1960. The U.S. military had got Elvis Presley in 1958, but its British ally would not get Jimmy Page or any of his contemporaries. Of all the changes going on in and around him in the late '50s, Page has conceded possibly the most crucial and definitely the most enduring: "My interest in the Occult started when I was about fifteen."[39]

Starting with rock 'n' roll and then delving into its blues roots, the young guitarist, whether he knew it or not, had also been caught up in a "revival" of folk and blues music gaining currency in Great Britain. America, the authentic birthplace of the genres, was going through its own boom of the folk motif via acts like Pete Seeger and the Kingston Trio, but the British had adapted it with a scholarly fervor. The purists among them (a high per-centage) could listen all the way back to its primordial home-grown sources in the Celtic, Renaissance, and Elizabethan lute and harpsichord music that had made its way to the colonists and slaves of the New World; now, transposed to the relatively recent vehicle of the guitar, it had come full circle. Rock 'n' roll and even skiffle were perceived as commercialized, dumbed-down offshoots of such styles—these were the genuine article. Their English champions included grown-up, self-consciously elitist figures like Alexis Korner, Chris Barber, and Cyril Davies in London and other promoters and aficionados further afield. None of them could foresee the direction the music would take at the hands of its steadily younger and more restless audience.

A more subtle but further-reaching cultural shift was coming via the waves of immigrants arriving in England from Common-wealth countries in the Caribbean and South Asia. Jamaicans, Pakistanis, and Indians could and did face resentment and hos-tility from native-born British, but in the decades to come their numbers—and their dress, their religions, their cuisine, and no-tably their music—would profoundly alter the social landscape of the nation. The last of these was due to alter the music of Jimmy Page in the coming years.

As much promise as the British music scene circa 1960 held, with its avant-gardes, underground interminglings, and newly adventurous listeners, the industry itself was still a cautious one. Radio and television programming was still sanctioned by government officialdom, and recording studios were still ster-ile, technocratic places ill suited for capturing the spontaneity and dynamism of skiffle, blues, and rock 'n' roll. The equipment was certainly there: stereo sounds were coming onto the market and into the control booths, and Les Paul's ingenuity with re-verb, multitrack overdubs, and other studio trickery (which so fascinated Page's friend Jeff Beck) was being taken up in more and more production houses. Solid-body electric guitars and basses, like Fender's Stratocaster, Telecaster, Jazz bass and Gib-son's mahogany single-cutaways, named after Les Paul himself, were showing up in music shops to be drooled over by neophyte instrumentalists everywhere. In 1958 and 1959, two specific Les Pauls, with their electric-buzz-neutralizing or "humbucking" pickups designed by Gibson's Seth Lover and Ted McCarty, rolled off the Gibson production line at Kalamazoo, Michigan—their eventual acquisition by James Patrick Page of Epsom, United Kingdom, would be a milestone in the history of electric music.

But the profession as a whole was slow to catch on to many of these advances. The live sound of a small ensemble in a nightclub or dance hall, for example, was pretty much determined by the energy of the performers, the attentiveness of the crowd, and the evening's temperament of whatever microphones and amplifiers were in use. Drums, the loudest acoustic instrument, didn't need mikes, and guitar amps turned too loud for too long tended to edge into a thick distortion that few players or fans could abide. Public address, or PA, systems were redundant when an act was really cooking, of course; the largest crowds of a few hundred or a couple of thousand people could hear everything well enough, and after all it wasn't as if the shows were being held in anything so outrageous as, say, a 20,000- or 30,000-seat sporting arena.

As 1959 became 1960 and Jimmy Page's sixteenth birthday loomed, the furthest things from his thoughts would have been the low fortunes of a bottom-of-the-bill outfit of amateur Elvis Presley, Little Richard, and Carl Perkins fans up in Liverpool who had called themselves the Moondogs and the Silver Beatles before finally agreeing on just the Beatles. Closer to home, he had yet to imagine the existence of a second group of earnest but unlearned blues buffs around Dartford, named with undeserved confidence Little Boy Blue and the Blue Boys, featuring Keith Richards on guitar and his friend Mike Jagger on harmonica, or that of a shy, painfully dedicated blues guitar acolyte from Ripley, Eric Clapton. But as Page's manhood approached, they and every other artistic, technological, intellectual, and economic element in the portentous atmosphere of his day would assume a pivotal import. Enjoying good times and bad times with male and female company, teaching himself new guitar runs all the time, buying and borrowing a greater collection of records, and more and more sure the stages of the youth clubs in and around Epsom were where he liked to be ("I used to play in many groups . . . anyone who could get a gig together"),[40] the solitary, reflective boy from Miles Road had begun to narrow his musical interests down from the fusion of skiffle, country, blues, and folk into just two: rock and roll.

That's the Way

1960-1968

Our spiritual consciousness acts through the will and its instruments
upon material objects, in order to produce changes which will result
in the establishment of the new conditions of consciousness which
we wish. That is the definition of Magick.

—ALEISTER CROWLEY,
CONFESSIONS

"I played in a lot of different small bands around," Jimmy Page
would say of his first public appearances in Epsom, "but nothing
you could ever get any records of . . . just friends and things."[1]
Though his skiffle showcase on the *All Your Own* show must
have been something of a coup in 1958, Page has never thought
it worth mentioning as an early step to success. In itself this ad
hoc, let's-start-a-group background is unremarkable for young
musicians in any circumstances, but Page was already ahead of
the pack in his attention to guitar technique and guitar equipment. At some point his Grazioso electric was replaced by its
American inspiration, a Fender Stratocaster—still considered
one of the great rock 'n' roll guitars (Buddy Holly, killed in a plane
crash in 1959, was its highest-profile exponent at the time)—and
Page's model preceded Fender's purchase by CBS, after which
many players insist the Strats' craftsmanship went into decline.

"Fenders got screwed up when they started making 'em in Japan, of course,"[2] Page opined.

That Page was getting hold of top-of-the-line instruments while still unattached to any full-time band shows a commitment to the music well beyond his years. "I just started exchanging and getting better ones. I think the second one I had was a Fender Stratocaster, and that was the first good guitar I ever had."[3] Playing a "good guitar" would naturally have improved his own skills at a juncture when many of his peers were stuck with knockoffs and utilitarian products that frustrated musical growth. Among his own small coterie of mates, school chums, and record collectors, Jimmy Page was a guitar hero at age sixteen.

And then he started getting noticed. Though there are no known recordings of Page's six-string abilities from this time, he must have been talented enough to stand out from the other musicians around him. One night in an Epsom dance hall, toward the end of 1960, someone spotted the slim, dark-haired lad's authority over his Stratocaster and commented on it to his sister. She later told her boyfriend, who sang and served as manager-cum-roadie for a gang of rock 'n' rollers led by Red E. Lewis and the Red Caps. The boyfriend's name was Chris Tidmarsh but was to go by the name Neil Christian. "They'd seen this kid get up with this amateur band in this Epsom hall," Christian has recollected. "They started doing this Jerry Lee Lewis number and it was damn good." Christian then went to hear for himself, catching another gig where Jimmy Page's act was booked to open for (according to one source) the Dave Clark Five. "I knew the boy had something,"[4] he confirmed.

Christian sought to recruit Page into the Red Lewis combo—"We started to chat and he asked whether I'd like to play in London, which of course I did,"[5] Page remembered—but his tender years made his parents nervous about sending their son, scarcely of school-leaving age, out into the nightclubs of southern England. "I talked to his parents," Christian later said, "because they wanted him to stay at school and not leave for some rock 'n' roll band, but I talked them into it."[6] Page admits that Christian's guarantees to Jim and Patricia Page were "quite a courteous thing to do. I was tailored in the mould to do what all young lads do, which was to go through school and pass exams. . . . He reassured my parents and said he'd keep a watchful eye on the young lad, and anyway the gigs were at weekends."[7] Neil Christian gives his own parallel account: "I went to his father and said, 'If I promise to pay your boy £15 a week, would you consider him playing in the group?' He said no at first. Jimmy was the only boy, his parents were lovely people. Jimmy was a nice kid—quiet, shy, well brought up."[8] The elder Pages relented upon Christian's pledge to bring young Jim home after every show.

Red E. Lewis and the Red Caps (the name was an obvious nod to Gene Vincent and the Blue Caps) were rather behind the curve in 1960–1961—they were playing old-fashioned rock 'n' roll just when the style's brightest lights were dimming. Buddy Holly and Eddie Cochran were dead, Little Richard had "retired," Jerry Lee Lewis and Chuck Berry were facing legal troubles or jail time, and Elvis Presley had set his sights on Hollywood once his army stint was over. Cover versions of Gene Vincent and Bo Diddley weren't the hippest sounds around, and the newest Red Cap, Jimmy Page, found out the hard way after a few weeks' worth of gigs. "Jimmy said that things weren't going well with Red E. Lewis," Neil Christian says, "and said, 'Why don't you start singing?'"[9] The Red Caps became Neil Christian and the Crusaders. Jimmy Page became, for some sets, Nelson Storm.

It was another tough slog. Despite their new names (the play on words was itself an echo of Johnny Kidd and the Pirates, famous for "Shakin' All Over" in 1960), Page and his bandmates, including Christian on vocals, "Tornado" Evans on drums, and "Jumbo" Spicer on bass, had a set list that was still old hat. "At that time," Page noted, "public taste was more engineered towards Top 10 records, so it was a bit of a struggle. But there'd always be a *small* section of the audience into what we were doing."[10] This was the fallow season of rock music in both Britain and the United States, a historic interregnum between the initial excitement of the mid-

'50s and the later explosion of the British Invasion. "In the group, playing Chuck Berry and Bo Diddley songs, nothing really happened at all," continues Page. "Nobody wanted to hear those numbers and that's all we wanted to do."[11] The English record charts were dominated in those days by the "trad jazz" of Acker Bilk and Kenny Ball, as well as Connie Francis, Percy Faith's "Theme from *A Summer Place*," and the tame tones of Cliff Richard and the Shadows. Seventeen-year-old rock 'n' roller Jimmy Page was in on the ground floor and paying his dues.

And gathering strength. "Jimmy lived and died by the guitar," Neil Christian swears. "Every time you went to see him he had a guitar around his neck."[12] Still based rent-free at his mum and dad's on Miles Road, bringing home a very respectable £15 or £20 a week, Page's Crusader spoils were being put back into new equipment. His Stratocaster was now joined by an orange Gretsch Chet Atkins Country Gentleman, not as sleek as the Fender—it was a single-cutaway semi-acoustic with painted f-holes—but another very playable, very classic rock guitar. Somewhere along the line he'd also learned to restring his guitars with an .008-gauge banjo string for a high E ("I'd get a set of Fenders or Gibsons and put their first string on the second and throw the sixth string away")[13] to facilitate the bends he heard his exemplars play. Again, Page was ahead of his time in linking his creative work with the technology in his arsenal, when most musicians of his age and tastes would play whatever they could afford and gave little thought to the way different instruments and accessories made different music. A fellow Epsom player named John Gibb would later tell of Crusader Page "trying out all the new gadgets and sounds."[14]

The Crusaders had no lack of gigs, and the boy wonder Jimmy Page was a big part of their attraction. In the style of the day, they would perform Shadows-like choreographed stage moves, including bending over backward ("All the silly things that groups used to do," Page later confessed),[15] but Page's mastery of rock 'n' roll standards was no joke. "He could play all this stuff as though you were listening to the record," Christian says. "After we'd been together a year or so, he started developing his own sound. Jimmy was so quick, other guitarists used to come and see him."[16] Highlights of his show included fast rhythm 'n' blues numbers, convincing renditions of Gene Vincent and Johnny Burnette hits, and even slower instrumentals like Santo and Johnny's dreamy "Sleep Walk" and their cover of George Gershwin's "Summertime," which Page played with a slide.

Eventual Page collaborators like drummer B. J. Wilson would report, "One of the finest concerts I ever attended in my life was Neil Christian and the Crusaders the night Chris Farlowe [another accomplice-to-be] got up and jammed with them."[17] Long before he became his studio associate and Led Zeppelin bassist, John Paul Jones (then just John Baldwin) had taken notice of the Crusaders' six-string gunslinger: "I rated Jimmy Page for years and years," he recalled. "I can remember people saying, 'You've got to go and listen to Neil Christian and the Crusaders. They've got this unbelievable young guitarist.'"[18] Jeff Beck, too, heard about his boyhood chum's progress and caught some Crusaders appearances. "Page was sort of raving around with a big Gretsch Country Gentleman. It looked big on him because he was such a shrimp—all you saw was this guitar being wielded by a pipe-cleaner man. He used to play really fiery sort of fast stuff, but nobody was listening, nobody wanted to hear him." Beck's story authenticates the Crusaders' occasional battles with unmoved audiences and their own concessions to popular demand. "He wasn't playing funky at all, it was just sort of [traditional Jewish folk song] 'Hava Nagila'—terrible, but it was impressive!"[19]

Although they had no records to promote, the Crusaders did travel the English club circuit, and it was here where Page, barely seventeen, began to feel the pressure. "We lived out of the back of a van, out of cafes"[20] is Neil Christian's recollection; "It was quite soul-destroying" is Jimmy Page's. "Rushing all over the place, and doing quite a physical set and then jumping into the back of the van in ice-cold weather. I was getting flu all the time."[21] No doubt it was all fun for a while, and there were extra-musical rewards to be had on the road (Christian: "We met different girlfriends along the route and stayed at their places. . . . Jimmy went down well, he had that lovely baby face"),[22] but in the year and a half Page was a Crusader emotional and especially physical exhaustion set in. "All those breakdowns on the M1 which were great in their own way but after a while it just starts knocking you out. I was getting ill, and I really thought, 'I just can't carry on.'" By early summer 1962, he had to have a break. "I remember one night walking outside a gig, and the next point waking up and I was laying on the floor in some sort of dressing room. I just collapsed and couldn't keep going, and it was just fatigue and exhaustion."[23] The isolated only child was now a fragile young man. He had contracted glandular fever, a form of mononucleosis common in teens and young adults, whose symptoms include extreme tiredness, sore throat, and swelling of the neck nodes. Page handed in his notice: "This went on over a couple of months," Christian concludes. "He came up one day and said, 'I need a change.'"[24]

Page's term with the Crusaders, short and difficult though it was, is an important aspect of his career. A teenager who'd only been playing guitar for four or five years, he had already been taken up into a working rock 'n' roll group and received an education in both the stresses of performing and the rigors of keeping his technique and his gear at a professional level. "That was jumping in at the deep end and not being prepared for it,"[25] Page realized with hindsight. He was also the Crusaders' single guitarist, which meant he acquired a showmanship and an instrumental versatility from being the de facto musical star of the act, a role he would play in at least two future bands. The Crusaders would carry on for the rest of the decade, and other guitar-heroes-in-waiting would fill Jimmy Page's slot—Page suggested Jeff Beck at first ("I tried him out in a club in the West End. . . . I didn't like him so I gave him a fiver to go home,"[26] Neil Christian chuckles), but rockabilly picker Albert Lee, Heston resident

Ritchie Blackmore (Deep Purple), and Mick Abrahams (Jethro Tull, Blodwyn Pig) all apprenticed in his wake.

Recovering from his bout of illness, Page was not about to forsake the guitar. One curious account mentions him accompanying poet Royston Ellis at London's Mermaid Theatre around the end of his Crusaders period, adding free-form acoustic fills between Ellis's English beatnik verses (the writer would later author travel guides and historical fiction under the name Richard Tresillian). He continued to build his record collection, too, and had begun to pay some attention to guitar virtuosi outside rock 'n' roll, among them jazz greats Django Reinhardt, Tal Farlow, and the inevitable Les Paul, and classical masters like Andrés Segovia. "I never fitted comfortably into jazz,"[27] he would disclose, but hearing flamenco music, like that of the Gypsy master Manitas de Plata, was an early revelation that powerful guitar players weren't necessarily plugged in.

Still, Page had other paths to pursue. "I was doing a lot of painting and drawing in what free time I had," he reflected, "and so I thought I'd go to art college, because a number of my friends had gone to art college, and I thought . . . maybe this is it, maybe this is my vocation."[28] His five O-levels certainly qualified him for the higher education the choice represented, and signing on at Surrey's Sutton Art College, he "really wanted to be a fine-art painter. I was sincere in that aim and when I went to college I kept quiet that I played guitar or else they would expect me to play it in the lunch hour."[29] Though no original visual artwork by Page has ever been seen publicly, his talents must have been sufficient for Sutton, and he recounted how he had also been accepted at another institution in Croydon. "I don't know how because I was a terrible draftsman."[30]

In the '50s and '60s, British art schools were not merely, or even primarily, places where painters and sculptors were trained. They were also alternatives to more formal education that appealed to clever but hardly scholastic young people like Jimmy

Page and a host of other musicians of his cohort: the Rolling Stones' Charlie Watts, Keith Richards, and Ron Wood; the Who's Pete Townshend, the Kinks' Ray Davies, the Beatles' John Lennon, and the Yardbirds' Keith Relf, Eric Clapton, and Jeff Beck are some of them. Decades later, Page pointed out their value to him and the rest of the British invaders: "Remember, just about any British band that came out of the Sixties worth its salt had at least one member that went to art college, which was a very important part of the overall equation."[31] "The art schools," critic George Melly wrote in *Revolt Into Style: The Pop Arts in Britain*, "were the refuge of the bright but unacademic, the talented, the non-conformist, the lazy, the inventive and the indecisive: all those who didn't know what they wanted but knew it wasn't a nine-till-five job."[32] They would impart a special sensibility to the singers, guitar players, and drummers who emerged from them, a feeling that playing rock 'n' roll was not just a way to make a few bob and pull some crumpet but might conceivably be some sort of statement—a vehicle for expression more vital than canvas, oils, and clay.

So Jimmy Page, art student, did not eclipse Jimmy Page, rock 'n' roll guitarist. Page attended Sutton Art College for about eighteen months, from 1962 to late 1963, and while he took care not to play on campus, he was still playing on Miles Road and still cultivating contacts he'd made while serving with Neil Christian. Page actually participated in his first quasi-official recording session in the autumn of '62, joining up with the rest of the Crusaders in the home studio of independent producer Joe Meek on Holloway Road; the result was a soon-forgotten single called "The Road to Love," in which his guitar could barely be heard under Meek's trademark overdubs. "Joe Meek laid so much over it no one could recognize anybody,"[33] Neil Christian has recalled. Road work had impaired his health, but just jamming with friends, catching other people's gigs, and sitting in on club sessions were well within Page's limitations as a full-time collegian.

The Miles Road affairs were good fun for all, including Mr.

and Mrs. Page, who indulged their only child with the run of their front room and an appreciation for the sounds he and his pals produced in it. "All the boys that Jimmy knew, Jeff Beck and the other lads, would come to the house," his mother reminisced. "You had to shut your mind to everything else and just get into it. . . . I really took to it."[34] Fellow Epsomian John Gibb describes the road veteran Page coming out of his shell among all the instruments and recording and hi-fi gear scattered about his parents' parlor: "Jimmy had a couple of funny sayings he used a lot—'Quim the nun' and 'Prick the bish.'"[35]

Jeff Beck's reappearance (or appearance—some say it was only at this point that the two eighteen-year-old guitarists actually got to know each other) in his circle was an opportunity for Page to compare notes with another semiprofessional musician and blues buff, who brought news of a rock 'n' roll groundswell building throughout the country. "I had been in a band that was playing Chess Records material, but there was no market for it, so I just packed it in and went to art school" is Page's appraisal of the changes afoot. "But then the Beatles happened in the north of England where they were playing Motown things like 'Please Mr. Postman,' and you had this heavy blues thing happening in the south, and before you knew it, I started playing again."[36] Page saw a not-yet–Fab Four show in late 1962 or early 1963—"They didn't go down too well and I actually heard John Lennon going past saying, 'Fuck these London audiences.'"[37] About the same time, he met up with bluesy bohemians Mick Jagger and Keith Richards on a trip to Birmingham to see the Folk Festival of the Blues, in company with a van full of other record collectors and musicians from his area. "I remember them vividly because Keith said he played guitar and Mick said he played harp."[38]

The chronology of these heady days for Jimmy Page and his peers is vague; no one could have guessed the eventual results of such a scattering of students, oddballs, and young dreamers then taking the stages of Britain and no one was taking notes. A very sketchy report has Page hitchhiking around Europe and even to

India during this phase, flying home when felled again with glandular fever, but Page later told William S. Burroughs, "During the period when everybody was going through trips over to . . . Morocco, going down . . . making their journeys toward Istanbul, I was at art college during that period and then I eventually went straight into music. So I really missed out on all that sort of traveling."[39] His more productive (and more authenticated) journeys of 1963 were to central London's major blues club, the legendary Marquee on Wardour Street. "I used to go up and jam on a Thursday night with the interlude band," he explained. "I just used to sort of sit in, actually; they didn't let you jam, just sit in for one number, two at the most."[40]

Page's Marquee sessions, apparently, began soon after his Crusaders term, and he actually had to back out of Marquee kingpin Cyril Davies's offer to join a new group, the R & B All-Stars: "I thought it would be awful to go with him and really start enjoying it and then getting ill again, but I did in fact play with them for a bit."[41] Committed to school during the day, in the evening Page became a regular on the small but growing London blues scene, getting up at Richmond's Crawdaddy and Eel Pie Island as well as the Marquee. His musical accomplices on these occasions, including Andy Wren and Nicky Hopkins on piano and Long John Baldry on vocals, were almost strangers to him—"We didn't really know each other outside the Marquee, we just used to meet there and get up and play."[42] Incipient Yardbirds and Rolling Stones were rubbing shoulders with him in the wings and on the boards. "Eric Clapton would be there," Page would look back, when Clapton was midway between faltering acts called the Roosters and Casey Jones and the Engineers and his breakthrough slot in the Yardbirds. Soon enough they were introduced. "Eric came up and said he'd seen some of the sets we'd done and told me, 'You play like Matt Murphy,' Memphis Slim's guitarist, and I said I really liked Matt Murphy and actually he was one of the ones that I'd followed quite heavily."[43] That became the beginning of a friendship, though not always a beautiful one.

But the Marquee experience was crucial for Jimmy Page's musical evolution. "I guess [the club] would hold about a hundred people," he said a lifetime later. "It seemed very big at the time to me, I'll tell you that! It was a big gig for me."[44]

Bigger than he could have known. Aside from eliminating the burdens of travel and "road fever," the Marquee sessions would also have benefited Page in their centrality—unlike the half-empty halls of the suburbs where he'd played with the Crusaders, people actually came to the venue as the prime blues hot spot of the nation's biggest city. These would include music fans and aspiring amateurs, certainly, but also industry professionals, sniffing around for new talent as the English rock and blues explosion ticked down. While there are conflicting stories of when and by whom Jimmy Page was tapped as a session musician, there is no doubt that his performances at the Marquee were where his potential was recognized. "Suddenly I got this offer to do studio work," remembered Page, not too clearly. "Someone came up and said, 'Well, look, do you want to play on our record and I can promise you more work?'"[45]

John Gibb, who was then under contract to EMI Records as Brian Howard and the Silhouettes, says he got Page to play on a pair of his singles, "The Worrying Kind" and "Bald-Headed Woman." Page has also named bassist Teddy Whadmore's "Feeling the Groove" as his first studio gig of import, although "I don't even know if it was ever released."[46] Ex-Shadows Tony Meehan's and Jet Harris' "Diamonds," released in early 1963, has frequently been listed as the guitarist's first appearance on record (it became a British number-one single), although less than perfect hindsight coupled with the commercially tempting knowledge of Page's future superstardom may well have distorted memories of his involvement. Tony Meehan, who produced "Diamonds," was introduced to Page via a young studio tea boy named Glyn Johns, who knew Page from South London. According to Meehan, Johns told him "that Jimmy Page was a great kid. . . . He was young but he needed a break. . . . I decided to give him a try."

Page showed up at IPC studios, was handed the notation for the song, and, Meehan says, "I knew right away he was faking it; he couldn't read the music I'd written out."[47] Jimmy Page: "What went wrong was they stuck a row of dots in front of me, which looked like crows on telephone wires, which was awful. I could have played it so easily, and it was so simple when another chap came and did it." Meehan demoted Page, then almost completely without formal musical literacy, from lead to acoustic rhythm guitar, where he fared better. "It wasn't so much a matter of a lost opportunity as a matter of pride—I felt really stupid," said Page. "I had no idea what it was about, so I wasn't seen again for a while after that."[48]

A subsequent offer from arranger Mike Leander connected him with John Carter, singer of a studio-based group called Carter-Lewis and the Southerners, in the fall of 1963. "I was really surprised," he admitted later. "Before this I thought session work was closed shop."[49] Here Page handled himself without embarrassment on a single, "Your Momma's Out of Town," which sold moderately, and after that, he says, "It was like, 'Who's the guitarist on that?' Right place at the right time, really."[50] This is no false modesty on Page's part, since, as he explains, "The session scene was still one generation before, so I was like the new pick on the block."[51] He has granted that, as his guitar work began to be linked—by producers and other musicians if not the listening public—to hit records, "That gave me the impetus to keep on doing it."[52]

It is in the low-profile but high-prestige world of the London studio scene that the legend of Jimmy Page really begins. "Session musician," as commonly understood, was a relatively new career in the early '60s. There had always been anonymous players and sitters-in who backed up featured singers or instrumentalists onstage and at record or radio dates, but as the industry began to expand the absolute amount of music being put down on tape meant trained players could make a living on studio assignments alone, providing almost generic backups for countless

scores, songs, advertising jingles, and other snippets of performance. Audiences were buying ever higher numbers of sound
tracks, LPs, EPs, and 45s; somebody had to be making them.
Moreover, the advent of pop stars and pop groups exposed many
pretty faces as inadequate when it came to actual musicianship,
and session players were often called upon to fill in for lesser guitarists, bassists, and drummers whose names and pictures were
then featured on work to which they had not in fact contributed. On other occasions producers just needed known quantities standing by in the control booth when some new band of
provincial scufflers sought to be the Next Big Things (George
Martin had the Beatles' new drummer Ringo Starr sit out some
takes of "Love Me Do," replacing him with veteran Andy White).
Proven competent, reliable, and reasonably intelligent, Jimmy
Page's self-taught skills in blues and rock 'n' roll playing caught
the ears of employers who needed younger, hipper artists to keep
their own sounds fresh.

"He was a fast player, he knew his rock 'n' roll and added to
that," John Carter has reminisced. "He was quiet and a bit of an
intellectual," whose between-takes conversation might take in
"all sorts of odd cult things."[53] Before Page arrived the mainstay
guitarists of English pop sessions were Vic Flick and Big Jim Sullivan, an older, large-framed country and rockabilly specialist
who also had a taste for jazz. "If it was country I'd do it," Sullivan
revealed, "if it was rock he'd do it. Every now and then we'd have
a swap 'round."[54] As 1963 turned over into 1964, Big Jim Sullivan and (to avoid confusion) "Little Jim" Page were gradually
established as the go-to guitar players for the record companies'
breaking wave of rock and blues production.

And as the jobs started to fill up his calendar, he made the
serious decision to leave art college: "I was missing lectures, taking days off and I finally had to make a choice."[55] Perhaps surprisingly, this won his parents' approval; they saw the musical
vocation as more secure than the artistic one. "I think they were
quite relieved to see something being done instead of art work,

which they thought was a loser's game,"[56] disclosed Page. "I always thought I could return to painting, but I don't think I've touched a paint brush since."[57] "In the music business, Jimmy didn't have anyone to introduce him around," his mother proudly reminded one interviewer. "But Jimmy was never the pushy type—he just sort of glided into such a good position."[58] With the Beatles an international phenomenon by early 1964, and the Rolling Stones, the Animals, Gerry and the Pacemakers, and the Dave Clark Five hot on their Cuban heels, Jimmy Page's gigs for other homeland hopefuls were piling up.

"Anyone who needed a guitarist either went to Big Jim or myself. . . . It was all just flooding in because they didn't have any other young guys playing guitar,"[59] Page would reflect. It is safe to say that most of Page's session recordings of this era were well within his musical range, enhancing songs without really distinguishing them, and he inevitably played on more misses than hits. So often highlighted for his performances with famous or soon-to-be-famous acts (rightly, to be sure), Page's strumming and solos on the Pickwicks' "Little By Little," the Primitives' "You Said," and "A Certain Girl" by First Gear are far less memorable, even to Page himself. "They didn't want you to change the sound, or even the mike positions," he has complained. "When I first started it was, 'Play what you want,' which was great, but then the amount of input that you had started to diminish."[60] Apart from the income, which was fairly secure and easier earned than his touring pay had ever been, he would gain a key understanding of how recording studios actually functioned—a mild-mannered, compliant youth taking in the nuances of mixing, microphone placement, overdubs, and arranging as it all went on around him.

As a full-time guitarist for hire, he kept his tools in good order. The Gretsch Country Gentleman was exchanged for a black Les Paul Custom (his first possession of the fabled Gibson) around this time, although he has also asserted that the Les Paul was bought outright for £185 (this sum may have been part of the same trade). "I was one of the first people in England to have one," he discovered, "but I didn't know that then. I just saw it on a wall, had a go with it, and it was good. . . . It seemed to be the best all-rounder at the time."[61] The three-pickup solid-body fitted with a Bigsby tremolo arm would be his prized electric guitar for several years. He also owned an acoustic guitar that came in handy for sessions (possibly a Harmony), and he plugged into a Supro amplifier. More than these, though, his secret weapon as an electric rock 'n' roller was his association with Roger Mayer.

A young art college guitarist and do-it-yourselfer who had found gainful employment in the electronics arm of the Royal Navy, Mayer had first approached Page when he, too, was still at school and gigging intermittently, on the cusp of entering the session environment. "I had just started to do a few sessions," Page recalled, "and he said, 'I work for the Admiralty in the Experimental Department and I could make any sort of gadget you want.' So I said why didn't he try to make me this thing I'd heard years before on this Ventures record, 'The 2000-Pound Bee.'" Since the time of Edison electronically amplified sound had been judged according to its clarity and faithfulness to the acoustics of the original instrument, but by the '50s and early '60s guitar players had begun to notice that overdriven amplifiers—tube technology cranked past its optimum level—could produce a stinging, "fat" timbre that was either sickeningly out of place for jazz melodies or strangely appropriate for rock 'n' roll. The Gibson guitar manufacturers had even produced a simple "fuzz box" outboard accessory to this end, but it had never really caught on except as a novelty, which is how surf music instrumentalists the Ventures had employed it on the record Page described for Mayer. "We had one in England, but it wasn't too good; in actuality it was a disaster," continued Page. "So I said, 'Why don't you improve on this with the Admiralty's facilities?' Which he did."[62] To Mayer such implements were simple enough, even obvious, but in Jimmy Page's hands (at his feet, rather) they became indispensable components of his sound.

Now Page could *control* distortion rather than have it emerge accidentally, and he was definitely among the first guitarists to use the effect as a musical, not comical, one. "I haven't got that kind of mind where I can think of a sound and put it into capacitors and resistors," he would say. "One has to try and find someone who you can explain the sound to and hope that they can understand."[63] Roger Mayer was that someone for Jimmy Page—in a few short years he became that someone, exclusively, for an American expatriate named Jimi Hendrix.

The year 1964 was likely Page's most productive and most positive as a studio guitarist. His uncredited work on largely forgotten A- and B-sides like the Nashville Teens' "Tobacco Road," the Sneekers' "I Just Can't Go to Sleep," and the McKinleys' "Sweet and Tender Romance" has been heard as anticipating his later Yardbirds and Led Zeppelin riffery, but he also left marks on longer-lived discs where his influence became an open secret, like Dave Berry's "The Crying Game." As a regular denizen of London's numerous recording rooms, he had no reason to be starstruck, since he would professionally or personally meet any number of acts to whom studios were intimidating places passed through in spare moments before going back to the boards—he had already shown Keith Richards, for example, an apt solo for the Rolling Stones' "Heart of Stone" that Richards happily copped for the band's 1964 single. He got to know producers and engineers like Glyn Johns, the Stones' Andrew Loog Oldham, and the maverick Joe Meek, who improvised his own echo, compression, and distortion devices and who was allegedly obsessed with space, horror movies, and the occult (Meek killed himself and his landlady in 1967).

Ever alert to unconventional techniques, Page was one of the earliest musicians in England to acquire a sitar—"I had a sitar sent over from India before any other people in pop," he claimed, noting, "I'd been to see Ravi Shankar years before he became fashionable.[64] . . . I explained that I had a sitar, but didn't know how to tune it. He was very nice to me and wrote down the tunings on a piece of paper."[65] The case has even been made that Page introduced the instrument to the Beatles' George Harrison, whose popularizing of its exotic drones would lead to the whole sub-genre of "raga rock." Toward the end of 1964, Page's services were called upon to help salvage a new single for a struggling Welshman; drummer Chris Slade had already been reduced to tambourine (Page and a much improved Slade would later be in the same lineup) while Page added steady, straightforward rhythms to Tom Jones's smash hit "It's Not Unusual."

The year wound down with Page working on three record dates that would result in classic rock 'n' roll. The Kinks, led by brothers Ray and Dave Davies, needed a success and were counting on Ray's latest, "You Really Got Me," to be it. Page attended the sessions at the behest of producer Shel Talmy and was not warmly welcomed by the Davies boys, who distrusted outsiders and feared hotshot session aces like Page would step in and take the honors for what was surely the band's most exciting 45. Dave Davies, and not Jimmy Page, played the fiery solo on the released take of "You Really Got Me," although Page did try some fuzz-boxed lead on earlier tryouts of the tune, and some have pointed out that even if it was only his rhythm guitar heard on the track, it is his part, and not Davies's solo, that is its signature or "hook" (Van Halen would give the song a righteously hard-rock makeover in 1978). "I didn't really do that much on the Kinks' records," Page would allow. "I know I managed to get a couple of riffs on their album, but I can't really remember—I know that [Ray Davies] didn't really approve of my presence."[66]

Similar bad feeling brewed when Page stood in while Ireland's Them, with vocalist Van Morrison, were launching their version of the blues chestnut "Baby Please Don't Go." Production assistant Phil Coulter would confess, "I don't think Van felt any intense long-standing loyalty to the guys in the group,"[67] including guitarist Billy Harrison. There is dispute over whether it is Page's piercing blues line that defines the song, if he only played a run Harrison had already devised, or if Page only backed up Harrison himself, but there is no denying "Baby Please Don't Go," released in January 1965, was a hit record and an indestructible boogie (AC/DC were later to cover it with just slightly more intensity). Page is also heard on Them's "Gloria" and "Here Comes the Night," but the Belfast natives weren't happy about his and other session players filling their posts. "It was so embarrassing that you just had to look at the floor and play because they were glaring," Page recounted. "It could have been the end of their musical career in one evening. . . . God, it was awful."[68]

In December 1964, Shel Talmy again had Page on hand while the Who laid down their debut, "I Can't Explain," engineered by Glyn Johns. Guitarist Pete Townshend cleverly withheld the use of his Rickenbacker twelve-string electric, thus keeping Page on rhythm-guitar duties, but Page took the lead on the song's B-side, "Bald-Headed Woman," deploying his fuzz box for the number. "It was so simple even I could play it,"[69] Townshend laughed over his solo—although he and Page were also competing for an older woman they both knew. "She'd obviously fucked him to death and then proceeded to fuck me to death," reported Townshend. "We were both kind of cross-eyed with this woman."[70] "All I managed to do was sneak a couple of phrases on,"[71] Page would say discreetly, although his rhythm does fatten up the ageless power chords of "I Can't Explain." "It was all Pete and he was roaring, man,"[72] enthused Page.

His link to such popular music as put out by Tom Jones, the Kinks, Them, and the Who meant Jimmy Page's studio spots into 1965 would increase in standing—which they did, most but not all of the time. He still took jobs throwing down simple bits for the DeWolfe music library, copyright-free "cues" used for films, and any British movie of 1964–1965 where no-name pop sounds are heard in the background may well feature his guitar. More upscale sessions were those for American songwriter Burt Bacharach, in London to record instrumental versions of the charming pop tunes he had already crafted for others, e.g., "Walk On By" and "There's Always Something There to Remind

Me." Page respected Bacharach's meticulous approach to rehears-
ing and recording, and Bacharach, in turn, admired the young
Briton's politeness and polish (Page might also have bumped into
bassist John Paul Jones at these gigs). Oddly, Bacharach's record
with Page, *Hit Maker!*, turned up in the 1997 film *Austin Powers*,
where the clueless title character, played by comic Mike Myers,
brings it with him from the Swingin' '60s to the Ironic '90s—few
moviegoers knew that some of the kitschiest sounds favored by
the "International Man of Mystery" were actually provided by
one of the coolest musicians of the '70s. By the middle of the
decade, at any rate, Page had already made an impression on the
British and (indirectly) American music scenes. Had he never
joined the Yardbirds or formed Led Zeppelin, he would arguably
still have become a cult guitarist on the strength of his performances in those months, as well as his blooming confidence in
the studio and his promotion of technological inventions like
the fuzz box and cultural artifacts like the sitar. It is just possible,
indeed, to say that some of the key advances and some of the
tightest and toughest arrangements in transatlantic pop music
during its heyday have one musician in common: Jimmy Page.

Into 1965, Page continued accepting studio assignments while
furthering his private musical studies and looking around for
freelance work on the other side of the control-booth glass,
where he could not be merely a hired gun but a session overseer himself. Long after this time, he divulged the truth that he
had taken some brief lessons with jazz expert John McLaughlin,
later of Mahavishnu Orchestra but then toiling in a guitar shop:
"I would say he was the best jazz guitarist in England then, in
the traditional mode of Johnny Smith and Tal Farlow.[73] . . . He
certainly taught me a lot about chord progressions and things
like that. He was so fluent and so far ahead, way out there, and I
learned a hell of a lot."[74]

Page was even more deeply affected by hearing a rising young
folk player who'd just arrived in London from his native Glasgow,
Bert Jansch. Jansch had a dauntingly original fingerpicking style

that went far beyond ordinary folk strumming, and his mastery of the acoustic guitar came as a timely reminder to Page that brilliant soloists didn't always play through amplifiers. "His first album had a great effect on me," he said. "It was so far ahead of what anyone else was doing—that was what got me into playing acoustic. I watched him playing once at a folk club and it was like seeing a classical guitarist. All the inversions he was play-ing were unrecognizable."[75] Over and above folk contemporaries John Renbourne and Davey Graham, Page would always point to Jansch's influence over his own technique—"He was, without a doubt, the one who crystallized so many things. . . . As much as Hendrix has done on the electric, I really think he's done on the acoustic"[76]—and the influence was not just an indirect one. Folk artist Al Stewart was another Jansch admirer, and Page was present when Stewart was recording the B-side of his own single. "While we were doodling around between takes," Stewart recol-lected, "I showed him what I thought was Bert Jansch's version of [traditional English folk melody] 'Blackwater Side.' He seemed to like it."[77] Stewart explained that the guitar was tuned not in the usual way (EADGBE, low to high strings), but to DADGAD, which drew a resonant, sitarish buzz from the instrument, re-quiring not the fixed chord patterns of normal tuning but looser, more independent fingering. Sometimes called "open tuning" (since the instrument needs no hands on the fretboard to sound a complete chord), Page would adopt DADGAD and other tun-ing variations into his own method in the coming years, and Jansch's "Blackwater Side" would be closely adapted into his solo acoustic spot on Led Zeppelin's first album.

Returning to his blues roots, in April 1965, Page got to play with American pioneer Sonny Boy Williamson. The blues re-vival that had centered around the Marquee Club had become a pervasive force in English music, and its Stateside originators were frequently invited across the pond to bring some of their authenticity with them: black, middle-aged, and an irascible lov-er of whiskey, Williamson was a genuine bluesman in a city full of fresh-faced white wannabes barely out of their teens. These casual recordings, abetted by organist Brian Auger, saxophonists Joe Harriot and Alan Skidmore, and future Jeff Beck accomplice Mickey Waller on drums, resulted in awkward cuts of "I See a Man Downstairs" and "It's a Bloody Life" where Williamson was audibly impatient with his young accompanists. Still available today (on numerous repackagings), they are of more interest as testaments to Page's education in electric blues than as first-class examples of the form.

But white boys' electric blues was very loud on the sound track of what was now the world's cultural capital: Swinging London. Jimmy Page, twenty-one-year-old prodigy of pop and hidden face behind hip hits, was known to all in the remarkably small and cliquey community of players on the streets from Carnaby and Soho to Savile Row. Working groups solicited his guitar playing as a full-time band member, but the sessions were just too lucrative (while he continued to reside with his parents in Epsom) and his health still too frail for touring schedules. Carter-Lewis and the Southerners had put him on display in press photos of the act (which had no permanent lineup to speak of), as did Mickey Finn and the Blue Men, who had also used Page on their recordings.

Page paused a little, though, when Giorgio Gomelsky, manager of the Yardbirds, asked if he wanted to replace the departing Eric Clapton on lead guitar. The Yardbirds were making a name for themselves in the manner of the Rolling Stones' raunchy blues shows; they prided themselves on more accurate Chicago covers and fast "rave-ups" that always got the miniskirts twirling. But Gomelsky wanted the Yardbirds to have Stones-style hit records and, as Page remembers, "What was being put to me by Giorgio was that Eric was giving them trouble, and I didn't want to have anything to do with it."[78] Clapton, a blues purist to his bones, was "very disappointed, disillusioned"[79] when the band began scoring with poppier numbers like Graham Gouldman's "For Your Love" in March of '65, and left them soon afterward. Page tactfully refused Gomelsky's bid of £25 a week (he was making three times that and more in the studios) but did recommend an old friend—Jeff Beck. Whereas Clapton played very supple, very tasteful blues licks with grace and precision, Beck was eliciting screaming, squawking noises out of his Telecaster that would push the Yardbirds to their commercial and artistic peak. "They said, 'You're coming with us. . . . You're gonna be in a top fucking band'" is Beck's memory of his perfunctory audition. "There were other guys auditioning, but I think they knew I was gonna be the one."[80] If he was good by Jimmy Page, Jeff Beck was good by the Yardbirds. Beck was forever in debt to Page for the connection—Page had also given him breaks by tossing studio gigs his way—and rewarded him with a finder's fee of his prized 1958 Fender. "That old Telecaster Jeff Beck gave me was a beautiful gesture," Page later said. "It was after he joined the Yardbirds. He came 'round one day, knocked on the door and said, 'It's yours.' It was really a beautiful instrument."[81]

Page and Eric Clapton grew close during this time, perhaps another factor in Page's unwillingness to fill Slowhand's Yardbirds space. "We'd meet and go out to dinner," he said. "We talked about various subjects, education—both having attended art schools—music, films, books, just about everything."[82] Page may also have noticed Clapton's attractive blond girlfriend then, Charlotte "Charly" Martin from France, who would eventually become his own wife and mother of his first child. Clapton had joined John Mayall's Bluesbreakers, an uncompromised blues act after the Yardbirds (Mayall had even sought Page himself for the gig, but Page again demurred, citing his preoccupation with studio jobs), and Page was impressed by Clapton's use of Gibson guitars with the new high-powered Marshall amplifiers. "I thought he played brilliantly then, really brilliantly. That was very stirring stuff.[83] . . . You get a Marshall with a Gibson and it's fantastic, a perfect match."[84]

Although the Bluesbreakers were assuredly not a pop group, they did hook up with the Rolling Stones Svengali Andrew Loog

Oldham, who had started his own record label and fancied himself an English musical tycoon in the mould of Phil Spector. Oldham already knew Page by face and reputation, having used him as both a guitarist and studio maven, and picked him to produce some Bluesbreakers tracks, an opportunity Page gladly accepted. "They were good sessions,"[85] he reflected. Clapton's work on "I'm Your Witch Doctor," "Telephone Blues," "Sitting on Top of the World," and "Double Crossing Time" was a high point of his early career: rich, thick blues guitar, played at high decibels—so high that the engineer on the session balked at the volume levels registering on the console's needles. "I told him just to record it, put the faders back up," Page continues, "and I'd take full responsibility. The guy couldn't believe that someone was getting that kind of sound out of a guitar on purpose."[86] But Page believed it, and would remember how to get it again, and record it, for himself.

Around the same time Page was producing him in the studio, Clapton visited his house in Epsom to have some private jams, which Page also recorded. "The Bluesbreakers were playing over in Putney and Eric came to stay at my house. I had a Simon tape recorder that you could DI into [*directly inject* electric instruments without first playing through an amp], so the two guitars went into the machine and I just did these tapes of Eric and myself playing."[87] The DI trick enabled a huge amount of distortion while the two musicians played around with different twelve-bar I-IV-V progressions. But Page let Andrew Oldham's Immediate label know about the tapes ("I was really championing Eric, as you would"),[88] and they were confiscated as part of both Page's and Clapton's contractual obligations. "I argued that they couldn't put them out, because they were just variations of blues structures, and in the end we dubbed some other instruments over some of them and they came out, with liner notes attributed to me . . . though I didn't have anything to do with writing them. I didn't get a penny out of it, anyway."[89] This rather exploitative move on the label's part—they were released when given rhythm tracks by

Rolling Stones Charlie Watts, Bill Wyman, and Mick Jagger play-ing harmonica—led to some mistrust of Clapton toward Page, and Page's own frustrations at not owning music he had made. It was a bitter lesson.

But on the personal front, Jimmy Page was doing well. In late 1964, he had done a session for a song called "Don't Turn Your Back on Me," by a lovely blond American singer-songwriter, Jackie DeShannon. Born Sharon Lee Myers in Hazel, Kentucky, in 1944, she had already broken into the male-dominated music business, collaborating with Jack Nitzche and Randy Newman in the U.S. and touring with the Beatles, before going to Britain, where her own material was covered by the Searchers ("When You Walk in the Room") and Stones moll Marianne Faithfull ("Come and Stay with Me"). "When I was recording in England I was looking for a really good acoustic player," DeShannon tells it today. "I heard there was this new kid who had been play-ing around a lot. So I played him . . . my little riff, which I was very picky about. . . . But Jimmy played it back to me, of course ten times better, and it was perfect."[90] Faithfull has written how Page, who occasionally backed up on her records, was "very dull in those days." But love or lust was in the air and Page and De-Shannon, young kids let loose in the magical world of the music industry, became an item, having what Faithfull called "a very hot romance" in an adjoining hotel room while she was on tour. DeShannon, said Faithfull (who would know), "was brassy and a bit tarty. . . . You could see from the moment you met her that she had been distorted and thwarted by show biz, like a beauti-ful woman who'd been forced into a corset and twisted in some way."[91]

Jimmy Page and Jackie DeShannon were together for most of 1965, it seems (something of an accomplishment in the bed-hop-ping whirl of Swinging London), and she even escorted him on his first trip to America, where he shopped in the paradisiacal music equipment stores of Los Angeles ("I was trying to meet James Burton if I could have done"[92] is his expurgated review of the adventure). She also introduced him to Dick Rosmini, who had produced a record titled *Adventures for 12-String, 6-String & Banjo*, which Page said was "the best-recorded acoustic guitar sound I'd ever heard up to that point."[93] He bumped into the young Californian slide guitarist Ry Cooder as well.

At her most persuasive, Page's muse encouraged him to record a single under his own name, which came out on the Fontana label in February 1965, titled "She Just Satisfies," backed with an instrumental called "Keep Movin'." "She Just Satisfies," with lyrics by Barry Mason, showcased Page on all instruments bar drums (he played guitars, bass, and harmonica while session pal Bobby Graham kept the beat); Page also sang lead on the tune, likely for the first and last time. His rather flat, nasally voice echoed the Kinks' Ray Davies's, and the song itself was built around a Kinks-like power-chord sequence that was lifted from their "Revenge," in whose construction Page had assisted the previous year, and embellished with Beatlesque screams and whoops. (Also known as *fifth* chords—A5, B5, etc.—a power chord consists of only the root, fifth, and octave notes, well suited for electric guitars.) "Jackie DeShannon helped me salvage the whole thing," he admitted. "The end product I suppose was a trip to the States to see her."[94] Despite earnest promotion that identified him as "the greatest guitarist in Europe . . . Jimmy Page is a phenomenon,"[95] and underscored his teaming up with Jackie DeShannon, the single went nowhere and Page later dismissed it altogether. "There's nothing to be said for that record except that it was very tongue-in-cheek. . . . It's better forgotten."[96] DeShannon herself would not be, by Page or the rest of the business: that year she scored a big hit singing Burt Bacharach's "What the World Needs Now Is Love," charted in 1969 with the flower-power immortal "Put a Little Love in Your Heart," and she wrote "Bette Davis Eyes," made into a monster single by Kim Carnes in 1981.

With 1966 on the horizon, Jimmy Page was beginning to chafe under the studio routine. A publishing company he had devised in orbit of Andrew Oldham, James Page Music, was dormant.

Pop trends shifted from month to month, and for the moment guitar-based rock 'n' roll was on a downswing. "A point came where Stax Records started influencing music to have more brass and orchestral stuff," Page would reminisce. "The guitar started to take a back trend with just the occasional riff.[97] . . . The sax players and violinists used to look at me as though I were some kind of joke."[98] One violin player, however, did deign to chat with the increasingly sidelined mod electric guitarist—this was a man named David McCallum, Sr., father of the *Man from U.N.C.L.E.* television heartthrob and an occasional player with both the London Philharmonic and Royal Philharmonic orchestras. He asked Page if he had ever tried to bow his instrument as a violin. "I said I didn't think it would work because the bridge of the guitar isn't arched like it is on a violin or a cello. But he insisted that I give it a try." Page borrowed his bow to make a few tentative sweeps of his Custom. The guitar, of course, has a flat fretboard compared to the rounded neck of a violin, making it impossible to play a single string at a time, but the effect, when amplified and otherwise manipulated, was compelling. "Whatever squeaks I made sort of intrigued me. I didn't really start developing the technique for quite some time later, but he was the guy who turned me on to the idea."[99]

Such satisfactions were becoming rarer for Page, though. For every musically challenging session, like John Williams's obscure *The Maureeny Wishful Album,* where Page added sitar (or sitar-sounding) tones to "Dream Cloudburst" and "Early Bird of Morning," there were several standard backings for the likes of Petula Clark, Johnny Halliday, Lulu, Herman's Hermits, Brenda Lee, and unknowns David Jones (later Bowie), Mickey Finn (who later played with Marc Bolan of T. Rex), and Nico (later of the Velvet Underground). Assisting Brian Jones on a sound track for German director Volker Schlöndorff's film *A Degree of Murder* was a one-time diversion. His ultimate letdown by 1966 was finding himself called to make out-and-out "atmosphere" music—"It was a great apprenticeship, until they started making me play elevator Muzak," he reckons. "I started seeing my friends like Jeff Beck and Eric Clapton making waves and I wanted to get out there! I wanted to play fucking *loud*."[100] He worried, as well, that his chops were deteriorating while his peers were getting to stretch out. "I didn't realize how rusty I was going to get until a rock 'n' roll session turned up from France, and I could hardly play. I thought it was time to get out, and I did."[101]

There was light at the end of the tunnel in May 1966. Jeff Beck, who was fighting to keep the Yardbirds airborne with shrieking solos on "Evil Hearted You," "Shapes of Things," and the devastating "You're a Better Man Than I," attempted to branch out with his own recording session that month. He and Page had jammed over some simple chords back at Miles Road, Page playing a Fender twelve-string electric, and Beck heard a bolero beat in the sequence. He recruited the Who's unstoppable Keith Moon to drum for them, and his rhythm section partner John "the Ox" Entwistle was to join him but couldn't or wouldn't make the session—both men were wearying of their role as foils for Pete Townshend and Who singer Roger Daltrey, and Moon arrived at IBC Studios incognito, in a Cossack's hat. Beck and Page had nodding acquaintance and musical respect for studio bassist John Paul Jones, who agreed to sit in, and keyboardist Nicky Hopkins, who also showed up.

The two days' work yielded "Beck's Bolero," a slow-burning electrified entity bearing little resemblance to the Ravel classic and which would not be released until the next year as an independent Jeff Beck single on the B-side of "Hi Ho Silver Lining." But at the time all the players—not least of all Jimmy Page—considered forming a permanent band. Page essentially produced the cut when Yardbirds manager Simon Napier-Bell "just sort of left me and Jeff to do it"[102] (to Beck's displeasure, Page would actually get sole songwriting credit—"Even though [Beck] says he wrote it, I wrote it.")[103] The ensemble considered hiring first Steve Winwood, then the Small Faces' Steve Marriott as their vocalist, until rebuffed by Marriott's manager, the shady

Don Arden (father of Sharon, future father-in-law of Ozzy Osbourne). "The reply came back from his manager's office, 'How would you like to have a group with no fingers, boys?' or words to that effect,"[104] Page said. Both Keith Moon and John Entwistle have gone down as wryly predicting the whole project would go over like the world's biggest lead balloon.

Meanwhile, the Yardbirds themselves needed direction. With a half-dozen decent hits to their credit and tours of the U.S. and Europe under their belt, they had been working hard—like so many groups in that frenzied period, too hard. Bassist and musical arranger Paul Samwell-Smith, whose short hair and stiff demeanor stood out in the armies of swinging moptops, was tiring of the treadmill; vocalist Keith Relf, too, though looking a leaner version of the Stones' doomed Brian Jones, had never been a strong singer and seemed to know how overshadowed he was by the act's succession of star guitarists. On June 18, 1966, Jeff Beck drove Jimmy Page to a Yardbirds gig at the May Ball of Queen's College, Oxford. Relf was drinking and started trying karate moves backstage with Allan Clarke of the Hollies, who were also appearing—he broke his fingers on a chair and was propped up onstage feeling no pain. In the audience, Page was amused by Relf's condition and his obscene insults lobbed at the posh undergrads ("Everyone's in monkey suits and he started to slag 'em all off"),[105] but onstage Samwell-Smith's patience was at an end. After the show (such as could be rescued) the bassist announced he was quitting the band, advising rhythm guitarist Chris Dreja to join him. Dreja held out, but it was the chance both Jeff Beck and Jimmy Page had been waiting for: at Beck's keen recommendation, he would join his old friend to fill the sudden vacancy in the Yardbirds.

On bass. This was a temporary measure, giving Dreja time to learn Samwell-Smith's parts in off-hours before letting the two superior guitar players perform together. The rest of the Yardbirds, Keith Relf and drummer Jim McCarty, were supportive of doubling the group's guitar hero component, and knew Page himself was happy to come on board: "He was very gentlemanly and accommodating, and quite well spoken," McCarty has said. "Very easy to get on with, very businesslike."[106] "He was very sweet and wanted to please," agrees Dreja. "He'd do anything for you until his ego got in the way."[107] The Yardbirds had all known Page as a session regular and blues devotee and had seen him casually for years. "I used to meet him outside, of all places, a tropical fish store in Tolworth," Dreja looked back. "Jimmy was a tropical fish enthusiast and he'd say something like, 'Hello, Chris, I've just bought a nice thermometer for my fish.' He was a strange guy, even then."[108] McCarty had met him when Eric Clapton was on lead guitar: "He came to a gig when Eric was still in the band and he was with Jackie DeShannon. He looked pretty cool, a bit of a rock star."[109] Now that he was an official band member—booked for what would be his first public gigs since 1963—Page was ready to dress the part. "He made a point of getting the right sort of clothes, getting these old military jackets," McCarty has noted, adding that "Jimmy seemed to be interested in perversions. He didn't talk about it very much. Every now and then he'd start talking about instruments of perversion and the Marquis de Sade."[110] Yardbird publicity photos of the era show the muttonchopped Page wearing German war surplus lapel pins of a swastika-brandishing eagle.

Page's first shows with the Yardbirds came just nights after the Samwell-Smith departure. Though inexperienced on bass (Dreja's model was an Epiphone), Page took to the instrument congenially—"I offered to play bass though I'd never played one in my life before. . . . I knew their act and what they were doing and learned enough to get through"[111]—and his fill-in spot may have given him a special appreciation for its low registers that would later come in handy. After a few weeks of gigs in the U.K., the quintet traveled to North America for their third tour of the continent, Page's first. The great distances and widely varying venues of the New World exposed the newest Yardbird to the fatigue of his bandmates, and in particular the erratic showmanship of Jeff Beck. "Jimmy was so professional and very fresh, as he hadn't been on the road,"[112] Chris Dreja acknowledged. Beck's lead guitar, promoted as the act's main attraction, could be dazzling at one concert and barely passable the next, and emotionally both he and Keith Relf were fraught. "I was pretty unbalanced when I joined the group," Beck would concede. "I was twenty, which is pretty young to be marched off from rags to riches. I got really sort of messed up."[113] Stumbling under tonsillitis and other health problems, and his mind on a pretty Californian named Mary Hughes, Beck temporarily dropped out of the Yardbirds on the western leg of the tour—on August 25, 1966, at San Francisco's Carousel Ballroom, Dreja switched to bass and Jimmy Page took over lead guitar. Impromptu though it was, it worked, and Page not for the last time acquitted himself well as the virtuoso instrumentalist of an electric English blues band.

Back in England the Yardbirds regrouped. Page and a recovered Beck now planned a twin lead-guitar attack, jamming over numbers like Freddie King's great "I'm Going Down" to perfect a back-and-forth effect they hoped would revive the band's fortunes. Their next single, "Happenings Ten Years Time Ago," featured the two squealing over a surreal, incessant boogie on the cutting edge of psychedelia '66, and Page played bass on its fast-rocking B-side, "Psycho Daisies," but the record did not hit. Another slew of shows around Britain saw them opening for Ike and Tina Turner and the Rolling Stones, with powerhouse stage showdowns between Beck's Les Paul and Page's Telecaster. To the mounting consternation of Beck, Page usually came off the winner. "I'd find that I was doing what I was supposed to," Page would analyze, "while something totally different would be coming from Jeff. That was all right for the areas of improvisation, but there were other parts where it just did not work."[114]

Simon Napier-Bell, a mostly hands-off manager for better or worse (he had taken over from Giorgio Gomelsky in April '66), had secured a film deal for the Yardbirds to appear in *Blow-Up*, director Michelangelo Antonioni's elliptical mystery set in Swinging London, starring David Hemmings and Vanessa Redgrave. Ultra-hip in the mid-'60s but badly dated today, the movie's best sequence is actually the Yardbirds' musical interlude when Hemmings wanders through a trendy discotheque while the group play the compulsive "Stroll On," a thinly disguised (for copyright reasons) version of their standout "Train Kept A-Rollin," which they had adapted from Johnny Burnette's Rock 'n' Roll Trio. Page is seen in medium shot playing his Tele before an improbably immobile clientele, nameless long-haired English pop yob. Antonioni was infatuated with the Who's self-destructing stage show and directed Jeff Beck to smash his Les Paul à la Pete Townshend ("Tell Mr. Antonioni to shove it,"[115] Beck returned), so a run of cheap Hofners were sacrificed for multiple takes at the Elstree Studios set. "The funny thing was that I'd once aspired to having one of those,"[116] Page thought, looking on.

There was no letup. In October the Yardbirds went back to America for an ill-considered Dick Clark "Caravan of Stars" package tour where they crisscrossed the nation by bus, alongside people like Gary Lewis and the Playboys ("This Diamond Ring") and Brian Hyland ("Mission Bell"). Page: "It was the worst tour I've ever been on as far as fatigue is concerned. . . . We didn't know where we were or what we were doing."[117] By the end of the month Jeff Beck cracked for good, throwing a malfunctioning amplifier out a window and threatening Keith Relf with his guitar in the dressing room. He stormed off from Harlingen, Texas, to the arms of Mary Hughes in Los Angeles, leaving Page as sole guitarist in the Decatur, Alabama, high school auditorium, the Paintsville, Kentucky, high school gymnasium, the Michigan state fair, and comparable high-class joints. Retreating to England in December, Napier-Bell and the rest of the Yardbirds dismissed Jeff Beck. They had no other options. Gigging and recording continued. There was still no letup.

As 1967 dawned, the now-four-piece Yardbirds had become more successful as a live act than as recording artists. Whatever the other members' attitudes toward it, Jimmy Page was up for their nonstop itinerary of concerts: he gave the Telecaster a homemade op-art paint job ("Everyone painted their guitars back then"),[118] rewired its pickups, and started to bow it in performance, changing the band's sound from raw white blues into something louder, more abstract, more distorted. He also did some songs with a Vox electric twelve-string, and he was plugged into bright Vox AC-30 amplifiers. The quartet journeyed throughout Britain and Ireland, over to Western Europe and down to Australia, New Zealand, and Singapore with Roy Orbison and the Walker Brothers (Page returned alone via Bombay, India; "I really busked my way through the trip")[119] before revisiting their most lucrative market—the United States. American audiences were receptive to the Yardbirds' souped-up, stretched-out electric boogie, and subsequently guitarists like Joe Walsh and Aerosmith's Joe Perry would cite Page's guitar spotlights of these tours as formative points in their own musical development. It was in the U.S. in 1967 that Page caught guitarist Jake Holmes doing a song called "I'm Confused," with its foreboding, downward-spiraling bass line, which Page appropriated for the Yardbirds' act, layered under fuzz and his latest effects acquisition, a wah-wah pedal. The onomatopoeic wah-wah allowed the musician to rapidly oscillate the pitch of notes between treble and bass, giving them their unique "underwater" tone. Page enjoyed America, where the most progressive groups, e.g., Vanilla Fudge, Captain Beefheart, and Moby Grape, were freed from the commercial and technical constraints of his homeland.

In London once again, however, the Yardbirds were typecast as a pop group who made singles, and even those, such as "Little Games," were barely scraping into the charts (despite its string arrangement by the ever-familiar John Paul Jones). Simon Napier-Bell, whose biggest feat had been scoring their *Blow-Up* platform, had few regrets over relinquishing management of the band ("Jimmy thought I was an inexperienced manager and that he knew more than I did—he was probably right!");[120] recording sessions from now would be handled by Mickie Most, a former singer and all-round impresario who had worked in the English and South African music businesses since the '50s. Energetic but creatively shortsighted, Most wrangled the Yardbirds into doing lightweight tracks like "Ha Ha Said the Clown" and "Ten Little Indians" that showed little indication of the free-form potentials Page had discovered in the ballrooms of the U.S. Catchy two-minute hits were Most's specialty. Page did manage to get one of his own pieces, "White Summer," on tape, an Indian-styled instrumental played on a Danelectro guitar in the DADGAD tuning he had heard Bert Jansch play. An inexpensive and un-sexy electric, the Danelectro was favored by Page for open-tuned work. The song itself was a recognizable interpretation of the English folk song "She Moved Through the Fair," earlier remade by Davey Graham.

"I'm not putting Mickie down," Jimmy Page has commented on Most's tenure in the studio with the Yardbirds, "because he was so good at his singles thing, but . . . it wasn't right for the Yardbirds." In fact Page, who by 1967 had learned more than a thing or two about record production himself, was appalled at Most's amateurishness. "He'd do the mono mix and go home and let the engineer do the stereo mix. But we knew that in the States it was about people listening to things on stereo head-phones.[121] . . . We weren't even allowed to hear playbacks."[122] This slapdash modus operandi was an object lesson for Page on what not to do, but, luckily, Napier-Bell's resignation had brought Most and his dubious musical direction on board with a partner who would handle the Yardbirds' business affairs. His name was Peter Grant.

Jimmy Page had first met Grant via Mickie Most, during his session days. Now the two had become financially bound to each other as performer and manager in a relationship that would last over twelve years and reap fabulous fortunes for both. Unlike Most, Grant made no claims to musical judgment; his personal tastes were for '50s stars like Elvis and Little Richard. His real ability was as a collector of earnings, a trade he had learned kicking around the fringes of British show business in the 1950s as a stagehand, bouncer, pro wrestler, movie and television bit player, acting double (for Anthony Quinn and Robert Morley), and tour manager for visiting American rock 'n' roll acts Gene Vincent, the Everly Brothers, Bo Diddley, and Chuck Berry. Grant found out early the crooked or dirty dealings behind the allure of stage and screen, where promoters and booking agents regularly cut corners and greased palms, and his fatherless, penniless childhood in Battersea, plus a formal education that ended at age thirteen, instilled in him a cold-hard respect for cold-hard cash. Over six feet tall and overweight to the point of obesity, he used his size to intimidate reluctant or evasive middlemen, and made verbal and physical aggression prime elements of his negotiating tactics.

At the same time Grant considered himself scrupulously honest and loyal in a profession that was usually neither, and he took great pride in winning for his clients (hitherto the New Vaudeville Band of "Winchester Cathedral" fame were his biggest) no more and no less than what they had coming. Jimmy Page and Peter Grant, waiflike middle-class rock 'n' roller and strong-arm blowhard dealmaker from the slums, saw an unlikely ally in each other. Simon Napier-Bell warned Grant that his new client, the smart Yardbird guitarist who'd saved his money working the studios and living with his parents, was a "stirrer in the band." Grant relayed this to Page, who didn't disagree. "Troublemaker? You're dead right. We did *Blow-Up*, four weeks in America and a Rolling Stones tour of Britain and we got just £118 each."[123] Chris Dreja confirmed the acuteness of Page's swindle antennae: "As a businessman he had quite a tough edge to him because he'd spent a lot of time around producers and had probably picked up all the vibes."[124] Soon enough Grant would come to the same opinion. "If you want to bump off Jimmy Page," he later joked, "all you have to do is throw tuppence in front of a London bus."[125]

The Yardbirds did some desultory recording and gigging in England and France through 1967–1968, preparing for what would likely be their final tour of the U.S. in the spring. Page was now leading the band with "I'm Confused" (somewhat rewritten and rearranged into "Dazed and Confused") and a fast number, "Think About It," marked by his flashiest electric solo to date. Full of quick bends and quicker blues licks, sounded through the high-pitched single-coil pickups of the Telecaster, "Think About It" would be grafted onto "Dazed and Confused" to produce Led Zeppelin's first showstopper. Taking the stage in colorful velvets and a carefully permed halo of black curls, the Fender now hanging lower on his thighs as he played, Page had remade this ultimate incarnation of the Yardbirds into a prototype of his next band, whether he knew it or not. At some gigs the openly psychedelic intervals would echo with taped blasts of Adolf Hitler's speeches and ferry whistles, Page's own *musique concrète*. In March the Yardbirds went to America.

Keith Relf and Jim McCarty were, by this time, just going through the motions. Worn out from nearly five straight years of playing and traveling, they were both interested in softer music; they were also partying hard. McCarty missed several concerts in the previous year's circuit and numerous stand-ins had to be recruited. "We were in LA, and I was really into what we were doing," Page remembered, ". . . we all got together in a room and Keith—who was drinking a lot and not a happy man—said that he and Jim wanted to go off and do something else."[126] Relf told Page that for him the enjoyment of being a Yardbird vanished with Eric Clapton. Even so, Page pushed the group to at least fulfill its recording and live contracts, bringing to Columbia Studios in New York City some new songs he wanted to get down, including a plaintive ballad titled "Knowing That I'm Losing You." Perhaps a wistful tribute to Jackie DeShannon (he was spotted with a brunette named Lynn Collins that trip), the Yardbirds' "Knowing" was never finished, but Page brought it out again with Led Zeppelin, where it became the beautiful "Tangerine." There was no personal animosity between the individual members: at one show Relf spotlighted Page as the "Grand Sorcerer of the Magic Guitar," and Page would avow, "They were a great band. . . . I was never ashamed of playing in the Yardbirds."[127]

He liked to play offstage as well. Relf and McCarty had taken to LSD and other drugs, and notwithstanding his professionalism it's probable that Page shared the odd toke or trip with his bandmates. In the next century the guitarist admitted, "For me drugs were an integral part of the whole thing, right from the beginning."[128] For this tour, in addition, Peter Grant employed Richard Cole, a young road manager with a hardscrabble background that matched his own. Londoner Cole had drifted into the English rock scene in the early '60s, hanging out with and then lugging equipment for Ronnie Jones and the Nighttimers, Unit Four Plus Two, and the Who, then graduating, under Grant, to the New Vaudeville Band and the Yardbirds. By all accounts a competent and fiercely protective tour supervisor who got his charges to hotels and venues on time and who shared his boss's sharp instincts for the fair cut, Cole also mixed liberal doses of sex and drugs with his rock 'n' roll. Outgoing, reckless, and quick to violence where Jimmy Page was frail and reserved, Cole became Page's willing enabler in many senses of the word.

The tour's end in Montgomery, Alabama, coincided with the assassination of Robert F. Kennedy, on June 5, 1968. Shortly afterward, Peter Grant, who accompanied his bands whenever possible, gathered the Yardbirds in a Holiday Inn and drafted an agreement whereby Jimmy Page would maintain possession of the group's name following the breakup. The amiable Chris Dreja was hanging on for the moment, although he, too, was "knackered" and had taken an interest in photography. A funereal performance at Luton Technical College on July 7 marked the terminus of the band in England (where they had become almost irrelevant), and from there Keith Relf and Jim McCarty went on to record together, eventually forming their own act, Renaissance. Their loose affiliation would be cut short in 1976, when the tragic Relf died of electric shock in his London home at the age of thirty-three.

Always in demand as a session player, Page made a successful re-entry into the studios helping bassist Chris Stainton and drummer B. J. Wilson find the right tempo for a Beatles cover they were working on with a boozy blues belter from Sheffield. Joe Cocker's "With a Little Help from My Friends" rode Page's guitar to glory, turning into a worldwide hit and launching Cocker's stardom, but by the summer of '68 lone Yardbird Jimmy Page needed a lot of help from friends he had yet to find.

Between his earnings as a hired guitarist and the money he'd made with the Yardbirds, Page could now afford his own home. He settled into a boathouse in Pangbourne, in Berkshire, near the head of the Thames River. Already collecting antiques—a hobby he shared with Peter Grant—the house was decorated with seventeenth- and eighteenth-century pieces he'd picked up in his travels and had a large four-poster bed. Stereo and musical equipment were everywhere. But the Yardbirds as a legal unit were still under obligation for dates in Scandinavia, and Page didn't plan to get comfortable. Grant recalled driving with him and asking him his next move. "We were in a traffic jam and I said to Jimmy, 'What are you going to do, do you want to go back to sessions or what?' And he said, 'Well, I've got some ideas.' He didn't mention anybody."[129]

Thinking over his experience with American audiences, he would have been aware that listeners were increasingly drawn to heavy guitar-dominated music, extended improvisational passages, and carefully plotted buildups and releases, high volume next to deafening silence. The Yardbirds, of course, had been only one of several groups pursuing this route, and hardly the most famous. The Who were proceeding with their awesome stage shows and guitarist Pete Townshend's compositions were becoming more ambitious, pointing the way to his dramatic "rock operas"; mollified for now, Keith Moon and John Entwistle had coalesced into an impregnable and *extremely* loud rhythm section that underpinned everything Townshend and Roger

Daltrey did over top. In 1966, Page's old mate Eric Clapton, following his work with the Bluesbreakers, had joined drummer Ginger Baker and bassist Jack Bruce to put the cream of British instrumentalists into a single band, named exactly what they were. Cream's "power trio" format, featuring long drum solos and guitars roaring out through a wall of amplifiers, had struck gold in both Europe and North America, albeit at an emotional cost to the temperamental musicians. Most of all, there was that left-handed colored American cat who had been brought to the U.K. in late '66 under the auspices of the Animals' Chas Chandler and then blew everyone away in California the following year, when he set his Stratocaster on fire.

Jimmy Page never saw Jimi Hendrix perform. "I was doing sessions when he first came over and Jeff [Beck] would come 'round and say, 'There's this wild man, he's fantastic, he does this and he does that...'[130] Well, being in the Yardbirds and then Zeppelin, it was always, 'Oh well, I'll see him next time.' And then there wasn't a next time."[131] He couldn't have missed Hendrix's music, however: solid blues chops that went through a battery of distortion, echo, sustain, and feedback before squalling out as sci-fi extravaganzas. Like Cream and the Who, Hendrix made high-voltage guitar the star of the show—no Mickie Most–style teenybopper ditties for him.

Page heard all three acts and came up with a blueprint, taking care to factor in his own creative and business preferences. "I had in my mind exactly what I wanted to try and get together.... I wanted to do the sort of work that I'd managed to expand around the Yardbirds' material . . . a lot of riffs of my own, and ideas, and passages, and movements and things. That, along with incorporation of the acoustic work[132] . . . I wanted Zeppelin to be a marriage of blues, hard rock and acoustic music, topped with heavy choruses."[133] He had Peter Grant on his side, too, to balance the books and enforce contracts with a heavy hand. "I wanted artistic control in a vice grip."[134]

Page had penciled Chris Dreja in as part of his lineup, but

the bassist's Yardbirds whirl had all but depleted him. Without explicitly backing out, Dreja stood by while Page put the word out that he was forming a band, and thus the sequence of enlistment into Led Zeppelin over July, August, and September 1968 is jumbled. Jimmy Page definitely knew and had cut tracks with John Paul Jones on numerous occasions (Jones even played bass on the Yardbirds' "Happenings Ten Years Time Ago," "No Excess Baggage," and "Goodnight Sweet Josephine"), but the pair had little social contact and Jones initially approached Peter Grant, who still shared an office with Mickey Most, to convey his interest. Jimmy Page did *not* meet Jones at the sessions for Donovan's "Hurdy Gurdy Man," as often retold—the guitarist there has been variously identified as Allan Holdsworth or an Ollie Halsell—although Page and Jones could well have played on other Donovan material.

Page's first concern was finding a vocalist: he needed someone stronger than Keith Relf, someone with a voice and presence akin to Joe Cocker's or Jeff Beck protégé Rod Stewart's. His and Grant's short list still numbered Steve Marriott, but Terry Reid, who had once sang with Peter Jay and the Jaywalkers on a bill with the Yardbirds, was the top choice. "I remembered him as being a really good singer," Page said, "so I told Peter that I wanted to start a group with Terry Reid."[135] Reid, though, had already signed a deal with Mickie Most (of all people) and Grant had misgivings besides—"He had a dreadful father who I had to deal with."[136] Begging off, Reid told Page and Grant of a singer he knew and liked, up around Birmingham. "[Page] said, 'What does this singer look like?'" Reid reported. "I said, 'What do you mean, what does he look like? He looks like a Greek god, but what does that matter? I'm talking about his singing.'"[137] Reid also spoke to Robert Plant, the singer in question, informing him that he could get himself under consideration as the Yardbirds' new front man.

Upon tracking Plant down via telegram and listening to one of his demo tapes, Page went north, Peter Grant and Chris Dreja in tow, to hear him in person. The vocalist was scheduled at a teachers' college, performing with his latest group Hobbstweedle. Between or before sets, Plant, wearing a University of Toronto sweatshirt, let the Southerners in the back door and Page nudged Grant, "Crikey, they've got a big roadie."[138] Onstage, the "roadie" let loose a soaring tenor moan and Page's first thoughts were that such talent had to come with a crippling personality handicap that kept him from already being a star. To find out, he invited Plant to Pangbourne to get acquainted.

Just twenty, the impoverished singer got off the train near Page's home only to be berated by an elderly woman over his long hair. "It was the real desperation scene, man, like I had nowhere else to go,"[139] he would recollect. Jimmy Page, established insider, and Robert Plant, starving artist, got along well, going through the host's record collection while Page described his ideas for a rock group that could do both hard rock and gentle folk—everything from Muddy Waters's "You Shook Me" to Joan Baez's "Babe I'm Gonna Leave You." "He had a demeanor which you had to adjust to," Plant would say. "It certainly wasn't very casual to start with."[140] Jimmy Page also let his guest know that there was a big market in the States for this type of thing; he'd been in the Yardbirds and had seen it firsthand. "I mean," thought Plant, "when someone comes along and says, 'Come with us, you're going to make a lot of money,' you think he's got to be joking so you say, 'Okay.'"[141] Brimming with excitement, Robert Plant left Pangbourne to tell an old friend about the gig.

With unplayed Yardbirds shows slated, Grant and Page continued to toss names around. B. J. Wilson of Procol Harum, ex-Bluesbreaker Aynsley Dunbar, session pro Clem Cattini, and Chris Dreja's associate Paul Francis were mentioned as drummers but found unavailable or unwilling. Robert Plant gushed to Page about his chum and sometime bandmate John Bonham, then playing with American Tim Rose, and a curious Page caught a Rose appearance at North London's Country Club. It may be that Jimmy Page had already heard *of* an unusually loud stickman from the Midlands who'd played with various short-lived bands, but had he heard him directly there would have been no forgetting it. Some portent of his future might have flashed through his ears and brain at the Tim Rose gig: "I wasn't ready for John Bonham, I must say. He was beyond the realms of anything I could possibly have imagined.[142] . . . When I saw what a thrasher Bonzo was, I knew he'd be incredible.[143] . . . It was immediate."[144]

For Page, not Bonham. Married, father of a two-year-old boy, and living in a trailer, the drummer was at last getting steady work with Tim Rose and beginning to field offers from name singers Chris Farlowe and Joe Cocker. His long-suffering wife, Pat, fretted about him teaming up with that hopeless dreamer Robert Plant again—"Every time you do anything with him you come back at five in the morning with half a crown!"[145] The Yardbirds, whether new or old, seemed like a dead end for him. But Page was persistent, sending no less than forty telegrams to Bonham's local pub (he had no phone) to arrange a meeting. Peter Grant was in San Francisco as Page began his persuasion, and was shocked to be called on the guitarist's bill. "Jimmy Page? Making an outgoing phone call to America? I knew something important had happened,"[146] he cracked. "I saw a drummer last night and this guy plays so good and so loud we must get him!"[147] exclaimed Page.

In time Bonham was won over. Page and Grant took him to lunch, spelling out what Page insisted was a "once in a lifetime"[148] opportunity, and now there was at least a tentative formation of musicians who could be billed as the New Yardbirds. It was then that Chris Dreja cast his lot with photography, and John Paul Jones, who had never had to prove himself to Page, was officially brought in. "He didn't need me for a job," Page knew, "but he felt the need to express himself and figured we could do that together."[149] A small rehearsal space was booked in London's Soho district, at Gerrard and Lisle streets near Leicester Square, and the quartet gathered for the first time on or about Monday August 19, 1968. Plant and Bonham had never met Jones and barely knew Page ("I didn't know Jimmy and I felt a bit shy. . . . He was the big star,"[150] Bonham later conceded); they were enclosed by instruments and amplifiers and were uncertain how to begin.

Jimmy Page suggested they try a Yardbirds favorite, "Train Kept A-Rollin'," the locomotive riff of G and A over the open low E string that had rumbled over many a crowd in North America. Plant and Bonham knew the number but Jones, cradling his Fender Jazz bass, didn't and was given a short tutorial. Then someone counted down and then, for a few bars in that stifling room in Soho in late summer, it must have seemed like the walls and ceiling melted away, as destiny closed in and the world opened up for Robert Plant, John Bonham, John Paul Jones, and Jimmy Page.

When the Levee Breaks
1968-1970

I cannot even say that I crossed the Abyss deliberately. I was hurled
into it by the momentum of the forces which I had called up.

—ALEISTER CROWLEY,
CONFESSIONS

The assembly of personnel who would form the performing and
recording group known as Led Zeppelin was a joint venture of
professional musician Jimmy Page and his manager, Peter Grant,
who held both short-term stakes in a nominal extension of the
Yardbirds' act and an open-ended interest in the transatlantic
market that had showed such tantalizing promise for the music
Page and the latter-day Yardbirds had begun to develop. The recordings and concurrent live appearances by which Led Zeppelin
established their commercial reputation were accomplished in
the space of eighteen months. Jimmy Page, the band's producer
and guitarist as well as its conceptual designer, was twenty-four
years old when Led Zeppelin was put together.

The immediate goal was to perfect a set of songs that could
satisfy the expectations of promoters in Sweden and Denmark,
where the Yardbirds had a modest but workable following. Since
Page owned the rights to that group's title, he and Grant were
within their lawful bounds in substituting Robert Plant, John
Paul Jones, and John Bonham for Keith Relf, Chris Dreja, and

Jim McCarty: trade papers and publicity handouts in August and September 1968 announced the imminence of the "New Yardbirds," or the "Yardbirds with Jimmy Page," or the "New Yardbirds featuring Jimmy Page." In days to come this sort of equivocation would complicate matters for, say, the Temptations or the Beach Boys, but there had never been any hiding the split of the "old" Yardbirds who were known to be, by then, a spent force.

Through August, Page, Jones, Plant, and Bonham rehearsed, at the Gerrard Street base and then at Page's home in Pangbourne. The chemistry was apparent from their first notes of "Train Kept A-Rollin'," and the players were, to a man, exhilarated by it. "At the end," Page said, "it was like, 'Shit! What was that?' Like the collective energy of the four individuals made this fifth element. . . . Everybody sort of went, 'Wow!'"[1] "The power of it was remarkable,"[2] agreed Robert Plant. John Paul Jones and John Bonham, each accustomed to an erratic range of rhythm section colleagues, listened to one another with mutual appreciation. "I realized he knew what he was doing," Jones described, "so I could immediately work on slotting in. Suddenly he looked up and thought, 'Hang on—here's someone else who knows what he's doing.'"[3] Besides "Train," the numbers the four got down that month included "Dazed and Confused," Yardbirds staples "I'm a Man" and "For Your Love," Plant's choice of Garnet Mimms's "As Long as I Have You," and blues gems like Albert King's "The Hunter" and Otis Rush's "I Can't Quit You Baby."

Before he and the others could embark across the North Sea, Jones himself owed some studio duties, so he won the New Yardbirds some paid run-throughs backing up P. J. Proby, a transplanted Texan who had been singing in England for several years. With Plant banging a tambourine, Jones, Page, and Bonham lit into a loose jam that ended up on record as "Jim's Blues." "I've got news for you," Proby informed them. "You're going to go down great."[4] Shortly following this, the quartet went to Copenhagen, Denmark, where they played in public for the first time on Saturday, September 7, at two local teen clubs. "We were disappointed it wasn't really the Yardbirds,"[5] a Danish photographer recollected. For another week they trekked around the Nordic lands with small shows in Stockholm and Göteborg ("They were so loud it almost hurt,"[6] ran a Swedish review), then returned to London to make a record.

With the Scandinavian gigs out of the way there were no more obligations to the Yardbirds card (although Chris Dreja was said to have requested the appellation be conclusively put to rest). Jimmy Page and Peter Grant had already registered a publishing company, brazenly listed as "Superhype," but what to call the act itself? Page had always remembered Keith Moon and John Entwistle laughing that the "Beck's Bolero" lineup would fail in earth-shaking proportions, and "Mad Dogs" and "Whoopee Cushion" were mercifully vetoed before the guitarist decreed that Moon and Entwistle's ironic expectations of going down like a lead zeppelin deserved a defiant revisit. Amusing as a once-heard joke, Jimmy Page and Peter Grant made it immortal with the deliberate misspelling, making sure no one (particularly in North America) would confuse the first word's meaning of "heavy metallic element" with the verb for "cause to go with one, esp. by guiding."

This shameless makeshift phonetics became hugely influential in rock music and its descendants: Def Leppard, Megadeth, Krokus, Ratt, Mötley Crüe, even Def Jam, Outkast, Heavy D and the Boyz, and Snoop Doggy Dogg. The article-less "Led Zeppelin," in contrast to the older, straightforward plural style of *the* Crickets, *the* Beatles, or *the* Doors, was itself anticipated by band names Iron Butterfly, Moby Grape, and Vanilla Fudge, and would shape the three- or four-syllable nomenclature of countless acts of the following decade, e.g., Lynyrd Skynyrd, Black Sabbath, Thin Lizzy, Uriah Heep, Iron Maiden, and Judas Priest. Finally, the Teutonic implications of the airship designer's family surname invested a gothic sensibility to the ensemble's work, subsequently envied by Nazareth, Kiss (incorporating the lightning-bolt SS logo), Van Halen, Mötley Crüe, Blue Öyster Cult, and Mötorhead.

Both Jimmy Page and Peter Grant had decided that the group would not rush to put out singles, and in any event they as yet had no record contract (as a Yardbird Page was signed to Epic in the U.S., but there were no claims to him as a member of any other band). They were turned down for a space in the Rolling Stones' upcoming *Rock and Roll Circus* music film, to no serious detriment. Grant had formulated the strategy early on, remembered by Simon Napier-Bell: "Peter thought that if you put a single out you were competing to get into the chart, and if you don't get into the chart, you are then a failure. If you don't put a single out, you can't be a failure."[7] Page wanted to likewise bypass the 45 format, hearing them as a two-minute artistic straitjacket. Albums, like Cream's *Wheels of Fire,* the Jimi Hendrix Experience's *Axis: Bold as Love,* and the Beatles' landmark *Sgt. Pepper's Lonely Hearts Club Band,* were the trend of the times. They cost more to make, and to buy, but the hip, affluent youth undergrounds in Britain and America had turned them from a high-overhead pop sideline to the coin of the rock 'n' roll realm.

In early October, Page reserved time at Olympic Studios in Barnes (southwest London) with his own money, most of it saved from his session jobs rather than the sparse nets of the Yardbirds, and hired longtime Epsom mate and studio staffer Glyn Johns to engineer the sessions. Page had chosen himself to produce an album of tracks, meaning he would be formally in charge of recording, mixing, and sequencing the music (which gave him the authority to request retakes and overdubs, to approve equipment used, and to keep an eye on the clock) and selecting its packaging. A bold conceit in the era—rather like an actor designating himself to direct a play in which he also starred—it would in retrospect be apprehended as Jimmy Page's masterstroke and effectively the culmination of his career. And though the group's rehearsals and its primary concerts had been encouraging, it was not until the microphones went live and the tape started rolling that the depths of his performers' talent, and his own, became clear.

The musician's musician in Led Zeppelin, John Paul Jones was born John Baldwin in 1946, in Sidcup, Kent. His parents were working entertainers (father a pianist and arranger, mother a singer and dancer), and he had seen them play on small-scale tours of England alongside wide varieties of other artists: "Jugglers, acrobats, trapeze, animal acts, as well as singers, dancers, etc."[8] Growing up in the '50s, he had taken to the sophisticated sounds of jazz, then rhythm 'n' blues and soul, before drifting into the London session scene at about the same time as Jimmy Page. He, too, had experienced the strains of touring, playing in the backing band of breakaway Shadows Jet Harris and Tony Meehan at age seventeen, alongside Page's one-time instructor John McLaughlin on guitar. "And those were the days when they used to scream all the way through the show,"[9] Jones smirked. Because of his wit, youth, musical literacy and fluency on both bass and keyboards, by the mid-'60s he was a London studio regular, working on many of the same postings as Page and many more besides: Dusty Springfield, Herman's Hermits, Tom Jones, Donovan, and the *Satanic Majesties*–era Rolling Stones.

"My reasons for joining up with Led Zeppelin were purely musical,"[10] John Paul Jones later stated. The medium was a valid vocation to him, not a starstruck fantasy. At ease with theory but tired of loaning out his skills to people who didn't much use them, Jones brought a dispassionate, pragmatic perspective to Olympic Studios that autumn of '68. As a seasoned bassist, pianist, and arranger in one of the capitals of the world music industry, he could write his own ticket and play with whomever he wanted; he just happened to have taken a specialist's interest in rock 'n' roller Jimmy Page's latest project. Electric blues, in fact, was one of the few musical genres in which he did not have a firm grounding, and consequently Jimmy Page's simpler songwriting or jamming notions would sometimes benefit from subtle John Paul Jones embellishments—funky grace notes, treacherous time shifts, and indelible bass fills. At the 1968 sessions, Led Zeppelin recorded two pieces that originated with Jones, "Good Times Bad Times" and "Your Time Is Gonna Come."

Unlike Jones, Page's selection as vocalist had been plucked from obscurity. Robert Plant, born in 1948 and raised in middle-class environs outside Birmingham, was a hungry twenty-year-old who had been knocking on doors since he was a teenager. Few opened. Employment in Andy Long and the Original Jury-men, the Delta Blues Band, the New Memphis Bluesbreakers, the Black Snake Moan, the Crawling King Snakes, the Tennes-see Teens, the Banned, Listen, and (most successful) the Band of Joy were among his amateur and semi-pro credentials—earnest English folk, blues, and R&B cover bands trying to sound more American than Americans and seldom getting far. In 1966, Plant actually managed a record contract and recorded a trio of singles with CBS Records, but sales were scant and he remained just another fringe player with big ambitions and small prospects. To the dismay of his parents and the indulgence of his girlfriend (soon wife), Maureen, he kept trying. "I decided that if I didn't get anywhere by the time I was twenty, I would pack it in."[11] When the star guitarist and his heavy London handler turned up to see Hobbstweedle, Plant was on the verge of his second decade.

But Robert Plant's engagements in so many small-time groups had paid off in one way: the revelation of his voice. Over six feet tall and narrowly built, he turned out to have been equipped with a strong set of lungs that blew out of his throat like a human foghorn, a sustained, almost operatic pitch that more than matched any of the acts' other instruments—including John Bonham's drums in the Band of Joy. Without any prescribed musical technique, he had a natural vocal control that needed no masking by rasps, slurs, or other affectations, and his projection was long and loud without being unintentionally raw. Singers like Rod Stewart, Roger Daltrey, Joe Cocker, and Ian Gillan of Deep Purple had parallel mannerisms to Plant, but none could top his power. "I just could not understand why," Jimmy Page wondered at his initial audience, "after he told me he'd been sing-ing for a few years already, he hadn't become a big name yet."[12]

Perhaps the answer was the most valuable quality that Rob-ert Plant brought to Led Zeppelin—sincerity. Unlike Page and Jones, who kept a certain measure of professional distance from their work, Plant was a wholehearted convert to rock 'n' roll. He really did cry over albums like Love's *Forever Changes*; he really did ascribe to the hippie visions of Buffalo Springfield and the Jefferson Airplane; he really was haunted by the pure emotional-ism of Robert Johnson and Muddy Waters. Offstage, Plant liked getting high and reading J.R.R. Tolkien's *Lord of the Rings* trilogy, which led him to nonfiction studies of Celtic and Norse mythol-ogies, spiritual explorations he and millions of fellow longhairs took very seriously. Above all, his love for the black music of Chicago and the Mississippi Delta was such that he knew the blues like a fire-and-brimstone preacher knew the Bible: quot-ing a line here, a verse there, and a chorus from somewhere else, the bitter poetry of lemons and trains, steady rollin' women and worried minds had been absorbed by him to a degree that it had lost its literal meaning or authorial attribution and became a music of its own. Robert Plant's intuitive blues feeling was not the collector's scholarship of Jimmy Page, but it would sound the cultural reference of Led Zeppelin.

It was Plant's mate John Bonham, however, who really distin-guished himself at Olympic Studios. Another Birmingham-area journeyman who had started early and sat in with provincial groups around the Midlands like Terry Webb and the Spiders (cf. Neil Christian and the Crusaders), A Way of Life, the Aveng-ers, the Blue Star Trio, Steve Brett and the Mavericks, the Crawl-ing King Snakes, the Nicky James Movement, and the Band of Joy, the big builder's son was well liked by other musicians but regularly hired and fired by them. (Curiously, Jimmy Page, Robert Plant, and John Henry Bonham were all named for their fathers.) Chums called him "Bonzo," after a lovable comic strip dog, and while he was a great lad to jam or share a few pints with, his drumming at gigs sometimes made him a liability, because he was just so crushingly, overwhelmingly *loud*. When Page found him playing with Tim Rose, Bonham's fortunes were on the rise—£40 a week!—but he never knew when he might be back hammering nails at his dad's construction sites.

He had always wanted to play the drums; even his name evoked the thud of a tom-tom. Bonham grew up admiring big band legend Gene Krupa, the Motown drummers of the anonymous "Funk Brothers" (Benny Benjamin and Uriel Jones), then acquired a taste for brother Englishmen like Keith Moon, Ginger Baker, and even the Beatles' metronomic Ringo Starr. At a young age, a neighbor turned him on to jazzer Dave Brubeck's Joe Morello, known for his digital dexterity and expertise with unconventional time signatures. But John Bonham liked drums best for their central purpose: "Someone once asked me what technicalities I applied to my playing. I said, 'Technicalities? What the hell are you going on about?' I said, 'This is my technicality,' and raised my hand into the air, and let it fall. Hand to drum, that's what it is, hand to drum.[13] . . . Hit 'em as hard as yer can."[14]

As tall as Robert Plant but stocky where the singer was slim, Bonham's imposing build was the real key to his drumming. He played large Ludwig kits—large in size of the drums, not in their number—and kept both heads (skins) on each piece when many drummers removed the bottom; he also rolled tin foil inside his bass drum to maximize its reverberation. In the same way that Jimi Hendrix's massive hands gave him an authority over the fretboards of his guitars, Bonham had a physical dominance behind the drums that put them all within easy reach, and he sat low on his stool so that his pedal action tended to be full-leg stomps instead of tapped toes. He tuned the big instruments tightly, again punching up their volume. "He was superhuman," asserted Jimmy Page. "Besides being one of the best drummers I've ever heard, he was also one of the loudest. . . . And his playing wasn't in his arms, it was all in his wrist action. Frightening! I still don't know how he managed to get so much level out of a kit."[15] At one practice Page needed to inform Bonham, "You're going to have to keep it a bit more simple than that," and was backed up by Peter Grant, "Do as this man says—or fuck off."[16] Once he harnessed John Bonham, Page had toned the band's metric muscle.

Then there was Jimmy Page himself. A guitar hero already, he had never shone as brightly as a studio player or as a Yardbird as he did on Led Zeppelin's debut. Still using the 1958 Telecaster hotwired through a Roger Mayer–built Tonebender distortion box and a Vox Crybaby wah-wah pedal then into a diminutive tube-driven Supro amplifier ("I like things with valves. . . . I like to see the thing burn when you hit a chord"),[17] he was free to play as fast and as hard as he could, and he did. "Good Times Bad Times," the album's opener, was first outlined by Jones on a Hammond organ but given its explosive crunch by Page, who also whipped off two furious solos for the song of which the second, a breakneck slalom down the E blues scale before the fadeout, was stunning in its virtuosity. Midway through "Dazed and Confused," Jones and Bonham changed into high gear as a runaway steamroller, but Page kept up with a run he had taken in the Yardbirds' "Think About It," now plunged with wah-wah and mimicked by the scat-singing Plant. "Communication Breakdown" was speed metal '68. Page tried the country music implement of a pedal steel guitar for Jones's "Your Time Is Gonna Come" like no honky-tonker had ever dared, and he borrowed an acoustic Gibson J-200 to play the proto-power ballad "Babe I'm Gonna Leave You" (nice Manitas de Plata flamenco flicks overdubbed), and his hyperkinetic reworking of Bert Jansch and the DADGAD tuning on "Black Mountain Side." (Tabla player Viram Jasani sat in with Page for the latter.) Screaming blues licks and bowed Tele strings marked "You Shook Me," "I Can't Quit You Baby," and "How Many More Times."

At the mixing console Jimmy Page's prowess was even more apparent. Glyn Johns was a smart and capable engineer who was turned down for a co-production credit, but Page was in command. "I put this band together," he said to Johns. "I brought them in and directed the whole recording process.... You haven't got a hope in hell."[18] His long-standing gripe as a session man had been careless recording that muffled dynamic performances into a flat midrange. "I was into ambience on the first album, I'll tell you that," he told it long afterward. "Hearing drums sounding like drums.[19] ... When I was playing sessions, I noticed that the engineers would always place the bass drum mike right next to the head. The drummers would then play like crazy, but it would always sound like they were playing on cardboard boxes. I discovered that if you move the mike *away* from the drums, the sound would have room to breathe, hence a bigger drum sound."[20] From this simple device of spacing out microphones to take in the studio acoustics like a human listener and not an electronic implement, Page achieved the vast three-dimensional wallop that was Led Zeppelin's genius. That he was taping John Bonham—the incredible bass triplets on "Good Times Bad Times" set a new standard for drum footwork—allowed him to expand the ambience into a frame of colossal stereophonic breadth. The twelve-inch speaker of the Supro allowed him to maximize its volume, knowing it would thus "record" more loudly than a bigger amp set to medium. Page also juxtaposed the album so that each tune stood out from those before and after it, hence the whiplash jump-cuts from the crescendo of "You Shook Me" to "Dazed"'s ponderous bass and guitar harmonics (Page bending strings behind the Telecaster's nut), and from the acoustic raga of "Black Mountain Slide" to the cranked electric riffing on "Communication Breakdown." Stoned headphone wearers were in for a very heavy trip.

Graphic artist George Hardie was commissioned to illustrate the album cover, from a photograph that Page had decided on: the flashpoint of the Nazi dirigible *Hindenburg*'s destruction at New Jersey in May 1937. Rendered down to a stark black-and-white, the former student of Sutton Art College had cannily picked an image that conjured both phallic potency and fascist cataclysm,

Led Zeppelin's visual shorthand ever after. On the back, the band photograph of the four musicians, average age twenty-one-and-a-half, was taken by Chris Dreja at Page's request. George Hardie himself became a much-sought designer of rock album covers during the medium's twelve-inch heyday, and the principal creator of Pink Floyd's iconic *Dark Side of the Moon* and *Wish You Were Here*, as well as Zeppelin's eerie *Presence*.

Titled only *Led Zeppelin*, the album would become a watershed of rock music and popular culture. Eric Clapton and Jimi Hendrix had played distorted electric blues guitar and Pete Townshend had slammed power chords against slabs of bass and drums, but Jimmy Page had distilled those sounds down to something like pure rhythm, pure riff. "Good Times Bad Times," "Dazed and Confused," "Communication Breakdown," and "How Many More Times" were all in the surly, snarling key of E, which let Page play them on the guitar's lowest open string for the hardest possible sound. Although Hendrix tuned his guitars down to E-flat, he only occasionally stayed there with really chunky patterns ("Little Miss Lover," "Fire," "Manic Depression"), more often moving up the neck for his signature licks. In Cream, Clapton had also come up with fat classics like "Crossroads," "Sunshine of Your Love," and "Born Under a Bad Sign," but he, too, preferred to wail away on the higher strings, while the Who relied on high-voltage chordal progressions ("Pictures of Lily," "Pinball Wizard"), not true blues lines. Jimmy Page broke down the basic blues scale into its component notes, then transposed them to the deep end of the guitar's natural range. He wasn't merely flailing at loud and fuzzed-out whole chords—as were raw American bands like Blue Cheer and the MC5—but *tight*, deadening the bottom strings just enough to give them a steady percussive attack while going over and over those primeval pentatonic minor intervals. In other words, "How Many More Times," "Communication Breakdown," et al.

Only one other guitarist had done anything like it: Jeff Beck. In October 1968, Beck released *Truth*, featuring himself and singer

Rod Stewart backed up by Ron Wood on bass and Mickey Waller on drums. Many would hear *Led Zeppelin* as Page's hurried bid to repeat *Truth*'s arrangements of tough blues and howling voice, as Beck himself did when Page played him an acetate version before release. While the proud Page urged him, "Listen to this, this guy called John Bonham that I've got,"[21] Beck thought, "This is a piss-take, it's got to be."[22] Both albums even contained a version of "You Shook Me" with John Paul Jones playing Hammond organ—"When *we* did it," Page avers, "Jonesy didn't say, 'Oi, I've just done this with Jeff,' because they were so different."[23] Beck's and Page's roots were close enough that both men had gravitated to the same musical styles since they had been playing together and some sort of accidental overlap was likely, but the truth is that *Truth* is a good guitar-based rock album and *Led Zeppelin* is guitar-based rock as a groundbreaking exercise in sculpted sound. Final word: *Truth* was produced by Mickie Most, and *Led Zeppelin* was produced by Jimmy Page.

Led Zeppelin put on their first show under that name in England on October 25, 1968, and commenced a small tour of the country over the following few weeks, appearing at clubs and universities in London, Liverpool, Exeter, and other towns. Fans expecting a revived Yardbirds were unprepared for what they saw—and heard. John Gee, manager at Page's old stomping grounds, the Marquee, was taken aback by their volume. "I thought they were overpoweringly loud for the size of the Marquee. Anyway, the lads received an enthusiastic, but not overwhelming, response from the audience."[24] Keith Altham of the influential *New Musical Express* weekly was not convinced, either. "I lasted the first few numbers and my ears were ringing. I couldn't stand it anymore, so I left." Altham's comments to Peter Grant were frank. "It's all improvised rock without any structure. I can't see it myself."[25] But Grant and Page were looking across the ocean.

Frequent flyers when the "jet set" was still elite company—they crossed the Atlantic the way other people crossed London—Jimmy Page and Peter Grant went to New York in late October to negotiate Led Zeppelin's record deal. Columbia Records' Clive Davis, whose holdings encompassed Epic, the Yardbirds' label, was dismayed and angry when Grant blithely told him that Page's new "solo" enterprise exempted him from Columbia's contractual reach. "Oh, no, we've already signed the Zeppelin to Atlantic,"[26] said the manager. Ahmet Ertegun and Jerry Wexler had scooped Page on hearing the tapes from Olympic, having first met him on his 1965 American visit and knowing too his résumé as a studio wunderkind and last of the Yardbirds' guitar heroes. R&B and soul aficionados from way back, as well as old-fashioned businessmen whose word was their bond, Ertegun and Wexler understood the growing public taste for album-oriented rock with blues pedigrees; they had earlier signed Cream and Iron Butterfly and had designs on the Rolling Stones, whose contract was coming up for sale in 1971. Then again, shortly after their winning Zeppelin bid, Atlantic blew six figures on someone named Cartoone, featuring guest guitarist Jimmy Page.

"Everybody in the band recognized that at first having Jimmy's name was a great help,"[27] John Paul Jones confirmed, although Jones himself was highly endorsed by Dusty Springfield to Jerry Wexler. Page's role as Led Zeppelin's in-house producer was a slight control issue for Atlantic, who hinted the Olympic tracks needed a remix job. "Jimmy said, 'What are they talking about?'" Grant recalled. "I said it's just politics. Tom Dowd [Atlantic production boss] was there and Jimmy foxed him with a few technical questions. That was an early battle we won."[28] Atlantic Records paid Led Zeppelin $200,000 for a five-year distribution deal, at that point a record amount for an unplayed act, with Grant and Page winning key concessions on artistic authority. The premiere album had cost all of £1,782 and thirty hours' effort in the studio.

Grant had scored a major coup, the consequences of which would reverberate throughout the industry. The previous generation of rock 'n' roll artists and managers had operated on the premise that single acts would have at best a couple of hit songs or a year of profitable touring before their popularity declined; men like Mickie Most and Don Arden kept in the black on a rotating stable of performers who were signed and dropped as their fortunes waxed and waned. But by the mid-'6os, steady sales of the Beatles, the Rolling Stones, and Bob Dylan had shown that fans would remain loyal as musicians matured, and indeed the gradual, spontaneous evolution from "She Loves You" to *Sgt. Pepper* and from "Blowin' in the Wind" to *Blonde on Blonde* was precisely what gave such figures their commercial cachet. Disposable pop groups and their Top 40 product were out, and heavy rock bands and their long-playing "statements" were in. As the last year of the '6os loomed, Atlantic Records' Led Zeppelin had made a very big entrance.

The skeptical reaction of British bookers to Led Zeppelin was forgotten in the lead-up to the group's first visit to America. Jimmy Page and Peter Grant had planned for the U.S. to be their main source of revenue, committing to a full schedule of concerts throughout 1969. It was to be a grueling year of almost nonstop travel, performing, and playing that would have tested the stamina of any act, but it would succeed. Led Zeppelin took off from England on Christmas Eve and made their first U.S. gig in Colorado's Denver Auditorium on Boxing Day. Seattle, Vancouver, Spokane, and Portland were visited over the next five days, followed by shows in Los Angeles's famed Whisky-a-Go-Go alongside Alice Cooper. Others who shared stages with Led Zeppelin these nights were the Move, the Wind, Zephyr, and Mother Blues, with Vanilla Fudge at the top of the bill. For now.

Of all the members of the band, Jimmy Page was the only one who had been to the U.S. and the only one who could be considered any kind of celebrity. Leaving his Yardbirds flame Lynn Collins behind, he arrived in L.A. a rock star (carrying on despite a high fever) and turned twenty-five the night Zeppelin played San Francisco's psychedelic capital, the Fillmore Auditorium. As Robert Plant looked back, "We couldn't believe we were in the

States; everything was new to us. Meanwhile, Pagey was walking around like a king, the King of the Yardbirds, with all these chicks."[29] It was ex-Yardbird, one-time Joe Cocker, Kinks, and Donovan backer-up Page who was mentioned front and center in Atlantic's press releases ("Jimmy Paige" in some entertainment listings), the unquestioned top draw of the latest English rock 'n' roll export to America.

Backstage, there was Richard Cole. Peter Grant's tactical liaison, he had decided to road-manage one act rather than juggle three or four, much as Grant had done as a business manager. Cole's reasons were less economic and more personal: "I'm fed up with fucking around with all these other bands you're sending me out with," he told his boss. "I want to stay with Zeppelin. They're going to be big."[30] In 1969, as the group made several circuits of North America's important rock venues, Cole basked in Led Zeppelin's reflected glory. In March they were back in Scandinavia and Britain for more club dates, but *Led Zeppelin* had been released and was climbing the U.S. charts and getting radio airplay. A second crossing to the States was made in April, commencing twenty-four gigs in five weeks, and Cole kept his clients, and himself, well lubricated. Sometime that spring he perpetrated the "shark incident" at Seattle's Edgewater Inn, in which an acquiescent female was defiled with a fresh-caught fish for the diversionary enjoyment of spectators, although Jimmy Page seems not to have witnessed this. But Page may have been around when a reporter from *Life* magazine who was covering the tour was manhandled and had her clothes torn by unnamed group members; hurt and humiliated, her tale added to the shark story and Richard Cole's ongoing ingenuity for excess to give Led Zeppelin a notoriety that had nothing to do with their music.

Days off were a rarity. Hotels, barrooms, swimming pools, airports, airplanes, limousines, and vans were about as much as the musicians saw of America and Canada—and stages. Now they were headliners of their shows with Vanilla Fudge, expanding their sets from the arsenal of *Led Zeppelin*—"Dazed and Confused," "How Many More Times," "I Can't Quit You Baby"—to other blues standards like "Killing Floor" and "Bring It on Home." While the Fifth Dimension's "Aquarius / Let the Sunshine In," Glen Campbell's "Wichita Lineman," and the Beatles' "Get Back" crackled from transistor radios, Led Zeppelin were shaking the rafters at the Kinetic Playground in Chicago and the Boston Tea Party. Monaural AM radio couldn't do them justice, and they'd groped and pawed away any chance of positive publicity from the mainstream press. What good name they would get had to be earned the old-fashioned way.

John Bonham and John Paul Jones were anchoring the act as its juggernaut rhythm duo, and Jones also played Hammond organ for "Your Time Is Gonna Come" and improvised spots. On the boards, Jones was wordless yet dependable, starting off near the footlights but soon gravitating back to the engine room, where he and his partner laid down the beat; his expression always suggested a faint disdain for the whole affair, as if he was missing a much more challenging assignment elsewhere and nothing Page or Bonham threw his way could faze him. Bonham frequently stole the shows with his catastrophic drum solos, playing lengthy passages with his bare hands, roaring and yelling like an animal, and blowing crowds away with his jackhammer energy. "Turning down?" Jimmy Page asked rhetorically. "No, we're getting louder. Our drummer is amazingly loud. I come off stage with my ears ringing."[31] Egged on by Richard Cole and far from his Midlands home, the percussionist was also becoming a troublemaker between gigs. And with his spine-tingling delivery, Robert Plant was developing an onstage persona that merged prophet with prima donna, full of grandiose hand gestures and supplications heavenward. Plant was not a dancer like Mick Jagger, but he took the Stone's style a few steps further, as a singer so confident in his masculinity he could afford to pout, preen, and strut, and puff his hair, sultan of rock 'n' roll sexuality and keeper of the rock 'n' roll flame.

But Jimmy Page remained the mane attraction. The raven-haired warlock to Plant's blond deity, he was already known to his bandmates and managers as being very conscious of his looks, his magnificent black tresses being a prime object of attention. Plant would reminisce about "driving around America in a station wagon with Bonzo and I talking about home and Page saying, 'Shut the window, it's messing my hair up.'"[32] Richard Cole watched him prepare for one appearance: "Jimmy was admiring himself in front of his hotel mirror . . . like a beauty contestant about to strut down the runway. . . . He had curlers in his hair, and after he removed them he spent fifteen minutes brushing his locks." Cole and Peter Grant joked over Page's vanity, but never to his face. "Tell the old girl that the limos are waiting downstairs," they would chuckle. "Isn't it time for the old girl to get dolled up for the concert?"[33]

His guitar work live and on record had won him favorable comparisons to the other stars of the day, singled out next to and over the recently disbanded Cream and the still-kicking Jimi Hendrix. "Jimmy Page ranks with the top pop guitarists," ran one write-up, adding that "Britannia will continue to rule the airwaves so long as new groups like Led Zeppelin continue to come up."[34] For this tour Page was still playing his Telecaster, but he had brought some English-made Marshall amplifiers over with him, after trading in some inferior Rickenbacker cabinets, which he hid under more desirable Fender grilles (a neat little scam akin to selling a Chevrolet body over an Edsel chassis). He had tried Hiwatt, Orange, and Vox amps, but the Marshalls became his model for the duration of Led Zeppelin and beyond. His bow solo during "Dazed and Confused," where the group laid out and he scraped the strings with the dramatic poses of a psychedelic Paganini, was a far-out freakout for the fans, although he had to defend the piece as more than a gimmick. "I use an ordinary violin bow on the guitar," he explained to one music journalist, "given a little more tension on the horsehair . . . plus a lot more rosin. It gives an infinite variety of sounds, ranging from violin to cello and from a whistling wind to a Boeing

707 taking off."[35] Unlike Hendrix, Page had no tremolo arm on his instrument and he was never much for feedback, nor did he smash his Fender as Pete Townshend might, and thus the bow was his limited but nevertheless unique claim to guitar theater.

More inventive was Page's theremin ritual. During the winter of '69 Led Zeppelin had shared some bills with American acid rockers Spirit ("I Got a Line on You"), who deployed one of the strange electronic gizmos in their sets, and Page was inspired to get one of his own. Designed in the '20s by an eccentric Russian émigré named Leon Theremin, the instrument consisted of an antenna that transmuted vibrating waves of air into high-pitched tones that pulsed from small speakers in a cabinet below. With careful, harplike plucking and stroking motions around the theremin's "wand" it was possible to extract actual notes and music from its wires and tubes, but over time the machine had lost its novelty (Theremin himself was forcibly repatriated by the Soviet government), and it became known for its otherworldly descants in '50s movies like *The Day the Earth Stood Still*. In pop music, the warble of a theremin was best heard underneath the Beach Boys' "Good Vibrations," Brian Wilson's idealized surf opus of 1967. It was with these spacey sounds that Page took the theremin out with Led Zeppelin, transmuted through his overdriven amplifiers to lay into audiences even more powerfully than the somewhat affected bowing segment. Coaxing demonic yelps and bleats from the weird antenna, waving his ragged bow over the heads of assembled heads at the Fillmore, the Whiskey, the Circus, or the Tea Party, possessed fingers dancing over the strings of his guitars, Jimmy Page cut a magical figure in 1969.

Each show broke down into a jam session, with Page trading six-string moans and groans with Plant's voice while the implacable Jones and Bonham cemented the vocalist's most derivative blues clichés and the guitar player at his most aimlessly noodling. One April night, though, somewhere in America, they were vamping around with "As Long as I Have You" when Page fired up one of his fat power chords and held on to a repetitive phrase: B-D, B-D-*E*, and again, B-D, B-D-*E*. As was his wont, Robert Plant sang the first thing that came to mind, in this case Muddy Waters's "You Need Love," while John Paul Jones effortlessly put a bottom on Page's already bottom-heavy E root. John Bonham didn't play for a few bars, either trying to find the time in his head or just letting the others stand out before his wrists and feet came in again on top of them all. He soon did, and the attendees at the Winterland or the Fillmore or the Rockpile or wherever it was were treated to the inception of Led Zeppelin's "Whole Lotta Love" and the genesis of heavy metal.

In June, the quartet returned to the U.K., but not to holiday. They did radio and, reluctantly, TV shows in Britain and France (during the Parisian *Tous en scène* television program, the seats were filled with middle-aged people and parents covering the ears of their young children; Page went in hopes of meeting Brigitte Bardot). They played Britain's Bath Festival on June 19 and at the Royal Albert Hall for the Pop Proms, the latter with the dirty blues merchants Fleetwood Mac, acoustic progressives the Incredible String Band and Pentangle (with Bert Jansch), and the Who. "When Led Zeppelin came on and played at a good ten times the volume of everyone else, the audience nearly freaked completely,"[36] observed *Disc* magazine. Then it was back on the runway for the long flight over to the States.

Led Zeppelin was a bona fide hit record—over 200,000 units had been sold in six months—and it needed a follow-up. There was no time to settle in at one studio, much less compose complete songs, so Jimmy Page found himself recording whatever the band had down at any point during their spring and summer travels. Some tracks were nailed at London's Morgan and Olympic Studios, others in what Plant said was "a shed in Vancouver,"[37] and still more in A&R in New York and Mystic in Hollywood. Page sought to avoid relying on one recording engineer—or, worse, be accused of such—so at different times George Chkiantz, Chris Huston, Glyn Johns's brother, Andy, and

Hendrix collaborator Eddie Kramer were on hand to work the dials and spool the tape.

Even more significant to his sonic battery was a show Zeppelin had played with the James Gang, including guitarist Joe Walsh. Walsh, who later joined the Eagles and made great contributions to their epic *Hotel California,* appreciated Page's playing and offered to sell him one of his own guitars, a ten-year-old Gibson Les Paul. (The Les Paul line had then been discontinued since 1961.) "I said, 'I'm quite happy with my Telecaster,'" Page remembered. "But as soon as I played it I fell in love. Not that the Tele isn't user-friendly, but the Les Paul was so gorgeous and easy to play. It just seemed like a good touring guitar."[38] Walsh may have wanted to relinquish the Gibson after having it worked on: "Joe brought it for me when we played the Fillmore. He insisted I buy it, and he was right. . . . It's possible that one of the reasons he wanted to sell me the guitar was that it didn't feel the same to him when he got it back from the shop." Its neck had been shaved down to a slim, extra-playable depth, fitted with low frets, and Page modified it anew with sealed Grover tuning heads. He knew that "with a three-piece like Zeppelin, you couldn't have slipping machine heads."[39] Later the guitarist installed push-pull rotating tone controls, which switched the interior wiring to achieve a "reverse phase" effect, what he called "a close approximation of the sound [Fleetwood Mac's] Peter Green would get, and certainly B. B. King."[40] Its distinctive "Honey Sunburst" coloring was a departure from the period's day-glo custom patterns—flamed, natural wood finishes would be highly prized by guitarists in the coming decade. Apart from cosmetic details, the Les Paul produced a richer, longer tone that didn't depend so much on special distortion boxes for its intensity the way the single-coiled Fender did: "The Gibson's got a stereotyped sound, maybe. . . . But it's got a beautiful sustain to it, and I like sustain because it relates to bowed instruments and everything. . . . When you think about it, it's mainly sustain."[41] Page subsequently acquired a nearly identical 1958 "backup" Les

Paul following his conversion by Walsh (leading to some confusion over whether it really was the '58 or '59 he was more often photographed with during the '70s), and brought his new axes with him to record the new album.

In the high summer of 1969, Neil Armstrong walked on the moon, Ted Kennedy was embroiled in a fatal car accident, Charles Manson instigated a pair of gruesome mass slayings in Los Angeles, 500,000 young people gathered at Woodstock, New York, for an enormous outdoor rock festival, and Led Zeppelin was again touring the continent. Page and Company were playing Southern California the night the entire Sharon Tate household were murdered by, it would emerge, a drug-soaked collection of flower children led by a charismatic guitar player obsessed with the occult; a week later, Peter Grant on behalf of the busy group turned down the opportunity to play alongside Hendrix, Ten Years After, Santana, the Who, and Crosby, Stills, Nash & Young up by Yasgur's Farm. Jimmy Page and John Bonham did consent to recording rock 'n' roll jams in L.A. with Briton Screaming Lord Sutch, a semi-comic performer who inveigled the two to help him produce a solo album. "To cut a long story short," said Page, "he rewrote all the tunes and put another guitarist on top. But, and this is where the criminal side of it comes in, he didn't put 'Extra guitar—So-and-so' . . . he put 'Guitar—Jimmy Page,' so everybody thought, 'Oh, Jimmy Page played on that heap of crap,' and it became more than an embarrassment."[42] The album, *Lord Sutch and Heavy Friends,* was a failure, and both Page and Bonham disowned it. Sutch committed suicide in 1999.

But the City of Angels had its satisfactions. By the late '60s, the traditional feminine adulation that had always been directed at famous and successful male entertainers had evolved into a socio-political movement that was not just about carnal brushes with greatness but a conscious propagation of free love. Rock stars sang how all you need is love, love is all around, asked let's spend the night together, love me two times, and now offered whole lotta love, but the new generation of young women who had grown up on rock 'n' roll were actually practicing what musicians just preached. Called *groupies* by the straight world but avoiding the term themselves, they made a point of guiltless, generous sex with performers who passed through their vicinities, for both their own empowered pleasure and the moral encouragement of those they serviced. Jimi Hendrix called them "band aids. . . . They are just innocent little girls trying to do their thing."[43] Homemakers away from home, den mothers, and concubines in equal measure, Los Angeles held a loose affiliation of such girls, promoted by the (monogamous) Frank Zappa as a kind of lighthearted complement to masculine rock groups: these were the Girls Together Outrageously, or the GTOs.

An organization like the GTOs made eminent sense in 1969. Guitarists and singers came and went (so to speak), but in America's entertainment capital the Girls were the local fixtures. GTO Pamela Miller was twenty years old, pretty, bright, a passionate music fan and just the teensiest bit spoiled, and could legitimately claim to have been temporary muse to Jim Morrison, the Flying Burrito Brothers, and Hendrix bassist Noel Redding. A hormonal adult with a teenybopper mind, her charm and beauty gave her access to wherever homes and nightclubs in Los Angeles visiting rock bands might gather. She first saw the hot new British quartet stop in her city in late April, following them to a groovy watering hole called Thee Experience, where Richard Cole and others in the Zeppelin party started a none-too-private orgy with some bolder women in attendance. Free love was in the atmosphere and sex was on and under the tables. Miss Pamela spied the group's guitarist across the sweaty room. "Jimmy Page sat apart from it all," she wrote in her memoir, *I'm with the Band*, "observing the scene as if he imagined it." Her friend Miss Mercy spotted him, too, warning, "Dangerous man."[44]

A working musician since his teens, Page knew of groupies from way back. "You look for certain things in certain towns," he enlightened one researcher. "Chicago, for instance, is notorious for sort of two things at once."[45] During the initial raids of Led

Zeppelin, he and his entourage had the advantage of anonymity as compared with more or less household names like the Rolling Stones, who also toured the U.S. in 1969. As far as outsiders could tell, Led Zeppelin were just another bunch of Limey noisemakers who needed a decent haircut; anyone who knew who they were would already have been potential friends, or lovers, with whom they could do as they pleased away from the glare of press and police. Jimmy Page made quite a few friends that year, and word of his tastes reached California before he did. He confided to Richard Cole, "My dream is to find a young Joni Mitchell lookalike: thin, angular features, long blonde hair . . . " According to the road manager, he had a default preference: "The younger, the better."[46] In Pamela Miller he found a winning combination.

Page and Miss Pamela began a torrid and, to her, highly emotional affair in August. He first jettisoned Catherine James, a previous L.A. conquest, then took her to an Everly Brothers show where he slipped "Miss P" a ring. "I wondered if I was going steady with the best guitar player in the world," she swooned. Miss Pamela discovered a collection of whips in his suitcase, but he soothed her, "Don't worry, Miss P, I'll never use those on you. . . . I'll never hurt you like that." Page only drank and took drugs in moderation, she saw, and fussed over his hair. Headed for other gigs throughout the States, he requested a special dispensation that she allow him to "do things" while traveling, to stave off boredom. She listened with him as he intently took notes over playbacks of what was to become *Led Zeppelin II* (she thought Bonham's drum solo was interminable), then cringed when he called her from the road to say that the "scenes" he was enjoying were no more than "eating hamburger." She met "Percy" Plant, "Bonzo," and "Jonesy," as well as the imposing "G" (Peter Grant), and even accompanied the band to spectacular shows in New York: "10,500 people just screamed for Jimmy," she wrote in her diary. "God, he drives me nuts, I can't fuck him enough." Finally they had a tearful farewell, after a glorious night where she swore she heard him say, "If I were to marry you, P . . ."[47]

'Twas not to be. Led Zeppelin returned to Europe for some high-grossing concerts in Paris and London, and Page put the finishing touches on their sequel to the first album, as Miss Pamela found solace in the arms of no less than Mick Jagger. When the foursome flew back to the U.S. for their *fourth* tour in less than twelve months (highlighted by acclaimed sets at Carnegie Hall), the romance had cooled—she walked with him while he shopped for rare prints by the Dutch lithographer M. C. Escher, and he pulled the old, "I don't deserve you . . . I'm such a bastard, you know." By the end of the year, Page wired her money to purchase some artifacts of the magnetic cult figure he perhaps newly identified with, and in a Hollywood bookstore Miss P found an original Aleister Crowley manuscript, which she lovingly sent to England. In thanks, he mailed her a gorgeous necklace and enclosed a holiday card, "With all my love at Christmas, Jimmy—XXXXXXX."[48]

On Halloween, 1969, *Led Zeppelin II* was released in America. Unlike its predecessor, it had not been put together over a quietly optimistic couple of weeks in London but during the frantic months of winning the continent with nightly assaults on the eardrums and brains of the Now Generation. It did continue *Led Zeppelin's Sturm und Drang* theme with a brown sleeve and cover art designed by David Juniper, in which the musicians and friends were doctored into a World War I photograph of "Red Baron" Manfred von Richthofen's fighter squadron. Demand was high—there were half a million advance orders in the U.S. alone—and with Jimmy Page again testing the limits of studio technology and his players' ability, it did not disappoint.

The E jam on "You Need Love" had been elaborated into the Olympian "Whole Lotta Love," the minimalist boogie riff and Plant's voice-as-instrument melding into the band's quintessential performance. Page and Eddie Kramer dropped a wildly abstract but somehow appropriate "bridge" into the song, a prototype of industrial rock and sound art, in which the yowling theremin and a variety of tape loops were panned back and forth across the stereo spectrum. It fit. "I told him exactly what I wanted to achieve . . . and he absolutely helped me to get it,"[49] Page praised the engineer. "It's a combination of Jimmy and myself just flying around a small console twiddling every knob known to man"[50] was Kramer's description of the single real-time "take." For a solo Page reeled off a declaratory string of Hendrix-like passages punctuated with barks of the home E5 power chord, played through a wah-wah pressed down to its treble position.

Drenched in reverb as it was, "Whole Lotta Love" featured Page's innovation of *backward* echo, which he had tried as far back as the Yardbirds and on the earlier "You Shook Me," against Glyn Johns's reservations that "Jimmy, it can't be *done.*"[51] This required physical manipulation of the recording tape to re-record an inversion of an already played phrase. "There were lots of different effects," Page discussed afterward, "but the backwards echo was definitely one of them. . . . You turn the tape over—you *did* turn the tape over in those days—and then record the echo which is obviously after the signal; you turn the tape back and it precedes the signal."[52] With that spooky, sliding resonance behind its chorus and its indivisible Page-Plant-Jones-Bonham songwriting credit, "Whole Lotta Love" was a compelling fanfare for the work that would tower over rock 'n' roll for the next decade.

Other tracks carried almost as much punch. "Heartbreaker" drove on what just may be the Killer Riff of All Time, a sinewy ascending blues line played low on the Les Paul, tossed to and fro over John Paul Jones's woofer-rattling bass. This came to a crashing, stop-on-a-dime halt, whereupon Page dropped in an a cappella acid rockabilly solo (recorded elsewhere at a slightly higher pitch) that laid out his claim to instrumental hero. Very provocative in its day, the format of an unaccompanied guitarist shredding his heart and hands out became a mandatory hard rock power trip. John Bonham deserved and got his own single spotlight, the leviathan "Moby Dick," bookended by another intricate Page workout on the Gibson, notable for its lightning-fast leaps from drop-D growl (bottom E string tuned down two steps) to squealing unison bends (one string bent up to the pitch of a note sounded on the adjacent one) far up the neck. Vaguely descended from a blues workout the act had played for BBC Radio, around Sleepy John Estes's "The Girl I Love She Got Long Brown Wavy Hair," even Jimmy Page himself wouldn't always be able to pull this lick off perfectly. And on the gentler "Thank You," Page strummed his Vox twelve-string for a lovely ballad he invited Robert Plant to try lyricizing, a warm tribute to his wife for her patience as he at last found his fortune in the music business.

The album as a whole was a group effort, with Jones's bass on the spacious "What Is and What Should Never Be," his Hammond on "Thank You," Bonham's Ludwigs and Paistes on the metallic-pastoral "Ramble On," and Plant's bluesy pastiches of "The Lemon Song" and "Bring It on Home" as standout cuts. Page's production once again was to the fore, giving the base material of a four-piece rock 'n' roll unit a larger-than-life clarion impact hitherto unthinkable—even the knockoff "Livin' Lovin' Maid (She's Just a Woman)" (characterizing a composite of their persistent Californian groupies) boasted a slick Telecaster solo and sounded like electric thunder. Very quickly, *Led Zeppelin II* surpassed the first LP in public demand on both sides of the Atlantic. Just over a year since the train started rollin', Jimmy Page was riding a runaway.

Then came the backlash. Ever since Page and Grant secured the $200,000 Atlantic deal, the rock critical community had its reservations about Led Zeppelin. Here was a group that appeared to have been formed in a corporate boardroom, not the back alleys of Liverpool or Memphis or Minnesota; here was an act built to be a moneymaker before anything else. The endless concert agenda of Page, Plant, Jones, and Bonham was lost in the news of their record-setting concert fees. When *Led Zeppelin II* had the temerity to displace the Beatles' *Abbey Road* and the Rolling Stones' *Let It Bleed* from the top of the U.S. album charts near the end of 1969—

Above: Jimmy Page with Neil Christian and the Crusaders in the early '60s. Although Page had moved on to session work by the time of this photo, he occasionally contributed to his old band's recording dates. *Photo courtesy of EMI Archives / Redferns.*

Left: Page (background), with Lulu, Keith Relf of the Yardbirds, and members of Herman's Hermits, around the time he was preparing to leave session gigs to play in the Yardbirds. *Photo courtesy of Emi Archives / Redferns.*

Page in the four-piece Yardbirds around 1966. From left, Chris Dreja, Jim McCarty, Page, and Keith Relf. *Photo courtesy of EMI Archives/Redferns.*

Left: Jackie Deshannon, the American singer-songwriter with whom Page had a musical and personal relationship in the mid-'60s. *Photo courtesy of Photofest.*

Right: Bluesman Howlin' Wolf's guttural inflections and quirky time patterns heavily influenc Page. *Photo courtesy of Photofest.*

ove: Page bows his psychedelic
ecaster in the latter-day
rdbirds. *Photo by Bob King / Redferns.*

ht: Now in the New Yardbirds,
ge with the recent addition
powerhouse drummer John
nham. *Photo by Jorgen Angel / Redferns.*

Above: Led Zeppelin—Rock and Roll. *Photo by Dick Barnat/Redfe*

Left: The Zeppelin and the Starship—John Paul Jones, John Bonham, Jimmy Page, Robert Plant. *Photo courtesy of Photofest.*

ge arrives in Hawaii with Richard Cole (foreground), Led Zeppelin's notorious road manager.
o by Robert Knight / Redferns.

e members of Led Zeppelin pose with Peter Grant, their intimidating, invaluable manager.
to courtesy of Photofest.

Above: Page manipulates spacey tones from his trademark theremin. *Photo court of Photofest.*

Middle: Roy Harper, eccentri poet and songwriter, became Page's creative alter ego. *Photo courtesy of Photofest.*

Bottom: Aleister Crowley, the sinister Edwardian occultist whose spiritual explorations inspired Page's own.

Facing page: Page owned two very similar sunburst Les Pauls. This model, seen at the Earls Court gig, is believed to be a '58. *Photo by Ian Dickson / Redfern*

Above: Page totes a Martin for Zeppelin's acoustic set at Earls Court, 1975. *Photo by Ian Dickson / Redferns.*

Left: With Robert Plant at Zeppelin's highest altitude. *Photo courtesy of Photofest.*

a presold formula elbowing aside the original heroes of the British Invasion—the knives were out. *Rolling Stone* magazine, which had dismissed *Led Zeppelin* as a cynical lift from Jeff Beck's *Truth*, was only one of many outlets that had little good to say about Jimmy Page and his band. *Creem* had a typically gonzo critique: "The songs are only redone joplinshake heavybody drughendrix . . . nothing to write or celebrate about."[53] For the remainder of their active career, Led Zeppelin would be relegated by the pop cognoscenti to the aesthetic backwaters of heavy metal. Reviews were not universally negative, but those that were had a nastiness that Page never forgot. "I may be a masochist in other regions, but I'm not that much of a masochist that I'm going to pay money to tear myself to bits—reading!"[54]

Zeppelin were not the "hype band" their opponents said they were (although they were advertised with slogans like "It's a Gas," "Now Flying," and "The Only Way to Fly" in trade and youth periodicals), but they did have that intimidating heaviness that put off some listeners. Much as groups like Metallica would sound in the '80s, Led Zeppelin came on so loud and so hard in 1968–1969 that they seemed to be only about volume and force, not grooving rock 'n' roll music but an aural endurance test. At one Boston Tea Party show, front-row fans were literally hammering themselves on the stage, in perhaps the first recorded instance of head-banging. Even fellow musicians like Eric Clapton were leery of what inspired such responses. "They were very loud—I thought it was unnecessarily loud," he said. "I really did like some of it, but a lot of it was just too much. They overemphasized whatever point they were making, I thought."[55]

What particularly galled rock critics on hearing the first two Led Zeppelin albums was their blues influence, which was not always properly credited. "Dazed and Confused" was spotted as a plagiarizing of Jake Holmes's "I'm Confused," ditto "Whole Lotta Love" from Muddy Waters's "You Need Love" (songwriter Willie Dixon), "The Lemon Song" from Howlin' Wolf's "Killing Floor," and "Bring It on Home" from Sonny Boy Williamson.

That most of these were heavily treated adaptations of songs themselves cribbed from a variety of sources (Plant's Muddy Waters lift was via the Small Faces) went unmentioned. "Every one of us has been influenced by the blues," Page protested, "but it's one's interpretation of it and how you utilize it.[56] . . . Robert was supposed to change the lyrics, and he didn't always do that, which is what brought on most of our grief. They couldn't get us on the guitar parts or the music, but they nailed us on the lyrics."[57] By the late '60s, rock writers had become very serious and very scholarly, affecting a more-authentic-than-thou purism that found in the freewheeling ad libs of Led Zeppelin a ripe target.

Irritated but undaunted, by November the foursome were in England again, putting down tracks for a third album in thirteen months. Jimmy Page and Peter Grant had stuck to their principles in refusing to issue a single version of "Whole Lotta Love" minus its free-form section. "We didn't release singles for the Top 20 stations in America, but we would release singles for FM album-oriented radio," Page explained. "We didn't have to create songs for a pop singles market; that would have been the kiss of death for us. But once people heard a new Led Zeppelin song on FM radio, they knew there was a new album."[58] With performance, record, and composer earnings piling up, Page and his bandmates splurged a little—he bought a Rolls-Royce Silver Cloud, only to get into a traffic accident on the way to London's Savoy Hotel, where Led Zeppelin was to receive an award from the British Parliamentary Secretary to the Board of Trade. The young Englishmen had just exported over £2 million in high-grade rock 'n' roll to the world.

The band's next project as 1970 opened was a selection of dates in Britain, France, Switzerland, Germany, Austria, Sweden, and Denmark. The tour was off to a strong start at London's historic Royal Albert Hall on Page's twenty-sixth birthday, January 9. "It was a magic venue," he remembered. "It was built in Victorian times and you go in there thinking about all the musical history that has preceded you. . . . So we were all really paying attention to what we were playing."[59] Backstage, Who singer Roger Daltrey had brought his companion, Heather Taylor, and her friend Charlotte Martin. Once matched up with Eric Clapton, the striking Mademoiselle Martin was now as unattached as Jimmy Page and the pair clicked. "Can you drive Charlotte and me to her apartment?" Page asked Richard Cole as the performers left the building. "It's not that far out of your way."[60] While the guitarist has always been silent on his relationships with women, his on-again, off-again involvement with Charlotte was to be one of his most fruitful. Her thin model's frame and Gallic hauteur represented his female inspiration and family center through much of the '70s.

Led Zeppelin cemented their European fan base that winter—although Page spat on an audience member in Göteborg, Sweden, who insisted on playing harmonica all through his solo on "White Summer" on the Danelectro—while Peter Grant arranged yet another North American jaunt for the upcoming season. Page alone made a rare TV appearance on BBC-2's *Julie Felix Show* in mid-March, filmed playing an acoustic "White Summer" and "Black Mountain Side." The act was now in enough demand that Grant and his U.S. booking agent, Premier Talent's Frank Barsalona, could request and receive as much as $45,000 per show, without the distraction of opening acts. Promoters in city upon city were aghast at the manager's price ("I have never seen anyone as vicious and money-minded,"[61] said Robert Chernov of Boston), but Grant held firm. "Promote it?" he sneered. "You don't have to promote Led Zeppelin. . . . Just announce on the radio that they're playing Madison Square and an hour later there won't be a ticket to be had. So what is the 'promoting' about?"[62]

A precedent-establishing hubris in 1970, this hard bargaining became another factor in Zeppelin's commercial and, in the long run, artistic triumph. By streamlining the connection between performer and audience (in contrast to the unwieldy Dick Clark Caravans into which the Yardbirds had been dragged), Grant ensured that ticket buyers got who and what they paid for without any unwanted frills. Thanks to him, rock concerts in the decade and beyond were hallowed events that spoke to the perceived integrity of the musicians on the roster. "In the old days everybody thought the artist worked for the manager," Grant was to look back. "You don't *own* artists. They hire you and give you a percentage of their money to do your very best for them. . . . If musicians are talented, why should they have to do a grease job on the media?"[63] Unlike moguls of later entertainment industry epochs, Grant and Frank Barsalona never made any pretense of supplying the product itself—that was Led Zeppelin's job.

In March and April 1970, the group toured Canada and the U.S., where attendance at their gigs often numbered 15,000 and up, and their name started to be noted alongside the dear departed Beatles' in drawing power. Their onstage presence had fused into an unbeatable balance of showmanship and musicianship, as related by John Paul Jones: "The main consideration was to give a dynamic shape to the whole show in terms of tension and release, a sort of macro version of what we would do when writing and arranging a single song. I feel that this holistic approach to the show gave Zeppelin the edge over a lot of bands at the time who were still subscribing to the 'wandering on and playing what they felt like' ethic. . . . [T]he audiences of 1969–70 simply didn't know what hit them!"[64] The bassist emphasizes the deft precision such sets necessitated: "Page always looked as though he was looking at the floor, but we'd watch each other's hand movements all the time. . . . We'd all go *bang*, straight into it. The audience would think, 'How did they do that?' It was because we were paying attention."[65]

America was still embroiled in Vietnam abroad and campus and inner-city unrest at home, though, and Led Zeppelin were unmistakably on the "counter" side of the nation's cultural chasm. In Los Angeles, Jimmy Page assured Pamela Miller of his faithfulness to Charlotte Martin ("which for him is a miracle," Miss P thought) and left with a warm hug and instructions for her to

"Be a good girl."[66] Below the Mason-Dixon Line things got ugly. "I grew up loving the music that came out of Memphis and Nashville," Page reflected. "But it turned out to be really depressing. We arrived in Memphis and were given the keys to the city . . . but I guess they didn't like the looks of us. . . . They didn't like the long hair at all, man. It was seriously redneck."[67] There was violence in the crowds and behind the scenes; a gun was pulled on the band in Texas. "I can't stand restaurants where they give you a bad time," Page told an interviewer after the tour. "Or trying to check into hotels where they don't like the look of you and don't want you messing up the swimming pool. It's just unfortunate that this is the age we live in, a very hostile age."[68]

They all had a holiday in May, in expectation of further recording and performing through the rest of the year. Jones and John Bonham returned to their English homes, but the vocalist and guitar player, who had formed an onstage empathy that transcended mere spectacle, stayed together. "The more you get into the bloke," Robert Plant found, "although he seems to be quite shy, he's not, really. He's got lots of good ideas for song writing and he's proved to be a really nice guy."[69] With his wife, Maureen, year-and-a-half-old daughter, Carmen, and dog, Strider, Plant invited Page and Charlotte Martin to spend time with him at a cottage in the Snowdonia region of Wales where he had spent time as a boy. Nestled in the Cambrian Mountains north of Aberdyfi, where legends of King Arthur and Merlin still held currency, the rustic location of Bron-yr-Aur ("Breast of Gold") was an idyllic scene for the couples to relax and replenish themselves after the frantic pace of the past year and a half. A small complement of Led Zeppelin roadies went along to help with chores—Page and Plant were rock stars, after all.

In that wild green springtime of his twenty-sixth year, far from Hollywood hotels and cranked Marshalls, Jimmy Page found a new musical direction. "No matter how cute and comical it might be now to look at," Plant said, "it gave us so much energy, because we were really close to something. We believed. It was absolutely wonderful, and my heart was so light and happy. At that time, at that age, 1970 was like the biggest blue sky I ever saw."[70] "The first couple of years we were touring all the time," Page expanded, "and that was the first official break that we had. . . . We were in a cottage with no electricity, just gas lamps. The only electricity was in the cassette recorders we had for reference. . . . I guess a lot of the acoustic songs came after tours, when you couldn't really go home and set up a 200-watt stack and just blast out, and consequently you just work out on the acoustic."[71] Wandering the eternal Welsh crags and pausing to sing and strum by the side of a waterfall on the River Dovey, the rock god and the rock magus were just two friends playing music together. Sometime that month, as night fell and the vacationers paired off, Page and Charlotte Martin retired to their room and conceived a child. But by 1970 Jimmy Page himself was already on his way to becoming immortal.

Over the Hills and Far Away

1970-1973

> Perhaps the most powerful magic words are those which the magician invents himself. . . . The magician should use only those words into which he can concentrate his entire being.
>
> —KATHRYN PAULSEN,
> *THE COMPLETE BOOK OF MAGIC AND WITCHCRAFT*

Following their rejuvenation at Bron-yr-Aur, Jimmy Page and Robert Plant reconvened with John Bonham and John Paul Jones for a resumption of their seemingly permanent regimen of stages and studios. But now there was a motivation and a confidence to their union that until then they had no opportunity to nurture. Now they had two hit albums to their name and the certainty that their hectic run of gigging had won them a loyal following in Britain, Europe, and especially North America; now they were secure in their aspirations to broaden Led Zeppelin's musical and continental range. Just after the summer solstice of 1970, the band played Reykjavik, Iceland, bringing their patented brand of hard rock to the land of ice and snow and the midnight sun, where the hot springs flow. The next few years would take them to even more exotic global and mental destinations and, under Page's leadership, to their artistic pinnacle.

With the countrified Plant and Page sporting beards and the guitar player wearing a woolen overcoat and "yokel's" hat, Led Zeppelin were the headline act at England's Bath Festival of Blues and Progressive Music in late June. Before almost a quarter of a million people—and after major stars like Santana, the Byrds, Country Joe and the Fish, and the Jefferson Airplane had finished sets—they announced their arrival into the front ranks of international rock 'n' roll. Ever the diplomat, Peter Grant preempted the penultimate spot by the Flock to ensure his boys were illuminated against a glorious summer sunset: "Hey, we haven't finished yet, man," spluttered the Flock's road crew as their gear was shut down and Zeppelin's Hiwatts and Marshalls were warmed up. "Oh, yes, you fuckin' have,"[1] Grant decreed.

Far down the bill at the Bath Festival was an English folkie called Roy Harper. Offstage, Jimmy Page and Robert Plant were introduced to the singer-songwriter and, recently returned as they were from their own bucolic retreat and aspiring to their own image of sensitivity, warmed to him as a kindred spirit. "He's just a very nice person," Page decided. "[H]e's a really talented bloke who's had a lot of problems."[2] Born in 1941, he had served in the Royal Air Force, done time in institutions penal and psychiatric, acquired a tasty acoustic guitar technique on street corners throughout Europe, and written yards of poetry. Part of the same coffeehouse league that included Bert Jansch and John Renbourn, Harper would graduate to the rock strata via associations with Pink Floyd and Kate Bush, and would be a kind of creative alter ego to Page in the coming years: the gifted, oddball folk picker whose thoughts were too deep to worry over cracking the Top 10 or selling out some football stadium in the States.

Work on Led Zeppelin's third album was already underway, with all four members hoping to challenge their critical and popular identity as relentless purveyors of overheated blues.

"The only heavy band I really dig is the Zeppelin—apart from that, I dig the mellower things,"[3] Plant revealed. "There was no conscious desire along the lines of, 'Oh, we've done Heavy, now we should look at Soft,' and thank goodness,"[4] put in John Paul Jones. "It's very difficult comparing this album with the others— there's a lot of acoustic stuff on it,"[5] John Bonham confirmed. "The fact was that Robert and I had gone away to Bron-Yr-Aur cottage in Wales and started writing songs," Page declared simply. "Christ, that was the material we had, so we used it. It was nothing like, 'We've got to do some heavy rock 'n' roll because that's what our image demands.'"[6]

For preliminary sessions they retired to Headley Grange, a dilapidated mansion in rural Hampshire, built in 1795, that had functioned as a workhouse in the nineteenth century and which had already been tried out by Fleetwood Mac—by driving up with portable recording equipment, the bands could rehearse and play in the homier, more intimate mood of an old stately home while feeding the signals into the state-of-the-art technology they brought with them. The consoles and tape decks were the Rolling Stones' sixteen-track mobile unit, operated by Andy Johns. "I've got to say that, right from the early days of working at Headley Grange," said Jimmy Page years later, "it was very, very spooky . . . I thought it was fantastic!"[7] Though lacking the absolutely sterile acoustics of professional recording rooms, Page discovered that the wide halls and stairwells of Headley Grange permitted him to record single takes of all four musicians playing live as they arranged themselves throughout the manor while keeping each other in view. "If you are just playing to headphones," he explained, "it's very hard to feel the rhythm. And that's the essence."[8] Some of the greatest ever Led Zeppelin tracks of the next several years would be captured in the resonant, resonating chambers of Headley Grange.

Many of the songs at hand were acoustic pastorals that had taken shape in the Welsh countryside, like "Friends," "That's the Way," and "Bron-y-Aur Stomp," but they had not wholly abandoned their roots. Among the most compelling new numbers was a fast and brutal Viking ode whose lyrical theme came to Plant on the Iceland visit: "Immigrant Song," with Page's fat, multiply-overdubbed Les Paul sitting on Jones's subterranean bass and Bonham's thumping right foot, took Zeppelin out of the cotton fields and the chain gangs and into the misty fjords and meadows of pre-Christian Europe, increasingly their spiritual center. Still metallic almost forty years gone, it must have seemed radioactive in 1970. The repetitive octave jump between two F-sharps (more of a chord fragment than a riff) was pure Jimmy Page and heralded one of his characteristic guitar devices. "Out on the Tiles" originated with Bonham and sounded like one of his raucous nights hitting the pubs of Birmingham—Page eventually panned the drums back and forth across an oceanic stereo spread. "Since I've Been Loving You," tried live as early as the Royal Albert Hall concert, took the traditional three-chord blues progression but inflated the key to an operatic C minor as Plant wailed hurt white-boy Howlin'-Muddy-Sonny Boy-Blind Lemonisms and Jones colored with a soulful Hammond organ. The solo demonstrated Page's mastery of the pentatonic minor scale, with none of his familiar thick riffing but instead choked-up flurries of pull-offs and hammer-ons (in which the fingers "flutter" over the frets to play notes faster than they can be picked) on the high strings—classic rock guitar at its most personal. Most bittersweet of all was the group's revisit of the Yardbirds' forsaken "Knowing That I'm Losing You," which became "Tangerine," credited solely to Jimmy Page. Strumming a sad A minor on his Martin D-28 and overdubbing a Fender pedal steel, he may have thought about Jackie DeShannon and those happy months when he and she were a queen and prince of Swinging London.

As these and other pieces were put together in Hampshire and polished in London's Island Studios on Basing Street near Notting Hill, and at Olympic Studios, Jimmy Page was considering a move. The Pangbourne boathouse, stuffed with art nouveau items (from shopping sprees conducted with Peter Grant) and now shared with Charlotte Martin, was becoming too small for him and too accessible; he'd had to change his phone number to fend off interruptions from strangers, and neighbor kids would tease him about his hair. By the end of 1970, he had made enough in Led Zeppelin's short life to spend £100,000 on a country estate on Ditchling Road north of Lewes, Sussex, called Plumpton Place. The flint-and-brick structure dated from Jacobean times but had been given a redesign and a special "music room" by the noted architect Sir Edwin Lutyens in 1928, as well as extensive gardens devised in tandem with horticulturalist Gertrude Jekyll. "It's moated and terraces off into lakes," Page told a reporter about his property, which apparently came with its own incorporeal inhabitants. "I could tell you things, but it might give people ideas. A few things have happened that would freak some people out, but I was surprised actually at how composed I was."[9] Plumpton Place would be handy enough to London for him to commute back and forth, but that year Page had found another place far to the north in Scotland, down from Inverness, overlooking Foyers Bay on Loch Ness. Significant less for its long, low layout than for one of its previous owners, this was the Boleskine House.

"My house used to belong to Aleister Crowley—I knew that when I moved in," Page divulged. "The house was built on the site of a kirk dating from around the tenth century that had been burned down with all its congregation. Nobody wanted it, it was in such a state of decay. I hadn't originally intended to buy it, but it was so fascinating. . . . All I'm saying is that it's a really interesting house and a perfect place to go when one starts getting wound up by the clock. I bought it to go up and write in."[10] Having long been gathering lesser pieces of Aleister Crowley paraphernalia, including books and clothing, the isolated Boleskine House was a final prize for Page. He had been captivated by the occultist since boyhood and had at last the means to literally follow in Crowley's footsteps. Throughout the '60s, Aleister Crowley's stature had risen with Jimmy Page's generation, as young Britons embraced the distant years of Victoria and Empire with proportional measures of irony and reverence. The prudery and jingoism of Britannia regnant prompted a reexamination of the period's freethinkers—D. H. Lawrence and Epsom's Aubrey Beardsley, for instance—and the formerly reviled Crowley could be seen as only a man well ahead of his time. "I read a lot of Crowley and I was fascinated by his ideas," Page stated. "But I was reading across the board. . . . It wasn't unusual at that time to be interested in comparative religions and magick."[11] In 1967, the Beatles had put Crowley's face among other "people we like" on the cover of *Sgt. Pepper's Lonely Hearts Club Band* (aptly enough between an Indian holy man and '30s sexpot Mae West), and Graham Bond, whose Graham Bond Organization had featured Ginger Baker before Cream, imagined himself Crowley's illegitimate son. Page was by then well versed in the subject. "After having read this ridiculous book called *The Beast* where the author hadn't the faintest idea of what Crowley was talking about and was totally condescending, I took it all from there. It's like there's this incredible body of literature . . . and it's like there's a diamond to be found at the end and it involves a life's study."[12] On crossing the threshold of Boleskine, he could tell himself, "I'm attracted by the unknown, but I take precautions. I don't go into things blind."[13]

Edward Alexander Crowley (he chose the "Aleister" on his own, liking the sound of it) was born in 1875 to an upper-middle-class family, heirs to a brewing fortune, who were also devout and rigid Christians. He learned more from his father's passionate faith than his mother's conventional piety and, from adolescence on, was drawn steadily toward mystical experience, through spirituality and art. The time was right, with the writings of Eliphas Levi and J. K. Huysmans inspiring a wave of occult awareness in England and France. *Tales from the Arabian Nights* delighted him, as well as poets like Shelley and Swinburne; while studying at Cambridge he began to experiment with varying rituals of Oriental and Occidental sorcery, and to compose lyrics of his own. An enthusiastic outdoorsman, he took up climbing, first in Britain and then the Alps—some of his ascents are still regarded as pioneering efforts in the sport of mountaineering. He never worked. Living on his inheritance (until his later years when he was alternately broke and indebted), he devoted his time to pleasure, excitement, and the pursuit of forbidden knowledge, either separately or, just as often, all at once.

Crowley did win notoriety during his life. Gaining little recognition for his poems (which are of some literary merit), he developed a standing as an incorrigible scoundrel, an affront to bourgeois morality labeled by the then-nascent tabloid press as "The Wickedest Man in the World." He left a string of wives and mistresses, several of whom committed suicide or were institutionalized; as a member of the Order of the Golden Dawn and his own Order of the Silver Star societies, he was a dedicated practitioner of "sex magick" with women and men; and he was a prodigious taker of hashish, opium, cocaine, and heroin long before they were even known to the general public. Closer to Oscar Wilde than Anton LaVey, he was a cultivated and keenly intelligent product of Victorian-Edwardian gentility, but known to be personally brutish, arrogant, and self-centered, a sadist and an egomaniac, and, at the end of his life, a rather pitiable drug addict. He was linked to the deaths and injuries of numerous associates, including the loss of five fellow climbers on a disastrous Himalayan expedition in 1905. His books, such as *The Diary of a Drug Fiend* and the erotic *Snowdrops from a Curate's Garden*, were denounced as obscene. By the time of his death in 1947, he was an occupant of the where-are-they-now file, a prototypical victim of fleeting celebrity and a fickle audience's appetite for shock.

For all that, Aleister Crowley was a genuinely unique and accomplished individual—in the era of Freud and Einstein he explored in his own fashion the limits of subconscious and cosmic reality. Critics acknowledge that, however distasteful he may have been as a person, he was a sincere scholar of unknown forces.

Frequently dishonest and disloyal, Crowley was nevertheless no fraud. A resident, at different periods, of London, New York, and a Sicilian Abbey (until expelled by the new regime of Mussolini in 1923), he also traveled widely, throughout Europe, North Africa, Egypt, India, the Far East, Mexico, Hawaii, the United States, and Canada. He was an acquaintance of the poet W. B. Yeats, the sculptor Rodin, and the novelist Somerset Maugham—the title character Oliver Haddo in the latter's *The Magician* is loosely based on him—and nearly all who met him agree that he was possessed of a magnetism that went beyond charisma and into a deep and somewhat sinister connection to supernatural power. "Do what thou wilt shall be the whole of law" was the motto Crowley believed had been dictated to him by the spirit Aiwass; he lived and behaved in the Nietzschean conviction he was a prophet of an emerging age, and for better or worse he was. Jimmy Page was a disciple and, unintentionally, Aleister Crowley's most famous evangelist. "Although I don't agree with everything he said, he was a visionary. I don't particularly want to go into it because it's a personal thing and isn't in relation to anything I do as a musician, apart from that I've employed his system in my own day-to-day life."[14]

After a quick summer circuit around Cologne, Essen, Frankfurt, and Berlin, in August and September 1970, Led Zeppelin were back in North America for a sixth tour. They faced same problems with corrupt cops and hick onlookers as they had in prior runs, but the music was stronger than ever. Now their concerts incorporated a sit-down acoustic interlude, where the shaggy-faced John Paul Jones, Robert Plant, and Jimmy Page moved to the front of the stage to perform the lighter songs they had been working on since Bron-yr-Aur. Page toted the Martin acoustic guitar for these turns, while the versatile Jones took a mandolin and Plant banged a tambourine. Once the laid-back segment was through—sometimes rendered inaudible by sound systems ill-suited to amplify folk melodies in packed halls—John Bonham joined in and the fans came alive again. Obliging and conscientious in the studio, the drummer was a wild man with an audience, and his pulverizing beats took the quartet's set lists to multiple climaxes. "You could rely on John, you could rely on that sort of power," Page claims. "He was listening to what [I'm] doing, he was listening to what Jonesy's doing. He's listening to the phrasing and he's phrasing *with* me. . . . It doesn't get any better than that, it doesn't."[15]

All four Zeppelin members were of a background where real music was considered something played before real people, and Jimmy Page has always spoken of his band's unpredictable qualities in front of paying customers. "If you heard us live, you'd know exactly where it was at.[16] . . . Nothing was ever static. Other bands at the time weren't able to do that; they didn't have the musical freedom and the freedom of collective spirit. Wherever we were and whatever year it was, we always went onstage determined to do our best, and I'll tell you what: Led Zeppelin's mediocre was better than anybody else's best."[17] During his solo turn in "Heartbreaker," for example, he might play not the Cliff Gallup appropriations of the recorded version but snippets of Simon and Garfunkel's "59th Street Bridge Song (Feelin' Groovy)" or Bach's Lute Suite No. 1.

While crossing the border into Winnipeg, Manitoba, in late August, Page's Les Paul Custom that had taken him through his years as a session player went missing. "Usually I never took that on the road because it was so precious. But things were going so well for us that I eventually took it over and it suddenly went. It got nicked off the truck at the airport when we were on our way to Canada."[18] Another disappointment that month came when Page made a trip to Memphis, Tennessee, where he completed mixing the latest album from tapes recorded at Headley Grange and in London. He had wanted to record in Memphis's Sun Studios, where Sam Phillips had committed the prehistoric strains of Elvis Presley to disc, but he had to settle for the nearby Ardent Studios with engineer Terry Manning. "I really wanted to get down there and cut some things in his sort of element and see how it worked out. But it didn't."[19] The American route concluded at New York's Madison Square Garden on September 19 as Led Zeppelin played for two and a half hours for 22,000 fans in a sold-out performance. The costliest tickets went for $7.50.

Led Zeppelin III was released almost a year after *II*, in October 1970. The title, or lack of one, continued Jimmy Page's presentation of eponymous albums in the manner of classical material like Symphony No. 5 or Ninth Sonata, and the LP was pulled out of a colorful sleeve designed by Richard Drew. A circular card inside was spun to display a collage of Page, Plant, Jones, Bonham, and other imagery through small holes in the cover. "It was my idea to have a revolving wheel," said Page. "I remembered those old gardening catalogues. You'd turn it to 'roses' to find out what kind of manure to use. . . . When you get fed up with the LP there is the added pleasure of ripping the cover apart to find out what's on the rest of the wheel."[20] The execution rather disappointed him, however: "There are some silly bits—little chunks of corn and nonsense like that."[21] To the surprise of many listeners, the music inside was as earthy as Page's cover concept. Along with the hard-driving "Immigrant Song," "Since I've Been Loving You," "Out on the Tiles," and a sliding "Celebration Day," there were distinctly rural ballads—the plaintive "Friends," a moving social and ecological protest called "That's the Way," "Tangerine," and a happily clomping "Bron-y-Aur Stomp." Public domain numbers were given new life in the form of "Gallows Pole" (with Page using six- and twelve-string guitars as well as a Vega banjo) and the album closer, "Hats Off to (Roy) Harper," a name-check for the folk singer befriended at Bath but a straight cover of Bukka White's country blues "Shake 'Em on Down" graced by Page's scratchy acoustic slide guitar in CGCGCE (low to high strings). "Friends" was picked in another alternate tuning the guitarist had conceived himself, CACGCE, and "Bron-y-Aur Stomp" showed off some good bluegrass fingerpicking in CFCFAC. Left off *III* but surfacing later were the rustic "Poor Tom" and "Bron-yr-Aur" (both in the C-tuning) and the country rock of "Hey Hey What Can I Do," found as a high-contrast B-side on the "Immigrant Song" 45.

Though the album was a big seller, it did not hit the heights of *Led Zeppelin II,* and the same critics who accused Led Zeppelin of being too heavy now said they had gone too far in the other direction: "Don't Zeppelin care anymore?" "1 . . . 2 . . . 3 . . . Zep Weaken."[22] Jimmy Page didn't pause to doubt himself. He and Robert Plant made another visit to Bron-yr-Aur in October and came back with more song thumbnails to bring to Island Studios in December, and later to Headley Grange. The acoustic tinge the springtime stay had imparted to their compositions remained but had darkened with the autumn weather. In January 1971, the four players moved to the old Hampshire mansion while Andy Johns manned the mobile truck and music began to ring through the age-worn wood and stones. "It was very Charles Dickens . . . I'm pretty sure it was haunted," Page opines of Headley Grange. "I remember going up the main staircase on the way to my room one night and seeing a gray shape at the top. I double-checked to see if it was just a play of light, and it wasn't—so I turned around pretty fast, because I didn't really want to have an encounter with something like that."[23]

The cold and wet mood forced Page and his ensemble to focus on recording. There was hashish and—a harbinger—some cocaine around, and they stocked up at the nearest pub, but it was not a party. John Paul Jones came with a tricky bass line he had devised after listening to Muddy Waters's *Electric Mud* record. Poorly received as a venerable bluesman's bid for psychedelic hipness, songs like "She's Alright" and "Tom Cat" impressed him for their long, rolling lines, which he extrapolated into a maze-like run of his own. "I wanted to write an original riff that had that same type of busy, yet plodding, feel,"[24] he said.

Baffling in its metric idiosyncrasy, he and Page arranged it into a call-and-response pattern heard on Fleetwood Mac's "Oh Well" while Plant scrawled a litany of blues idioms; even the mighty John Bonham was unsure how to accompany it. Was it 4/4? 5/4? 9/16? After much rehearsal they nailed "Black Dog" (after an actual Labrador retriever that ambled in and out of the Grange) as no other musicians would ever quite manage. "What, shifting the goalposts . . .?" Page smiled in retrospect. "I'd say [such quirky time patterns came] from Howlin' Wolf, because I found his riffs would cut across the time and regular 4/4 . . . I was extremely influenced by that stuff."[25] Generations of "Black Dog" listeners wonder if Page is stumbling over his move from B back up to E on the Les Paul, but in fact he and his rhythm section stay in the whiplash tempo throughout. Completed at Island Studios, Page's guitar was direct-injected three times to produce its withering triple-layered distortion.

In a related feel was "Four Sticks," whose equally erratic cadences annoyed Bonham so much he stopped one take to bash away at his hi-hat, doing Little Richard's old "You Keep A-Knockin'." Page, Plant, and Jones fell headlong into a I-IV-V boogie (in which lurk shards of Roy Orbison's "Oh, Pretty Woman" riff) that boosted the producer to change course. "That's how it was going back then. If something felt right, we didn't question it."[26] A few more takes and they had the basics of "Rock and Roll," Led Zeppelin's paean to their own genre and most recent addition to their catalog of electric overtures: "Communication Breakdown," "Whole Lotta Love," "Heartbreaker," and "Immigrant Song." Ian Stewart, the shy "sixth Stone" and superb pianist, provided barrelhouse eighty-eights.

From Wales came the lilting chimes of "Going to California," Jimmy Page and Robert Plant's devotional nod to Joni Mitchell, whose *Blue* LP and exquisite modal touch both had found deeply moving. With Jones's fine mandolin in the lead, Page plays an open-tuned acoustic guitar (DADGBD) with thumb and fingers to denote the sighs of the woodland breeze through the hills of Bron-yr-Aur, where the western edge of the New World was far over the horizon. With no percussive backing, "California" wafted past "Thank You," "Tangerine," and "That's the Way" to be

Zeppelin's most graceful folk song. Its close rival was "The Battle of Evermore," a sylvan duet borne of Page's unschooled trials of Jones's Harmony mandolin while at the Grange. "I suppose mandolin players would laugh because it must be the standard thing to play those chords but possibly not with that approach."[27] Plant's story recounts a mythical conflict he had conjured through his readings on the Anglo-Scottish border wars of 1296–1603; Fairport Convention's Sandy Denny was asked to trade off her high English intonation with his storytelling to portray the medieval clash. And Plant's heartfelt defense of cannabis freedom was supported by the monumental authority of "Misty Mountain Hop," which Jones began on electric piano before Page and Bonham quickly locked down the groove.

Engineer Andy Johns was alone with John Bonham at Headley Grange when the two absently tried Bonham's second drum set, hitherto stashed in the front hall in part of the building called the Minstrel's Gallery. Johns hung a pair of microphones from the staircase and wired them out to the truck where the recording gear, including Page's Binson echo chamber, was readied. As the signal of Bonham hitting his Ludwigs in the cavernous space came through his headphones, Johns called, "Bonzo, you've gotta hear this!" "*That's* what I've been hearing!"[28] whooped the drummer as the playback ran. Jimmy Page, on listening to the sample, knew this was his distance-makes-depth principle taken to its apex. "Everyone has gotten so carried away with EQ [equalization] pots that they have forgotten the whole science of microphone placement.[29] . . . The acoustics of the stairwell happened to be so balanced that we didn't even need to mike the kick drum."[30] Over Bonham's seismic beat, they put down a moaning Delta number Plant first heard by Memphis Minnie and Kansas Joe McCoy, as Page played an electric Fender twelve-string tuned to open G for further blues tones. He pushed "When the Levee Breaks" to its extreme by slowing it down in the final mix, deepening its swampy bottom below sea level. "If you slow things down it makes everything sound so much thicker," Page understood. "The problem is, you have to be very tight with your playing, because it magnifies your inconsistencies."[31] Haunted with echo effects and squalling with Plant's harmonica, the four members of Led Zeppelin were very tight in the Minstrel's Gallery. But there was one more stairway they had to work with.

Like Led Zeppelin itself, "Stairway to Heaven" was conceptualized by Jimmy Page well before its component parts were assembled. "Dazed and Confused" stood out in concerts for its duration and its jamming potential, and "Babe I'm Gonna Leave You" had its "light and shade" acoustic-electric arrangement that showed off the group's stylistic reach—why not create a new song merging the qualities of both? During his and Plant's second Welsh holiday, the opening arpeggios for this may have taken shape, but it was not a rush job. As early as April 1970, he had confided to a journalist, "Insomuch as 'Dazed and Confused' and all those things went into sections, well, we want to try something new with the organ and acoustic guitar building up and building up to the electric thing."[32] Decades afterward he testified, "I'd been fooling around with my acoustic guitar and came up with the different sections, which I married together. But what I wanted was something that would have the drums come in at the middle and then build to a huge crescendo."[33]

Some have heard "Stairway"'s chromatically descending A-minor introduction as a theft of Spirit's "Taurus" (Zeppelin and Spirit had been on the same touring routes in 1969), but the older piece begins with a first-position chord voiced down in single steps from A to F, whereas Page played at the jazzier second position (fifth fret), then moved from A minor to A minor (add 9) / G-sharp to C / G then to open D. More speculatively, the melody line has been linked to the eighteenth-century blind Irish harpist Turlough O'Carolan's "Carolan's Dream." At the other end, the remorseless aeolian climax of "Stairway to Heaven" (A minor–G–F) is said to resemble the i–♭VII–♭VI progression of the Dylan–Hendrix marathon "All Along the Watchtower," although

Page himself thought it sounded like Ray Charles's "Hit the Road Jack." This common sequence can also be found everywhere from the Four Tops' "Bernadette" to Del Shannon's "Runaway." No proof has ever been found that would suggest Jimmy Page's most celebrated achievement is anything but wholly original.

Once the song's arrangement had been formatted with John Paul Jones, Page entrusted Robert Plant to come up with lyrics. While Page, Jones, and Bonham practiced, Plant wrote down the title and bulk of verses for "Stairway to Heaven," a fortuitous stream-of-consciousness outflow that conclusively won him the confidence of his guitarist. "I contributed to the lyrics on the first three albums," Page reported, "but I was always hoping that Robert would eventually take care of that aspect of the band. And by the fourth album he was coming up with fantastic stuff. . . . It was really intense. And by the time we came up with the fanfare at the end and could play it all the way through, Robert had eighty percent of the lyrics done. It just goes to show you what inspired times they were."[34]

The eternal puzzle of "Stairway to Heaven"'s meaning derives from Plant's recent perusals of Celtic lore and pagan ritual, and from his own roots in the wild English Midlands. "You don't have to have too much of an imagination or a library full of books if you live there," he shrugged. "On a murky October evening, with the watery sun looking down on those hills over some old castle and unto the river, you have to be a real bimbo not to flash occasionally."[35] Lyrically, "Stairway" is an insoluble warren of folk symbolism—forests, the piper, the May Queen, a brook, rings of smoke, etc.—that leads to perplexing false starts and dead ends, and its regular syntactical motif of *There's* a lady, *there's* a songbird, *there's* a feeling, if *there's* a bustle, *there* are two paths, *there* walks a lady, conveys an archaic balladeer's sensibility. The lines are "pretentious" only in that they remain elusively obscure while openly allusive at once—T. S. Eliot for the rock generation. It is significant to point out that, while Jimmy Page holds the reputation of Led Zeppelin's mysterious maestro, the most evocative Zeppelin song owes its ambiguity to the outgoing, heart-on-his-sleeve Robert Plant.

As with the other Headley Grange cuts, the final takes of "Stairway to Heaven" were honed in London. Jones added bass recorders over the introduction (played on the Harmony acoustic guitar), then Page moved to a Fender electric twelve-string before Bonham made the behemoth entry Page had wanted, sounding like God waking up with a hangover, and the final riff was driven home on the '59 Les Paul. For the guitar solo, Page went to his 1958 Telecaster, which had lain dormant since *Led Zeppelin,* put it through his Supro amp, and threw down three takes of which the first was judged best. "I had the first phrase worked out, and a link phrase here and there, but on the whole that solo was improvised,"[36] he disclosed (the repeated four-note "sighing" lick near the end was punched in afterward). Jimmy Page has frequently been criticized for his "sloppy" lead guitar parts that sometimes lose their melodic fluidity in awkward clusters of bends and rockabilly pull-offs, but the "Stairway" solo is an almost flawless torrent of blues-based and Aeolian intervals, and its last spray of E-C-A hammer-on triplets at the seventeenth fret is where Page earned Plant's commendation as "the Wagner of the Telecaster."

Eight completed songs were to be mixed down and sequenced for the upcoming album (other sketched-out numbers would turn up on later collections) and in February 1971, Page took Andy Johns's advice that this task be done in Los Angeles's Sunset Studios. The producer, engineer, and Peter Grant went to L.A. in time for a moderate earthquake that reminded Page of a line from "Going to California" ("Bloody hell, I'm not taking any chances—I'm going to mix that one last!"). Played back at Olympic Studios in London, it seemed that the Sunset tapes had been equalized unnaturally low, giving a washed-out, muddy sound that threatened to ruin all the effort of the previous months. "I still don't really know what happened," Page wonders. "Maybe the monitors were giving us a totally false sound picture, because

Sunset Sound had these real state-of-the-art monitors that were able to reproduce a big stretch of frequencies. Who knows?"[37] Re-remixing at Island Studios, Page and a chastened Johns restored the tracks to their true brightness.

Then it was time to go back on the road, for a series of one-nighters at small venues throughout the British Isles, a generous "back to the clubs" gesture before the more remunerative amphitheaters of North America opened up in the late summer. Several of the new songs were taken out as yet unreleased on album and received positive responses. "Black Dog," "Rock and Roll," "Going to California," and "Stairway to Heaven" were performed for the first time in Belfast, Dublin, Leeds, Canterbury, and elsewhere that March. The complex structure of "Stairway" stimulated Page to get a special instrument that could accommodate its varied parts, and he chose an unusual twelve- and six-stringed double-necked Gibson for its live performance. Of course, the song *can* be played on a single set of strings (the similarly patterned "Babe I'm Gonna Leave You" had been presented with the Telecaster, with the volume turned down for the "acoustic" sections), but Page wanted a more faithful approximation of the piece's chiming textures and ordered a custom-made EDS 1275 6 /12. "They were really good about that because they weren't making them anymore," he said. "[Bluesman] Earl Hooker played the first one I saw. I always wanted one but you just couldn't get them."[38] (Hooker's was shown on the cover of his album *Two Bugs and a Roach*, while Elvis Presley, bizarrely, was seen sporting a Gibson double-neck in his 1966 movie *Spinout*.)

The cherry-red solid-body had a sonic identity all its own, making it not just two guitars stuck together but a single eighteen-stringed piece of craftsmanship. "When you just play the six-string neck," Page pointed out, "all the other strings start ringing in sympathy like the strings on a sitar. . . . It can sound like a harp."[39] (Some roadies groused over its tendency to pick up electronic interference and called it "the TV aerial.")[40] A tangible display of his multitalented guitar techniques, the double-neck became Jimmy Page's most iconic axe and prompted numerous other players to show off with EDS 1275s of their own: the Eagles' Don Felder, Rush's Alex Lifeson, and Page's old tutor John McLaughlin. Serial number 911117, it remains in Page's care and has been valued at £50,000, although it is more accurately priceless.

The British tour concluded at the Marquee on March 23, and from this step back into his past Page went into his future the next day, when Charlotte Martin gave birth to Scarlet Lilith Eleida Page. Aleister Crowley referred to all his female companions as his "Scarlet Woman," Lilith was a mythical demon who had been Adam's first wife before the creation of Eve, who was rejected and went on to mate with fallen angels (Crowley's first daughter was named Nuit Ma Ahathoor Hecate Sappho Jezebel Lilith), and Eleida may have been a feminized form of Aleister. Despite this doomy nomenclature, Scarlet was a healthy little girl, although her parents' relationship was less so. After a short month discovering the joys of fatherhood, Jimmy Page went out on another European excursion in May 1971. On July 5, Led Zeppelin barely escaped a riot at Milan's Vigorelli Stadium when police started tear-gassing fans and the shaken band retreated to a nearby bar. "[Italy] is a word never mentioned in my hearing," Page uttered. "It causes a big argument, or a nervous breakdown."[41]

Four weeks of concerts were given in Canada and the U.S. over August and September. Crowds and grosses were very large. Peter Grant was vehemently opposed to the relatively novel practice of bootleg-recording (in the days before downloads and file-sharing) and smashed up a microphone and tape unit in Vancouver, only to learn it was not a pirate operator's but a citizen from the Noise Abatement Society, there to monitor volume levels. Awfully sorry, mate, how much do we owe you? Jimmy Page later claimed (on no specifics) that the group's first stints of traveling in the U.S. had to be limited to no longer than six months before the four young migrant workers would be eligible for the national draft: "You know, they do keep an eye on people."[42] He had a hurried reunion with Miss Pamela in Los Angeles, telling her of Charlotte and his infant daughter. "They haven't gotten married and have lots of disagreements,"[43] Miss P wrote in her journal. "Stairway to Heaven" was being debuted to North Americans at these shows, and the unfamiliar creation won even stronger approval than it had in Europe. "I remember playing that at the LA Forum," its composer recalled. "I'm not saying the *whole* audience gave us a standing ovation, but there was this sizeable standing ovation there. And I thought, 'This is incredible, because no one's heard this number yet. This is the first time they're hearing it!' . . . And that was at the LA Forum, so I knew we were on to something with that one."[44]

After wrap-up gigs in Honolulu, Led Zeppelin broke fresh ground in Japan, at Tokyo's Budokan Hall, and at Hiroshima (played as a benefit for atom bomb survivors) and Osaka. The rowdiness that had always characterized their offstage behavior was accelerating, and Page admitted, "We did things [in Japan] that you just wouldn't believe. . . . Night after night after night we had all of this stuff going on, and we got away with murder. In retrospect, our Japanese hosts were probably completely horrified, but they were so polite they just kept bowing to us."[45] The guitarist himself was sometimes subject to intraband pranks, as when Bonham, whose instincts in that field ran to the scatological, defecated in Page's delicate lady friend's purse. "Who the fuck did this?"[46] Page raged when he found out. The Japanese tour spread the act's name to the Far East, but when the revenues and expenses were tallied, their indulgences left them at a financial loss. With Richard Cole and Robert Plant, Jimmy Page returned to Britain via Bangkok, Thailand (and its brothels), and Bombay, India. They shopped for antiques and trinkets, and Page jammed incognito with local players who were surprised at his ability. The Englishmen were humbled by the munificence of their poverty-stricken Indian guides after the money-mad tears through America and Japan.

In time for another short track around theaters in the United

Kingdom, Led Zeppelin's fourth album was released on November 8, 1971, its production problems finally surmounted. With this disc, Page (supported by Peter Grant) took his music-should-speak-for-itself code to its furthest extent. Though the lacquer pressings had been mastered by late summer, he insisted that the record's cover be a wordless package with no ascription to Led Zeppelin. "We wanted to demonstrate that it was the music that made Zeppelin popular; it had nothing to do with our name or image."[47] Page had never recovered from critical carps that he led a "hype band," but he met resistance from Atlantic Records, concerned that an untitled work was, in effect, un-hypeable. "So we said they couldn't have the master tape until they got the cover right."[48] Often cited as a brave innovation for the group, by late 1971, there had already been a trend in the pop music business for minimalist sleeves far removed from the toothy portraits of the enclosed artists so widespread in the '50s and early '60s: Bob Dylan's *Self Portrait,* the Band's *Music from Big Pink,* Joni Mitchell's *Ladies of the Canyon,* and the Velvet Underground's eponymous premiere, among others, had all featured low-key, "arty" graphics and were hardly flops. Page had selected a cover image integrating an old painting Robert Plant had discovered when accompanying him on an antique-hunting excursion to a junk shop in Reading, Berkshire. "So we decided to contrast the modern skyscraper on the back [the Eve Hill tower blocks, in Dudley] with the old man with the sticks—you see the destruction of the old, and the new coming forward.[49] . . . The old man carrying the wood is in harmony with nature. . . . His old cottage gets pulled down and they put him in these urban slums, old slums—terrible places."[50] Later he elucidated, "Our hearts were as much in the old ways as they were in tune with what was happening, though we weren't always in agreement with the new."[51]

More enigmas were inside. Jimmy Page's friend, one Barrington Colby, was commissioned to illustrate the gatefold, based on Pamela Colman Smith's graphics for the Arthur Edward Waite Tarot deck, originally issued in 1910 (the American

Ms. Smith was, with Waite and Aleister Crowley, a member of the Order of the Golden Dawn, and had done stage design for W. B. Yeats). "The Hermit," explained Page, was "basically an illustration of a seeker aspiring to the light of truth . . . a symbol of self reliance and wisdom."[52] (Was "Barrington Colby" Page's obscure alias?) The ninth of the Tarot's greater arcana, the Hermit card is said to represent "prudence; also and especially treason, dissimulation, roguery, corruption." (Tarot cards later were viewed on Blue Öyster Cult's *Agents of Fortune* and Dylan's *Desire*.) The complete lyrics of "Stairway to Heaven" were reprinted on the record jacket, in a typeface chosen by Page from *Studio,* an English journal of the Arts and Crafts movement, suggesting their collective pride in Plant's words. The definitive conundrum was the quartet of symbols utilized as the album's designation.

"At first I wanted just one symbol but since it was our fourth album and there were four of us, we each chose our own," detailed Jimmy Page. "I designed mine and everybody else had their own reasons for using the symbol selected."[53] In fact Page seems to have shown the others samples to pick while he had already invented an entirely unique one, or, as John Paul Jones recollects, "[Page] showed us [German typographer Rudolf Koch's] *The Book of Signs* and said we should each choose a symbol. So Bonzo and I did this, though later we discovered Jimmy and Robert had gone off and had their symbols specially designed, which was typical."[54] The vice-tight (and not terribly interested) rhythm section chose two runes that were, appropriately, almost geometric obverses of the other: Jones's was three ovals meeting in a circle, while John Bonham's was three circles merging to form three ovals. Robert Plant's feather in a circle derived from the mystical Rosicrucian cult's belief in a lost continent called Mu (possibly a variation of the Atlantis legend) and was found in author James Churchward's *The Sacred Symbols of Mu.* "I like people to lay down the truth—no bullshit. That's what the feather in the circle is all about,"[55] he laid down.

Page's icon (not technically a rune) was and is still the most inscrutable. "A lot of people mistook it for a word, 'Zoso,' which is a pity because it wasn't supposed to be a word at all but something entirely different. Basically the title thing was just another ruse to throw the media into chaos."[56] Subject to in-depth research and wild guesswork—and no firm answers from Jimmy Page—"Zoso" has been interpreted as standing for the alchemical logo for electrum (an alloy of gold and silver); the Scandinavian symbol for Thor, or perhaps Jupiter; the astrological sign of Capricorn (Page was an astrology connoisseur and a Capricorn); or a combination thereof, as well as more esoteric cryptology. It most resembles a sigil for Saturn from a 1557 document, *Ars Magica Arteficii*, by J. Cardan. The joint importance of the four symbols was to reinforce the rock 'n' roll ideal of fans' favorite bands as not merely teams of compatible musicians but mystical bonds between cosmic forces momentarily taken hold of long-haired, dope-smoking English guitar players. Sometimes referred to as "Four Symbols" but for purposes herein named *Led Zeppelin IV,* Led Zeppelin's fourth album received friendly reviews and excellent sales in 1971 (it was shipped to record stores in large numbers and with promotional material that made clear its authorship)—over three decades on, it has sold approximately 25 million copies in different formats and is considered one of the supreme documents of the rock era, with it and "Black Dog," "Rock and Roll," "When the Levee Breaks," and "Stairway to Heaven" permanent fixtures of pop best-ever lists. Outside its field, it may even stand as one of the landmark artistic achievements of the twentieth century.

Upon completion of the English tour in December '71, marked by their headlining the "Electric Magic" extravaganza at London's Wembley Empire Pool, the band took a Christmas holiday. By February 1972, they were back in the air and on the road, taking in the antipodean summer with a long trip to Australia and New Zealand, where they played six unruly indoor and outdoor gigs in Perth, Adelaide, Auckland, Sydney, Brisbane, and Melbourne.

They were raided by police in Perth, but somehow no drugs were found; the quasi-police state of Singapore wouldn't let Led Zeppelin in because of their long hair.

Home again, with *Led Zeppelin IV* still high on the charts, recording sessions for a fifth album commenced, using some ideas that had been roughed out over the past year. For these Jimmy Page accepted Mick Jagger's offer to take the Rolling Stones' mobile unit to Jagger's own country estate, Stargroves, near Newbury in Berkshire. While the absented mansion was more hospitable than the dank Headley Grange, the songs would once more be given their finished sound at recording studios in London (Olympic) and New York (Electric Lady, designed by the late great Jimi Hendrix). It was springtime, Robert Plant was about to become father to a new baby boy, and Page, Plant, Jones, and Bonham were on top of the world, dancing together on the sunny English lawn as engineer Eddie Kramer played back a cut of their ebullient new "Dancing Days."

By June the time had come for another North American run. Peter Grant was now scooping a full *90* percent of show grosses for him and his boys, to the helpless rage of promoters. "The days of the promoter giving a few quid to the group against the money taken on the door are gone," Grant advised them, not in so many words. "I thought the musicians should be the people who get the wages. We take the risks. . . . That's the way big names are made these days. Not by the press, but by people seeing them and making up their own minds."[57] Those were the days. Richard Cole leased a Dassault Falcon executive jet for Zeppelin, and arranged for a line of limousines to be available at Detroit's Cobo Hall, the Boston Garden, at the Nassau, Portland, Seattle, and Denver Coliseums, and all the other sites Plant thought of as "houses of the holy." Determined to get the attention of the music media and recognition for their popularity—four hit albums and more triumphant tours in not quite four years—Grant and Page hired publicist B. P. "Beep" Fallon, a likeable Irishman who'd assisted Marc Bolan's glittery rise (one account even has

Page himself giving Bolan guitar lessons), to spread the word to the world at large.

"We always seemed to play better when we were in the States," asserted Jimmy Page. "We were cocky and we'd show off, and it was fantastic."[58] Ready to rock 'n' roll for their most devout adherents, the band were bringing a burgeoning two-, three-, or four-hour set list of crowd-pleasers with them—"Communication Breakdown," "Heartbreaker," "Dazed and Confused," "Moby Dick," "Immigrant Song," and "Whole Lotta Love," with its long medley of Elvis, Fats Domino, and Chuck Berry standards woven throughout. Live, "Dazed" could elongate into a full fifteen or thirty minutes, every bar of the original recording blown apart into a mini-riff of its own or a wild excursion into hippiedom with Scott McKenzie's glorious "San Francisco (Be Sure to Wear Some Flowers in Your Hair)." In 1972, Page was also coming back with the known quantities of "Rock and Roll" and "Stairway to Heaven" well on their way to blockbuster status. Shorn of his beard and with recently tidied hair, the guitarist had a cool new look to go with the music. "Page and I were from the old school of, 'It's a show so wear something different,'"[59] John Paul Jones detailed. In the past, Page had worn anything from T-shirts and jeans to sweater vests and plaid trousers onstage, but Page now dressed in a special, customized outfit of black pants and a tight black shirt, embroidered with an ornate floral design. Now Jimmy Page would saunter and strut over the boards as the incarnation of what Keith Relf had hailed him years before: the Sorcerer.

"Those were the days of pure hedonism," Page was to remember. "LA in particular was like Sodom and Gomorrah, but it always had that vibe, even going back to the Golden Age of Hollywood in the '20s and '30s. You just ate it up and drank it down. Why not?"[60] The reliable Miss P was waiting for him there, and had her own perspective: "He was getting real high by then, and I happily joined him in never-never land."[61] At twenty-three Miss P was then an elder stateswoman of Los Angeles's celebrity followers. The '60s romanticism of the GTOs had fallen to a more aggressive cadre of girls who were more strictly interested in famous musicians than being rock 'n' roll Florence Nightingales; they were also younger and more jaded by exposure to wealth and power.

B. P. Fallon, a willing accessory to the Led Zep lifestyle, had shown Page photos from a rock magazine called *Star,* among them a nubile flock of Angeleno models of which one especially caught Page's eye. Lori Mattix (sometimes spelled *Maddox*) was a doe-eyed brunette, long and thin, full-lipped, and topped with luscious waves of dark hair. She was already known among L.A.'s upper ranks of groupies and para-groupies—nicknamed Lori Lightning—although she claimed never to have had dreams of meeting Led Zeppelin. Checked in to his suite at the Continental Hyatt House hotel (known as the Riot House when Zeppelin were guests), Page had Lori contacted through Leee Childers, a local rock insider and photographer. Escorted by Richard Cole, she was ceremoniously brought before Page in his lair, where he told her she looked lovelier in person. She was fourteen years old.

"He had this very calm and kind demeanor about him," Lori would reflect on her meeting with the guitar god twice her age. "You just immediately fell in love with him." They became intimate, while Page reassured Lori's either very naïve or very liberated mother with gifts of flowers and his soft-spoken English manner. "We were madly in love" is her reminiscence of the affair, and although she pleaded sexual innocence before knowing Page, she could not have been entirely ingenuous if she was posing provocatively as a teenage model and hanging around the Sunset Strip. Transient and statutorily illegal as his attention was (she remained his paramour in Los Angeles only), she felt their relationship was "the most beautiful thing ever."[62]

Despite the undeniable commercial and musical sensation of the 1972 American tour, and the efforts of B. P. Fallon, Led Zeppelin was drowned out that summer by the Rolling Stones, who were also on the road in America, for the first time since their 1969 visit, which had wound up at the tragedy-stricken Altamont debacle. The Stones were media darlings, aristocrats' playthings, ten-year veterans of the industry, and were treated as Important by writers like Truman Capote and Terry Southern—Jimmy Page and his bandmates had come along after the '60s rock consensus had crumbled and, to their chagrin, were usually lumped in with the likes of Grand Funk Railroad. "Look, we've just toured the States and done as well if not better than the Stones, but there was hardly anything about it in the British press," grumbled John Bonham. "All we read was the Stones this and the Stones that, and it pissed us off."[63] "But the thing is," Page philosophized, "the press have always been into images rather than music."[64]

After further mixing and recording in New York and a summer holiday, in October the group went to Japan once more for concerts in Tokyo, Osaka, Nagoya, and Kyoto. Taking a break in Hong Kong, they all sampled some Asian heroin (on the assumption it was cocaine) and became ill, a first frightening taste of the hardest of all narcotics. On the return to the U.K., Jimmy Page and Robert Plant again stopped in Bombay, where they recorded themselves and Indian players with Page's portable Stellavox equipment. "We heard one guitarist who was really good," Page said of these informal sessions. "He frightened me to death by saying, 'Oh, I practice for eight hours every day,' and you could see that he did, too."[65] The alien modes and scales of the subcontinent, worked into adaptations of Zeppelin tunes "Friends" and "Four Sticks," were compelling, and Page would adopt more of them into his own style in the future.

Following two dates in Montreux, Switzerland, Led Zeppelin barnstormed their way through a winter tour of the U.K. over December and into January 1973—100,000 tickets for these performances were sold in a single day. "The trouble is, you can't seem to please everyone," Page realized about playing these municipal auditoriums. "When we play large stadiums they complain, and when we play small clubs they moan about not being able to get in. You just can't win."[66] At home in Plumpton Place, he had furnished one room as a studio space and was trying out an early synthesizer for demo tapings on a New Vista eight-track recorder and a mixing console. "It's best used for feeding the signals on to tape, rather than as a studio-quality mixer," he explained, "but it's well capable of handling a full range of sounds."[67] To another interviewer he admitted, "I've set myself certain goals in life and I just haven't reached them yet, not by any means. Having a studio has helped a lot, mind you; I've been working on a film track which was another challenge."[68] This cinematic venture was a contribution to *Lucifer Rising*, directed by Kenneth Anger.

Born Kenneth Anglemyer in California in 1927, Anger was a pioneering underground filmmaker whose short works wandered a gray area between surrealist avant-garde and Times Square sleaze. As a boy he had appeared as the Changeling Prince in a Hollywood version of *A Midsummer Night's Dream*, but child stardom eluded him and he seemed to nurse a permanent grudge against show business convention, and every other kind, ever more. He had chosen his pseudonym well. His *Fireworks* and *Scorpio Rising* were bizarre collages of Nazism, sadomasochism, and homoeroticism, edited in with "found" footage and pop culture iconography, and his nonfiction book *Hollywood Babylon* became a tell-all classic. Bobby Beausoleil, a young musician and drifter who would wind up a convicted murderer through his close connections with Charles Manson, was one of Anger's discoveries and the ostensible star of *Invocation of My Demon Brother*. Constantly hustling funds for his projects, he had wandered from the U.S. to Europe and back, and in the late '60s he had found himself in the orbit of English rock 'n' rollers who toyed with him as a darker, more desperate Andy Warhol. Mick Jagger had been credited with the music for *Invocation*, and Anger had been a regular of the Stones' druggy circle until they got bored; Jimmy Page was to be his next patron.

By 1972, Page could claim to have one of the largest collections of Aleister Crowley material in the world. At a Sotheby's auction in London he outbid Kenneth Anger for a Crowleyan relic and Anger introduced himself afterward, impressing Page with his own self-taught erudition on Crowley and the occult. Page invited the auteur up to the Boleskine House and was somehow persuaded to provide music for his prolonged *Lucifer Rising* production (Anger had received a state grant from the British National Film Finance Corporation). The rich leader of Led Zeppelin didn't ask for payment, and in any event Anger was unlikely to supply any. "I felt it quite an honor that he'd asked me," declared Jimmy Page. He made it clear that his band was his first priority but offered the filmmaker as much time and music as he could spare, and Page was even briefly photographed for the picture as part of its fragmented visuals. "It's a very small part that I play and in no way sensational."[69] His accompaniment was to be more abstract tones than songs, achieved by "messing around" with his six- and twelve-string guitars and the synthesizer: "That's basically what I'm into— collages and tissues of sound, with emotional intensity and melody and all that."[70]

Jimmy Page's association with Kenneth Anger was symptomatic of a new trend in rock music, as the genre began to creep into some of the weirder corners of the counterculture. Erstwhile messengers of love and sunshine, both the Beatles and (more directly) the Beach Boys had had their names dragged through the blood of the Manson trauma. The Stones had sung "Sympathy for the Devil" and were popularly perceived to have been responsible for the bad vibes that had brought the '60s to such a violent end at Altamont; with "The End," "Riders on the Storm," and "The Unknown Soldier," the Doors had brought sex, dread, and death to the same perverse party; Cream had done a wicked version of Albert King's "Born Under a Bad Sign," and the damned bluesman Jimi Hendrix had the ghostly "Voodoo Chile (Slight Return)" as one of his best tracks. In America, Led Zeppelin's old Whiskey a-Go-Go stage rivals Alice Cooper were heralding a subcategory of "shock rock," and a foursome out of Birmingham England, Black Sabbath, were scoring chart success with their own brand of malefic boogie. Into 1973, Led Zeppelin had inherited the mantle of infamy and danger from the Stones, who were now jet-setters and fashion magnets—they got the mainstream press coverage, but Zeppelin, more than any other artists on the scene, had become the subject of whispers, innuendo, and conjecture.

Led Zeppelin IV was a prime source of the rumors. Its ancient lettering, inexplicable cover art, and the murky depths of "Stairway to Heaven" and "When the Levee Breaks" had fans divining *any* kind of meaning from the album. Early pressings of *Led Zeppelin III,* too, had borne a peculiar adjuration etched on the inner groove: *Do what thou wilt—So mete it be.* The very fact that Jimmy Page and his group were well out of the tabloids' eyes made them all the more interesting in the teenage wastelands of Illinois or Florida or Ontario, and in those pre-five-hundred-channel, pre-Internet years, what little could be gleaned about Led Zeppelin had to pass through word of mouth from record shops to high school smoking areas to suburban basements. Repeated and exaggerated, the stories grew into scary tales. For those who had actually seen and heard them in concert, or met any of the musicians afterward, the mystique was not dispelled.

Of the four, Page was the most unknowable. Robert Plant sang and introduced the songs and came across as a beatific beamer of sex appeal and certainty, while John Bonham and John Paul Jones were the trusty backup, a party-animal drummer and family-man bassist keeping the rhythms. The black-clad, black-haired guitarist who took the incredible solos, played the freakish twin-necked instrument, and who had instigated the whole phenomenon was another matter. What people had heard about him was not reassuring. He was known to follow the precepts of a strange English magician and live in a castle by a lake infested with sea monsters. Women had accounts of him keeping whips and handcuffs for his very personal use, of lighting small fires in his hotel rooms for ritualistic purposes. His Los Angeles girlfriend was underage. The blackest legend of all concerned the basis of Led Zeppelin's accomplishment: Jimmy Page, in exchange for talent, allure, money, and fame, had sold his and his bandmates' souls to Satan.

The Rover

1973-1980

Thus, even thus, (good Gentlemen, and my deare friends) was I
inthralled in that Satanicall band, all good desires drowned, all pietie
banished, all purpose of amendment utterly exiled, by the tyrannous
threatnings of my deadly enemy.

—The Historie of the Damnable Life and
Deserved Death of Doctor John Faustus

Entering the middle years of the 1970s, Jimmy Page had a good
case to be leading the world's biggest rock group, in a day when
such a title was hotly contested and carried a serious cultural
cachet. Without ever becoming a household name or a multime-
dia fixture, Led Zeppelin was an indisputable success within the
music industry and among the teeming youth market. The band's
fourth album had marked their creative zenith and they showed
no signs of slowing down or breaking up. Yet by the end of the
decade, a series of injuries, lawsuits, and deaths would shatter
their unity, and Jimmy Page would not be steering Zeppelin's artistic course but pondering his very livelihood and fighting for
his physical and psychological health.

In early 1973, such a denouement was unthinkable. Page was
with Charlotte Martin and father to little Scarlet, rounding off
a short tour of Britain with Robert Plant, John Paul Jones, and
John Bonham, and busy completing the quartet's next album, to

be designated not "Led Zeppelin V" but *Houses of the Holy.* The guitarist always maintained that, away from his work, he lived the sedate and secluded life of a landed gentleman. "We really only socialized when we were on the road," he held. "We all really came to value our family lives. . . . Our families helped keep us sane."[1] At home in Plumpton Place, Page began to try his hand at vegetable gardening, hung Afghan hangings in his rooms, and continued to manifest what he called his "affinity with the ideals of the Pre-Raphaelites."[2] Far to the north at his country seat of the Boleskine House, he had been locally active in fighting the proposed erection of power lines along the shores of Loch Ness. "If I wasn't into rock," Page told a journalist, "I would be living somewhere like Wales in a commune."[3]

But he was into rock, and deeply. Whatever his ideals of domestic tranquility, Jimmy Page was married to Led Zeppelin. As the act's producer, it was his responsibility to choose studios and engineers, oversee cover art (the colorful *Houses* package had unforeseen printing complications), and approve master tapes; the others contributed their songs and their performances, but Page was the one who opened early and stayed late. "We all wanted to see the music get better. And part of the reason things ran smoothly was that I had the last decision on everything."[4] And though Peter Grant and Richard Cole had overseen their large-scale tours of North America, Europe, and the Far East, the fact was that Led Zeppelin never went more than a week or two without one-off gigs, rehearsals, recording sessions, interview dates, awards presentations, or other routine professional duties. Besides Grant and Cole, the band employed a semi-permanent road crew of drivers, sound and lighting technicians, and instrument handlers (at various times Joe "Jammer" Wright, Ray Thomas, and Tim Marten were responsible for Page's guitars; they gave him the nickname "Led Wallet" for his parsimony). "I'm sure people aren't aware of this," explained Page in April '73. "I'm sure they think we sit on our arses all day long, but we don't. All I know is I haven't stopped for three years. If it gives you any indication, I haven't had a holiday ever since the group started."[5]

Whether he knew it or not, the psychic dislocation of his experience would be one from which he would never really recover, and nor would Plant, Jones, or especially Bonham. Pumping out a recurring set list of hard rock—"Rock and Roll," "Communication Breakdown," "Whole Lotta Love," "Dazed and Confused," and others—followed by an adrenaline-dousing cascade of alcohol or other substances before jumping into the limo or the van or the plane was a nightly strain that was slow to catch up with them, but when it did, it came with a vengeance. They and their handful of peers lived in a peculiar kind of isolation from, and even ignorance of, the everyday world. In some things they were very knowledgeable: the mechanics of professional recording studios, of putting on concerts for thousands of people, of first-, second-, and third-class travel arrangements, and of top-level pop musicianship, for example. They had known irreplaceable moments of adulation and had ventured into some of the deepest recesses of human indulgence and gratification. Yet they were also men not yet thirty years old whose formal educations had ended early, whose household affairs were attended to by assistants and minders, and who had spent their entire adulthoods pursuing an almost infinitesimal prospect of personal success. To their eternal wonder, they had realized it. They would never be the same.

Led Zeppelin toured Western Europe in March and early April 1973, playing some twenty-two shows in twenty cities and eight countries in just under a month. A major U.S. tour was planned for the spring and summer. *Houses of the Holy* was released on March 26 and capitalized on its four classic precursors and the artists' hard-won renown to enjoy strong sales and, soon enough, the number-one spot on the American charts. *Houses* was actually the band's widest departure from their blues-rock roots, and its undeniable musical sophistication masked an ambitious compositional stretch that didn't succeed quite as well as earlier or later efforts. "The Song Remains the Same" and "Dancing Days" were grandiose, self-mythologizing anthems of conquest and triumph, while "The Rain Song" (all three credited to Page and Plant) was a lavish ballad ornamented with Jones's mellotron strings. The latter was inspired by a meeting with George Harrison, who teased John Bonham over Led Zeppelin's avoidance of slow songs. "I'll give him a ballad!"[6] thought Jimmy Page, and even nudged at the Beatle's "Something" in "The Rain Song"'s opening chord shift. More effective were Page's acoustic hammer-ons and pull-offs introducing "Over the Hills and Far Away," a smooth segue of idiosyncratic folk picking and arena rock histrionics in the vein of "Stairway to Heaven." But "The Crunge" was an ill-conceived joke around James Brown–style funk, whose strangled treble Stratocaster chords and zigzag beats fractured anything resembling a groove. "D'yer Mak'er" was a better but still unlikely fusion of heavy metal volume with reggae moves that listeners found either charming or embarrassing. Page thought it was "just a giggle,"[7] but John Paul Jones claimed that Bonham "hated it, and so did I."[8]

Jones himself was behind "No Quarter," a foggy descent into keyboards and distorted guitar that is one of the album's standout cuts. Page employed the same slowed-down effect he had used on "When the Levee Breaks" to stretch and deepen the morbid arrangement, and his slurring wah-wah chords carry a subtle menace. All four members wrote "The Ocean," the one really high-powered riff in the collection, showing off their effortless mastery of 4/4 against 7/8 time. "The Ocean" goes from Page's incomparable electric slam (doubling its fretted A note with an open A string) to snakelike shuffle to doo-wop climax and became a concert favorite that year—it was, indeed, about the seas of heads and hands greeting them as they took the stages of the world. *Houses of the Holy* came packaged in a luminous sleeve of fairylike children (in fact a composite of siblings Simon and Samantha Gates) climbing the ancient stones of Giant's Causeway in Northern Ireland, with a gatefold of one being held in offering by a mysterious adult, all of which assured Led Zeppelin's occult standing. As with *Led Zeppelin IV,* there was no lettering on the cover, although its protective plastic wrap did bear its title and band name, this time in the gorgeous art nouveau font (designed by Bush Hollyhead) that would become Led Zeppelin's official emblem.

Then it was time for the sprawling two-legged tour of the U.S. and Canada over the spring and summer. There would be no competition from the Rolling Stones in 1973, and Peter Grant had hired the young PR representative Danny Goldberg to spread the word that Led Zeppelin faced no competition from anyone else. It wasn't a hard sell. From the opening shows in Atlanta and Tampa where concertgoers numbered close to 60,000, one-act attendance records set by the Beatles eight years before were decimated, and Mr. and Mrs. Middle America began to realize what their sons and daughters had already known: this was a big, loud, and wildly powerful rock group.

Jimmy Page was still leading the charge. A frighteningly talented soloist bedecked in his black suit, his Les Paul was draped down almost to knee level as he ran and leapt over the boards to the volcanic entry of "Rock and Roll." Wearing the heavy guitar that low put a strain on his back and seriously compromised the chording leverage he could get from his left forearm, but audiences detected no handicap. Page even confessed to being unable to play a proper barre chord, where the index finger spans all six strings: "I'm using my thumb [on the low E string] which is right out, technically."[9] In Los Angeles, in June, he hurt a finger of his right hand on a wire fence while chatting with some fans at the airport. "Now, think about it this way— you've played gigs for a whole month and then suddenly you can't touch the guitar for a whole month. . . . That was just a to-tally horrifying experience."[10] He remained a guitar hero, battle scars and all.

His presence onstage and off was now such that extra security was hired to protect him from the lunatic fringe to whom he had become a star of rock 'n' roll dreams and rock 'n' roll nightmares. "I was once informed that someone was set on killing me when I was in the States," Page recounted to Nick Kent of *New Musical Express*. "The guy was a real crazy and had all these photographs on the wall with circles around them. It was a real Manson situation. . . . Eventually this guy was tracked down and got carted away to a hospital. He would definitely have had a try, though."[11] For comic relief, he could hang out at the Hyatt House in Los Angeles with members of the Monty Python troupe, who were also touring the continent—Led Zeppelin would invest in the Pythons' first feature film, *Monty Python and the Holy Grail*—and the Flying Circus's Eric Idle fondly recalled his Riot House days and nights with "all those mad Led Zeppelin people."[12] And for romance, there was Lori Mattix, although she had a rival in the much older (twenty-four) Miss Pamela, who thought of her as "a giggling pubescent."[13] "I just view it all with amusement," Page laughed over his female stalkers. "The competition thing out there is incredible and you've got to keep out of the middle of it, or else it gets to you too."[14]

For the '73 tour the band traveled in grand style. Instead of the small executive jet that had shuttled them the previous year, Led Zeppelin flew in the *Starship*, a customized four-engine Boeing 720B airliner that was rented out to the very few entertainers able to splurge $2,500 per hour of air time on luxury-class accommodation between hotels. Even in an era of oil shocks and gas-station lineups, the aircraft made logistical sense in enabling the performers and their friends to hop short distances back and forth from strategic bases as opposed to packing up to new locations every night. Inside, among the shag carpet, private bedroom, and shower, sexy stewardesses named Suzee and Bianca kept the drinks flowing, there were porn movies flickering on the novel video monitor, and John Paul Jones played "I've Got a Lovely Bunch of Coconuts" on the keyboard for in-flight entertainment. "We weren't the only band that had its own plane," *Starship* passenger Jimmy Page remembered, "but we were the only ones that had a grown-up plane." His preferred seating? "I did have the bedroom. . . . I did like the idea of a horizontal takeoff."[15]

Even on the ground, Page was flying very high that tour. By 1973, cocaine was the intoxicant of choice for the rock jet set: unlike alcohol or cannabis, the stimulant was a lift, not a depressant or a psychedelic, and provided an exciting rush of confidence and energy to hard-working musicians while storming the arenas of the Midwest. First noted by Spanish explorers for its invigorating effects on South American natives in the Andes, cocaine had been illegal in the United States since 1914 (replaced by caffeine as a prime ingredient of Coca-Cola) and was mostly a luxury for the rich and elite until it began to be imported into America in large quantities in the late '60s, where a new generation of hedonists took to it as the next mind-altering thrill. A social drug, cocaine did not impair ability or perception, and had no tell-tale fumes to alert police. In flight and backstage with Led Zeppelin, it was administered quickly and discreetly—and frequently—followed by a sniff of cherry snuff and a dab of 1966 Dom Perignon champagne to offset its cold metallic aftertaste. The stewardesses on the *Starship* later joked that they made great tips pocketing the rolled-up hundred-dollar bills Jimmy Page and his entourage left behind. "That might've been true," said Led Wallet, "but I'll tell you one thing—they never got any of *my* money!"[16]

The aspect of cocaine least understood by its users in the mid-'70s was that it was highly addictive. There were nervous giggles about the flake being "God's way of saying you have too much money," or that "After a line, I feel like a new man—and the new man wants another line," but, until the highly publicized crashes of comedians John Belushi and Richard Pryor in the following decade, few knew just how habit-forming cocaine could be. Regular intake of cocaine reduces the number of dopamine receptors in the neurons of the brain, thus leading to steeper come-downs and a consequent need for more of the drug to trigger the pleasurable effects brought on initially. Led Zeppelin in 1973 were enjoying quantities of cocaine as only the most successful rock bands could afford, and as a result Richard Cole, Peter Grant, and John Bonham all became dangerously heavy abusers. But Jimmy Page may have been the heaviest abuser of all.

"Oh, everyone went over the top a few times," Page hinted to Nick Kent after the tour. "I know I did and, to be honest with you, I don't really remember much of what happened. The thing is that even when we were totally wasted we'd somehow be able to perform on stage."[17] Publicist B. P. Fallon corroborated, saying, "Jimmy just used to sit there sometimes looking pretty whacked, and he's really a fragile geezer, and suddenly he'd be on his feet shouting, 'Right, over the top!'"[18] Like other musicians of his renown, the sheer thrill of performing for thousands and thousands of people was the ultimate buzz, albeit one that needed constant reinforcement by other means: "I felt like a kettle with a cork in the top," Page admitted. "I'd stay up for five nights on the trot. It didn't seem to affect my playing, but I'd come off stage and I was just not leveling off at all, not turning off the adrenaline, I couldn't.[19] . . . Everything was so exciting—why would you want to go to sleep? You might miss something."[20]

The latter shows of the '73 outing were filmed for a Led Zeppelin documentary Peter Grant had envisioned. American director Joe Massot was an acquaintance of Page's partner, Charlotte Martin, and had seen the group's 1970 appearance at the Bath Festival, after meeting Jimmy Page and visiting the couple at their Pangbourne residence. In 1972, Massot had approached Page at Plumpton Place with the idea for a cinematic record and was referred to Peter Grant, who eventually agreed to fund the enterprise on the condition that Zeppelin have artistic control and legal ownership of the product. Coverage was fitful (the camera operators included Ernie Day, who had filmed David Lean's *Lawrence of Arabia* in 1962), and the group, though friendly enough, were not very enthused over movie work. Massot and his crew did capture their Madison Square Garden performances and the unintended crisis of a $200,000 cash robbery from their hotel. "If the tour had been a bummer, that would have been the last straw," Page thought, "but it wasn't."[21]

Massot's plan was to intercut live concert sequences with personal footage of the band members at their homes, and "fantasy" scenes interpreting their music. This material was shot back in Britain during the fall, once the American run had finished. Of all the players, only Jimmy Page was pictured alone (the others were seen with their wives and children)—he is first encountered on the verdant grounds of Plumpton Place, where he is having a solitary idyll by its moat where a pair of black Australian swans paddle about. Playing an obscure hurdy-gurdy and his acoustic guitar lying by his side, the camera approaches him from behind until he turns to the viewer and his eyes glow a haunting red, which he confirmed was accomplished through special effects, no doubt to the disbelief of many fans. "All my sections are related to the eyes, the eyes being the mirror of the soul,"[22] he explained. Over two cold nights in December, Massot filmed Page outside the Boleskine House under a full Scottish moon with Loch Ness in the background, as Page had asked. To be accompanied by the bowing passage from a live "Dazed and Confused," and re-enacting the gatefold of *Led Zeppelin IV*, Page doggedly ascends a cliff where a hooded "hermit" stands with a lamp. The hermit turns out to be an aged, bearded version of Page himself, who then reverses through time to childhood and infancy (via makeup and family pictures of a very young James Patrick Page) and then to a *2001*-like embryonic state. "I really had to do all my yoga training for that," said the neophyte actor. "I was exhausted by the end of it because I had to stand up all the time, absolutely rigid.[23] . . . It wasn't done in one take—that was the trouble!"[24]

Page continued occasional work on the sound track for Kenneth Anger's *Lucifer Rising* at his home studio at Plumpton Place, but there he also began demoing songs for the next Led Zeppelin album. There were enough pieces left over from previous sessions that a two-record set could be assembled, with new cuts recorded at Headley Grange and overdubbed at Olympic, as engineers Ron Nevison and Keith Harwood manned the faders. One of the first run-throughs was taped in late 1973 with just Page and John Bonham going over an electric progression in his DADGAD tuning—the drummer and guitar player collided into a droning groove that pushed raga rock to its limit. Robert Plant later arrived with lyrics inspired by his own holidays in North Africa in the wake of the American circuit, while John Paul Jones held off, reconsidering his role in the band and the strain it placed on his home life. "He was a family man, was Jonesy,"[25] Peter Grant recognized, promising to ease the Zeppelin itineraries for the bassist. Recording and mixing extended into the new year, all four musicians back together, and the Page-Plant-Bonham opus called "Kashmir" anticipated a strong collection.

In January 1974, Led Zeppelin's five-year contract with Atlantic Records expired, and Grant renegotiated with Ahmet Ertegun for high value and creative license that reflected the act's proven and expected earnings potential; a subsidiary, group-owned record label was included in the deal. "Sometimes I'd take Jimmy into Atlantic in New York and everybody would hide in their offices because they thought he was going to put a spell on them," chortled the manager. "He was very good at intimidating them."[26]

Very rich, Jimmy Page could now afford a third residence, and he surpassed David Bowie to pay £350,000 for a place on Melbury Road in London's Kensington district. Purchased from the actor Richard Harris, the Tower House was Page's dream home, combining the urban centrality he needed for business with the aesthetic qualities incorporated into his art. Its designer and first occupant was William Burges, who was to architecture what Pre-Raphaelites like John William Waterhouse were to painting, and the Tower House was a neo-medieval (it was completed in 1881) imagining of haunted castle and fairy tale. The rooms were conceived around mystical "themes," with the

entry as Time, the dining room as Fame, the library as Literature and the Liberal Arts, the drawing room as Love, and the
master bedroom laid out as an undersea kingdom for Burges's
opiated enjoyment. Page, who was an admirer of Burges, kept
up the household tradition.

Also in Kensington, Page was in the process of buying the
Equinox, at 4 Holland Street. This was a small bookshop that
specialized in the occult, which he acquired not as a business
venture but simply to have access to its library. "There was not
one good bookshop in London with a good collection of Occult
books and I was so pissed off at not being able to get the books
I wanted,"[27] he told an interviewer. Along with carrying astrology and tarot material, the Equinox would also publish works,
including Aleister Crowley's translation of *The Book of Goetia*
and *Astrology: A Cosmic Science* by Isabel Hickey; numerous au-
tographed copies of Crowley books were also for sale. The inten-
tion was never to turn much profit but to provide otherwise rare
or inaccessible volumes for the public and for Page himself.

In the spring, Peter Grant and Led Zeppelin officially announced the formation of Swan Song records, their own recording company, whose roster would number Scottish blues mistress
Maggie Bell as well as a new quartet, Bad Company, which rose
out of the ashes of Mott the Hoople (guitarist Mick Ralphs) and
Free (singer Paul Rodgers and drummer Simon Kirke), with
Boz Burrell of King Crimson stepping in on bass. "Having gone
through what appeared to be interference on the artistic side by
record companies," said Jimmy Page, thinking of his Yardbirds'
struggles and Atlantic's resistance to the untitled fourth Zeppelin album, "we wanted to form a label where the artists would be
able to fulfill themselves without all that hassle."[28] "Swan Song"
was picked as a corporate title after a long acoustic guitar piece
Page was developing. At first the name of the song, then an entire
album, "All the vibes started and suddenly it was out of the LP
and onto the record label."[29] The avian logo of the company was
based on the fowl of Page's Plumpton Place, placed over Ameri-

can artist William Rimmer's *Evening: Fall of Day,* a nineteenth-century watercolor found in the Boston Museum of Fine Arts. For all the big things envisaged for Swan Song—and the speedy success in June of hard-rocking Bad Company's eponymous debut—Page was no businessman and had no plans to become one. "I'm not personally involved with the business side of it because I'm so involved with the production of the records. . . . There are finite points where the two cross and I get involved then, but apart from that I don't really pay much attention to what's going on behind the scenes."[30]

Swan Song's all-important American launches took place in New York and later in Los Angeles, in May 1974. All the Led Zeppelin members arrived and typically imperial celebrations were staged, with the assortment of associates and label mates (Peter Grant, Richard Cole, and tour chum Roy Harper), plus incongruous celebrity guests (Rolling Stone Bill Wyman, Monkee Mickey Dolenz, and Marx Brother Groucho). In New York's Four Seasons restaurant, John Bonham, Cole, and Page gathered in a corner and took turns around a heaping plate of cocaine; in L.A., Page and his bandmates were ushered into the hotel room of the King himself, Elvis Presley. Jimmy Page had come a long way from Miles Road and "Baby, Let's Play House." "It was a little awkward at first," he looked back on the meeting, "because his music meant so much to us."[31] But auto buff Bonham struck up a conversation about a hot rod Presley had driven in his movie *Loving You* ("I've had one, El, that kicked back *real* hard,"[32] said the Midlands drummer), and the rock 'n' rollers relaxed into easygoing conversation. "He was wonderful, a fantastic man,"[33] Page concluded. Just over three years later, Elvis was dead.

In California, Page began a dalliance with model Bebe Buell, sometime partner of guitarist Todd Rundgren. Buell was taking the place of the bitter Miss Pamela and brokenhearted Lori Mattix, who were kept at bay by Zeppelin's security team when the couple paraded in front of them at the Rainbow Bar and Grill. Jimmy Page himself was a veritable King of Rock, flanked by goons who could, and would, pulverize unfriendlies who came too close ("It was a little like hanging out with the Mafia," thought Bebe Buell),[34] but he was uncomfortable in the spotlight and with hangers-on like the self-appointed "Mayor of the Sunset Strip," Rodney Bingenheimer. "I mean you walk in and the next thing you know there are cameras everywhere and you're ducking under the bar to get away. . . . The last time I was in L.A. there was this incredible groupie feud which was getting down to razor blade sandwiches."[35] Untroubled by his L.A. exes, Page escorted Bebe back to New York. She heard him assure Peter Grant and Robert Plant, "She's not a coke whore,"[36] which she took as high praise, and he implied to her that his future with Charlotte Martin in England was uncertain. She held on to Todd Rundgren, for the moment, while he returned across the Atlantic.

Back in London the Led Zeppelin film project was languishing and Grant was demanding to see what footage Joe Massot had assembled—at a private screening John Bonham cracked up when he saw Page in "Hermit" guise and Page thought the images of him climbing at Boleskine were unflattering. Massot was unceremoniously bounced from the project, and Australian filmmaker Peter Clifton, whose cameras had previously been trained on Otis Redding, Jimi Hendrix, Cream, and Pink Floyd, was hired. Clifton was wary of the group's reputation and his fears were well-founded. "As individual human beings Led Zeppelin were extremely sensitive and considerate, but as a group they were bloody difficult, if not impossible," he recalled. "It was Jimmy's band and what Jimmy said—or rather what Peter Grant said on Jimmy's behalf—was the way it was. . . . Peter made me swear that if I was going to make the film, if anything went wrong I must remember that Jimmy was the first man into the lifeboat."[37] His major task in July and August was to reshoot some of Page's "mountain" fantasy at Plumpton Place, and then to replicate concert sequences in Shepperton Studios. In the final film, scenes and music of the live Madison Square Garden shows from 1973 are mixed with close-ups taken with no audience, and there are some continuity gaps between Jimmy Page's hair and stage costume from either venue; at Shepperton, John Paul Jones wore a wig that is even more of a giveaway. But their performance for Clifton was real, and electric. "They were so hot and tight and fuelled up with you-know-what."[38]

Bebe Buell arrived in Britain in September, ostensibly to accompany Todd Rundgren on a promotional tour but with secret hopes of carrying on her romance with Page. Despite Rundgren's warnings as to his character, she soon found herself at the Tower House in Page's bed. "Maybe it was the music," she considered in her account, *Rebel Heart*. "Maybe it was his Satanic Edwardian quality. Maybe it was the medieval Sir Lancelot vibe. I didn't know and I didn't care." The two took mescaline together, which gave her hallucinatory perceptions of Page's endowment: "I needed to pull myself together and realize that it was an average-size penis."[39] So much for Moby Dick. She noticed that fans and passersby kept their distance from the rock star in a way they never did with, say, Mick Jagger. "I think it was because they were genuinely afraid that he was Satan, that he had some sort of evil allure."[40]

In London again, in November, for modeling assignments, Buell planned to meet Page once more, but when she went to the Equinox to track him down, the store's manager gently revealed that the upstairs apartment was being occupied by Charlotte Martin and Scarlet Page, after a swinging party between Jimmy Page, Charlotte, and soon-to-be Rolling Stone Ron Wood and his wife, Krissie, went awry. "Didn't I tell you he's a devil?" Mick Jagger soothed her at Wood's (now) bachelor pad. "You're just not kinky enough for him, not weird enough."[41] Page, Wood, and Keith Richards were all matey, however, and spent some very late nights together recording instrumental music, including a jam dubbed "Scarlet." Jimmy Page and Charlotte Martin resumed their relationship, although Krissie Wood was not entirely out of the picture herself. Afterward, Bebe Buell received a final phone call from Page in England when she was in New York, in which he promised her he would send "a sign" that evening. At midnight, she and a friend were up in Rundgren's Woodstock retreat when they were startled by a noise and found a big antique mirror in the upstairs bathroom had fallen and crashed to pieces.

The heedlessness with which Jimmy Page and his rock star friends slipped in and out of liaisons with women is part of their legend, but as time passed and their careers lost momentum, and as some of them became more interested in drugs than sex, that cavalier attitude would fade. Even in a pre-AIDS era, brief attacks of venereal disease were an occupational hazard of famous musicians, and the fickle attentions of girlfriends and groupies to which Todd Rundgren and Ron Wood could attest caught up with nearly everyone. Bebe Buell herself went on to affairs with Aerosmith's Steve Tyler (which served Page right, since his '60s fling Lynn Collins had been snatched from under Tyler's then-unknown nose) and New Waver Elvis Costello. *Rolling Stone* journalist Cameron Crowe, only in his teens when authoring sympathetic profiles of Led Zeppelin, recalled the atmosphere when he became the director-screenwriter of the 2000 film *Almost Famous,* his autobiographical composite of '70s rock groups and their followers. Though he only names one name in his recollection, it is clear who the real subject is: "What I was trying to capture in the script was the elaborate denial that the girls buy into. They talk about themselves as muses, they talk about bands as puppets. . . . But when you get with the rock stars, you realize [the girls] of course are the trinkets themselves. . . . As the years went by I would run into the guys in the airport, or see someone I once wrote about to ask them for music for one of the movies or something, and when we'd get alone they'd ask me a question like, 'Have you seen Lori?' I'd say, 'No, I haven't seen Lori since back then.' And they'd get a wistful look, where you realize later the power of those trinkets. They missed those girls, and when the success moved on a bit, or the years moved on, it's funny how they remembered those girls as a great symbol of their years of popularity."[42]

By the end of 1974, Page and the rest of his band were impatient for more road work. The guitarist had sat in for impromptu jams with Bad Company and Crosby, Stills & Nash, and guested on albums by Roy Harper and Maggie Bell, but it was time for another Zeppelin mission. Their new two-disc package, called *Physical Graffiti*, was almost ready and promised to bring in plenty of revenue for Swan Song Records; rehearsals were staged for a show that would feature spectacular new sound, lighting and laser elements, as well as the usual deafening array of amplification, now jacked up to 70,000 watts' worth. Warmed up with gigs in Rotterdam and Brussels, the foursome set off for America in the winter of 1975, a compromise with John Paul Jones and the other fathers in the act so as not to miss their children's summer holidays. But as Jimmy Page was stepping off a train at London's Victoria Station, he caught the ring finger of his left hand in a door and his playing was temporarily impaired ("I was just totally numb—numb with shock");[43] ditto Robert Plant's voice after encountering the January cold of Minneapolis and Chicago. The casualties of the campaign would mount further.

Page had once spoken of musical influences ranging from Gustav Mahler and Krzysztof Penderecki to Bert Jansch, but as the tour proceeded, the injured guitarist confided to Cameron Crowe an appreciation for American guitarists like Amos Garrett, who'd played on Maria Muldaur's "Midnight at the Oasis," Elliott Randall of Steely Dan ("Reelin' in the Years"), and said Little Feat was his favorite U.S. band. "We've lost the best guitarist any of us ever had, and that was Hendrix,"[44] he attested. Even with the aerial comforts of the *Starship* close by, Page was slogging through shows in Chicago, Cleveland, and Indianapolis on the strength of banana daiquiris, cocaine, and Jack Daniel's whiskey, normally meant for sipping but guzzled straight out of the bottle by Page in an iconic backstage photograph taken during these weeks. "He took this big swig and held it up in the air," cameraman Neal Preston remembered. "I took one frame and there it was. . . . He seemed to have a bottle around more often than not."[45]

In Detroit, Page laid a furious verbal assault on an English newspaperman who'd disparaged his craft. "You don't want to know about my music—all you care about is the grosses and the interior of the plane. You're a communist!"[46] In Philadelphia, Page was tempted to bash overzealous security guards on the head with his Gibson double-neck when they descended on a fan near the stage—"I saw this incident happen and I was almost physically sick."[47] In Los Angeles, a strangely insistent young woman was deterred from meeting Page and had to be satisfied with leaving a handwritten message for him, which was soon forgotten; shortly afterward, she was charged with pointing a gun at U.S. President Gerald Ford and discovered to be Lynette "Squeaky" Fromme of the Charles Manson family. In New York, Page was interviewed by novelist William S. Burroughs, who had written *Naked Lunch*, *Junky*, and other Beat books, and discussed Aleister Crowley, magick, and crowd control. "There *is* a responsibility to the audience," the musician told the writer. "We don't want anything bad to happen to these kids."[48] And while John Paul Jones kept well to himself ("If it was fun you joined in, if it wasn't you didn't"),[49] Robert Plant claimed, "I love my work, which is communication on a vast level,"[50] and John Bonham dressed and behaved as a droog from *A Clockwork Orange*, Jimmy Page was pierced with the white-hot laser of heroin.

Heroin. The downfall of Charlie Parker and Billie Holliday had always been on the fringes of the pop world, the deadliest and most seductive of all the pleasures available to itinerant musicians plying their trade from town to town. Page's old Surrey mate Eric Clapton had only just overcome his addiction, and Keith Richards was still in the grip of one that had begun in the late '60s. He had a connection at the hip London shop Granny Takes a Trip, and Page became a regular at the scene himself. On the road, heroin was dispensed by the network of opportunists and hangers-on who haunted the dressing rooms, promoter's digs, and hotel lobbies where rock groups congregated, a subtle hook offered from Nobody to Somebody (heroin can be snorted like cocaine) in exchange for the thrill of partying with the stars.

Heroin was not a social drug, though, and the already private Jimmy Page took to spending more time in seclusion dulling pain he never knew he had before.

Physical Graffiti was in the stores on February 24, 1975, and within days was the number-one album in the U.S. and the U.K. One million copies flew off the shelves immediately, adding over $10 million to Led Zeppelin's bank account, and the demand had the corollary effect of pulling all five of their previous albums back on the sales charts. Its cover did not fold out like *Led Zeppelin IV* and *Houses of the Holy* but revealed a haphazard collection of illustrations and snapshots (band members and associates, burlesque dancers, devils, a zeppelin, Queen Elizabeth II) seen through cut-out windows in a frontal photo of New York City's 96–98 St. Mark's Place. The music inside was just as eclectic, from brand-new numbers recorded in 1974 to older songs left off past discs, encompassing all the Eastern and Western, electric and acoustic, light and shade the band had to offer. To many, it is Led Zeppelin's best work.

The scattered studio sources of the material (including Olympic, Stargroves, Headley Grange, and Island), and the assortment of material itself, meant *Graffiti* did not have the crystalline sonic impact of *Led Zeppelin I* or *Led Zeppelin IV,* but the songs had an imaginative authority all their own. "Kashmir" turned up at the end of record one, side two, and was clearly their heaviest and most successful appropriation of the Indo-Arabian modes Jimmy Page had been drawn to since the '60s, combining the ersatz sitar timbre of "Black Mountain Side" with the heft of "When the Levee Breaks" and the majesty of "Stairway to Heaven." Bonham's drums, run through an Eventide phaser by engineer Ron Nevison (who had worked on the Who's *Quadrophenia*), are at their minimalist maximum, as Page's Sisyphean climbs up D5, D (sharp-5), D6 to D7 and back mesmerize. "In My Time of Dying" was similarly huge, returning to the blues with an eleven-minute destruction of Blind Willie Johnson's "Jesus Make Up My Dying Bed," as Page drew out an authentic slide guitar with his Danelectro tuned to open A. The opening cut, "Custard Pie," was another Delta flood, lifting Bukka White's "Shake 'Em on Down" and other standards to the sweaty floors of the Continental Hyatt House. And the overlooked and under-heard "The Rover," though begun as an acoustic sketch in 1970, had grown into Herculean hard rock with Page's wicked pentatonic riff in E that rises to a passionate aeolian in F-sharp under Robert Plant's pacific visions. Page's favorite console man, Keith Harwood, helped rebuild "The Rover" when Ron Nevison inadvertently erased its fattest guitar tracks: "I thought he should change his name to Ron Nevermind—because after *Physical Graffiti*, that was what I thought of him."[51]

Stretching out, Zeppelin got *very* funky in "Trampled Underfoot," showing much more soul than "The Crunge" had suggested; Page's bootylicious wah-wah accompaniment of John Paul Jones's quasi-disco clavinet was based on his familiar octave pulses (first noticed in "Immigrant Song") as Plant's suspiciously energized coda repeated how he couldn't stop talkin'. More octave jumps, likewise in G, were heard in "The Wanton Song," Page's taut single-note riff hurling at and caroming off Jones and Bonham's stop-start velocity through maelstroms of backward echo. "In the Light" and "Ten Years Gone" grew out of Page's home studio trials and demonstrated his interest in guitar orchestration, piling on layers of overdubbed electric and acoustic takes to build symphonic six-string opuses, whereas "Boogie with Stu" and "Black Country Woman" were loose jams captured at Headley Grange (with the Stones' Ian Stewart on piano) and the warm lawn of Stargroves, respectively. Any double album has a complement of throwaways, but "Houses of the Holy" (from the sessions for the record of that name), "Night Flight," and "Sick Again" were fully realized songs that would have been prime cuts on anybody else's single disc. Taken from the time of *Led Zeppelin III*, Jimmy Page's solo acoustic turn was "Bron-yr-Aur," a summery reverie in his patented C tuning (CACGCE) that was his most melodic instrumental yet and marked the softest end of the band's mellow range.

Well warmed up after the 1975 U.S. and Canadian tour, Led Zeppelin next announced a series of gigs in London's Earls Court arena—tickets for all five shows sold out within hours. This time they brought the set list and stage show from North America with them to the relatively midsized (capacity 17,000) site, including the laser showers that bathed Page during "Dazed and Confused" and giant TV monitors to show close-ups of the musicians. An L.A. seamstress named Coco had sewn for Page his new "dragon" outfit, bearing his star signs and "Zoso" sigil at the guitarist's instruction. "I'd just gone through a divorce," Page recollected (he and Charlotte Martin had never been legally wed but were slowly splitting up), "and those were the last shows of the 1975 tour."[52] He was also shorn of ties to his home country, thanks to the punitive tax regimen imposed on English rock stars and other wealthy entertainers by the Labor government of Prime Minister Harold Wilson. For the men of Led Zeppelin there were few loopholes in which to hide their earnings (just their instruments could be written off) and they could therefore only keep what they made by forsaking residence in their homelands. Jimmy Page owned three homes and had played music for people in four continents, but he now had no fixed address. "I remember I decided to travel, because there was nothing really keeping me home."[53]

He had numerous options. The resort town of Montreux, Switzerland, was a haven, and he could conduct Swan Song business and continue work on Zeppelin's film sound track (to be titled *The Song Remains the Same*) in New York; he made a visit to Brazil with Jim Capaldi, drummer for the band Traffic ("Dear Mr. Fantasy") and married to a local woman who gave them a tour of Rio de Janeiro's slums, to which Page would one day return. "The actual master plan," the unbound Page was considering at that point, "was to maybe do a tour through the Far East, going through Egypt and Bombay, then on to Thailand and all the rest of it, and then recording in those places."[54] By June he joined up with the likewise exiled Robert Plant (with his wife Maureen) in Morocco, beginning a holiday season they expected to conclude with more U.S. dates. They attended a folk festival in Marrakesh, then went way off the tourist trail into the desert wastes of North Africa, where being the two stars of Christendom's biggest rock 'n' roll act mattered little. What they saw and heard on their trek stayed with them. "It's trance music, basically," Page realized of the hypnotic beats and melodies and countermelodies he encountered through Casablanca and Tangiers. "When you see the sort of things that are done by the power of music as such, one couldn't help but sort of reassess what one thought one knew already."[55]

In August, Page was on his own in Sicily looking into purchasing a villa near Cefalù on the island's north coast, where, in the early '20s, Aleister Crowley had established a ragtag colony of decadents, expatriates, and believers—one of the party died there after drinking either impure water or the blood of a sacrificed cat. But on the Greek island of Rhodes, Plant met with disaster when he, his wife, their two children, and Page's daughter, Scarlet, were in a car accident that broke the singer's ankle and nearly killed Maureen. Page intervened immediately. "Jimmy came 'round very quickly, about 2:00 or 2:30 in the morning to see me," Plant said. "He was drunk and sat on my foot as he was moving a video machine around in my little room in the hospital."[56] His family was flown back to England to recuperate, but Plant himself was forced to reside in the offshore locale of Jersey in the Channel Islands to avoid the Inland Revenue. Still bound in a leg cast, from there he journeyed over to California where—against any reasonable expectation and in the teeth of their worst physical and mental circumstances—Led Zeppelin began to rehearse their next album.

There was to be no tour; Robert Plant risked never being able to walk again. But the four tax exiles were coming off the popularity of *Physical Graffiti,* the well-received American and Earls Court gigs, and the influences of Morocco, and they were moving beyond their proven blues 'n' boogie expertise into a taut rhythmic method all their own. "It's astonishing, the ESP between us,"

Jimmy Page reflected. "There'd be cues, sure, but there were so many times we'd just hit together spontaneously.[57] . . . The four of us were locked in musically like a tight fist."[58] The adventurous new music was one thing, but the deteriorating health within the band was quite another. Page was renting a house in Malibu that the roadies called "Henry Hall," after the English slang for heroin. His old lover Miss Pamela was around, now married to singer Michael Des Barres, and learned that Peter Grant had quashed any prospects of Page producing Des Barres's band, Detective, due to Page's Henry issues. Richard Cole added that Detective were not to ask Page to jam with them at a Los Angeles club as, Pamela quoted, Page was "very sleepy." "Uh-huh. Okay, Richard, no problem."[59] Elsewhere, she watched him "take twenty minutes to crawl across the room to get to a black bag full of pills. He kept toppling over, and everyone else in the room pretended not to notice."[60]

Through the fall of 1975, Led Zeppelin honed their songs in the U.S., then flew back to Europe for recording at Musicland Studios in Munich, West Germany (staying too long in any one country would have made them eligible again for taxation). Musicland was not a homey setting like Headley Grange or a familiar haunt like Olympic, and they could only reserve the popular room (in the basement of the Arabella Hotel) for three weeks in November and December as the Rolling Stones were booked immediately following. Munich was cold, the heroin was warm, and Jimmy Page was working long hours playing and mixing the music and propping up his injured vocalist. "All our pent-up energy and passion went into making it what it was," Page expressed. "That's why there was no acoustic material there.[61] . . . We had just finished a tour, we were non-resident and Robert was in a cast, so I think everybody was a little homesick."[62] The results were the claustrophobic and druggy *Presence*, Zeppelin's least accessible but in many ways most compelling collection.

Besides his Les Pauls, Page had acquired a pre-CBS Lake Placid Blue Fender Stratocaster with a vibrato arm, whose stabbing high notes and plummeting tonal drops made a distinct addition to the album's sound (this Strat had been debuted at the Earls Court shows). Though all but one of seven songs were credited to Page and Plant, Jones's bass and Bonham's drums carry the entire suite, in a telepathic lockstep with Page's serried ranks of guitars that can be described as either industrial funk or proto-techno-trance. "Achilles Last Stand" was ten minutes and twenty-six seconds of precision-timed arabesque, with Page's aeolian scales never more appropriate, and the cocaine warning "For Your Life" displayed the g-force pitch dives of the Stratocaster's vibrato arm pressed down to full depth. "Royal Orleans" and "Hots on for Nowhere" played very hard, Plant's jaded phrases of misadventures in Louisiana and California perched atop impossible swings and shuffles, with Page taking a full-on rockabilly break in the latter. "Candy Store Rock" was an even more authentic tribute to Scotty Moore and Cliff Gallup—albeit with the unforgiving rhythmic kick that runs throughout the album—and "Nobody's Fault but Mine" took a Blind Willie Johnson blues (once covered by Page influence John Renbourn) and remade it into a reverbed electric lament, like a sped-up and coked-out "When the Levee Breaks."

Presence concluded with the heartrending "Tea for One," Plant's candid call to his wife, who could only visit him from England on weekends, and his reevaluation of rock stardom, incapacitated and far from home. The music was a slower version of "Since I've Been Loving You," a three-chord blues in C minor (the same key as Beethoven's "Pathétique" sonata) that emerged as a rock "One for My Baby": brooding, nostalgic, and inconsolable. Jimmy Page's guitar in "Tea for One" is one of his finest performances, full of emotion-wracked bends and arpeggios, breaking down for two agonized, flamenco-style *rascuedos* and a final solo lick at the eighteenth fret as beautiful as anything he ever played. "I'm really pleased with the solo," Page beamed. "It's so held back. Seven minutes long and at no point does it blow out."[63] All the guitar solos, in fact, were recorded in one marathon fourteen-hour session ("Jimmy worked like a Trojan, no two ways about it,"[64] affirmed Plant), with Page and engineer Keith Harwood mastering the final mixdown together, spelling each other off as they took turns passing out at the console. In September the following year, Harwood was killed driving home from a Stones' session at Stargroves.

Jimmy Page continued to crisscross the Atlantic into 1976, making unannounced appearances with the rest of Led Zeppelin in a small Jersey nightclub in December, in England for Christmas, and then back to New York and Los Angeles to refine the mix of *The Song Remains the Same*. In L.A., he was driving with Richard Cole to the airport for another flight to London to see his daughter, Scarlet, now almost five and only slightly injured in the Rhodes auto accident. "For Christ's sake," Page sighed to the road manager, "don't get into this shit . . . I think I'm hooked."[65] Cole was using heroin regularly himself, though, and John Bonham had acquired his own habit. Bad influences were everywhere.

With Robert Plant still on the mend, Page could only wait out the year with sporadic recording and mastering work. *Presence* was released on March 31, 1976, in another cryptic cover whose square Technicolor portraits of straights (including one of the children from *Houses of the Holy*) were confounded with a surreal "object" front and center. Designer George Hardie gave the object its Escher-like twist at Page's suggestion. "You can put a number of interpretations on it," Page evaded in an interview, "so it's best to leave it as an open book situation."[66] Loyal audiences quickly sent the album to the number-one tier in Britain and North America, but its status fell soon after—the complex, negative feel of the songs and their epic duration were too much for casual fans. A new sound was on the horizon.

Punk rock broke in Britain in 1976, with the scandalous emergence of the Sex Pistols, Siouxsie and the Banshees, the Clash, the Buzzcocks, and other outrages in that and subsequent years. Much as young Jim Page had taken to skiffle in the '50s, thousands of disaffected British youth were drawn to punk's basic musical form of three chords and 4/4 time, a welcome return of rock 'n' roll simplicity and attitude after the sagging self-importance of Pink Floyd, Genesis, Yes, Queen, Jethro Tull, and, not least of all, Led Zeppelin. Sex Pistol Johnny Rotten laid down the gauntlet in denouncing what he called "the entire superband system,"[67] thus fixing forever the critical truism that successful prepunk acts like Zeppelin were old, out of touch, and hopelessly pretentious dinosaurs of no interest to alienated kids of the recessional United Kingdom. Punk had a crudely satiric quality that even tongue-in-cheek numbers like "D'yer Mak'er" and "Black Country Woman" had never neared—no one ever said Jimmy Page was much of a jokester—and the amphetamine-powered anger of punk performances was a sharp contrast to the stoned lethargy of the long solos of "No Quarter," "Moby Dick," and "Dazed and Confused." Jimmy Page, for one, became intrigued by punk. He took to the Damned, whose "sheer adrenaline music"[68] he later lauded (he even jammed with their drummer, Rat Scabies), and would admit that, "When the rock scene was becoming mellow and boring, [punk groups] came back bringing that fury and urge of primitive rock again."[69]

At the same time Page could not unlearn the musical skills he had already acquired, and, like many listeners (though fewer critics), he was wary of how punk's theoretical limitations amounted to an ongoing in-joke around little talent and bad taste. "The ones who want to stick to that original format are probably getting a bit hackneyed.[70] . . . A lot of younger people who I'd never really have expected to have got into [Led Zeppelin] have said that they got really fired up by the energy of the New Wave bands—and they still like the New Wave bands—but they got interested in the actual musical content and wanted to go one step further, which is how they discovered bands like us."[71] For all their excesses as instrumentalists, Page and his peers had the virtue of playing what they chose to instead of merely what they could, and maintained faithful followings for precisely the virtuosity punk's defenders sought to discredit. Eventually, the straightforward classic rock of Led Zeppelin proved to have enduring populist appeal, and the bohemian affectations of punk sounded far more pretentious than "Stairway to Heaven."

Page had more pressing problems as well. Part of his agreement with Kenneth Anger allowed the filmmaker to use the basement of the Tower House as an editing room for *Lucifer Rising*. But Anger was annoyed with Page's delays in providing a suitable sound track for the film, and also with not being selected to direct *The Song Remains the Same*, and following an altercation with Charlotte Martin at the residence, he found himself locked out and unwelcome. He went public in his snidest *Hollywood Babylon* fashion, holding a press conference to denounce Page as being dominated by his spouse, "dried up as a musician," and sapped by drug addiction. "I'm all ready to throw a Kenneth Anger curse!"[72] he threatened. Page refused to rise to Anger's bait, shrugging, "I've lost a hell of a lot of respect for him,"[73] and countering that he had indeed lived up to his side of the deal: "He had other music that I'd done, instead of the stuff that I'd delivered, which he said he wanted to use."[74] Anger, in truth, was constantly fidgeting with his picture and blamed Page for stalling an endeavor that was already in difficulty. He had even begun offering unauthorized tours of the Tower House in lieu of working there. Eventually he went back to Bobby Beausoleil, now doing life for murder in a California prison, for his sound track (Beausoleil, coincidentally, had met Miss Pamela in San Francisco in 1967 and played in an early version of Love, Robert Plant's favorite band). Page's half hour of *Lucifer Rising* contributions later found their way onto bootleg albums, full of swooping, scratching synthesized descants, and when the movie was finally shown in 1980, Jimmy Page appeared in Anger's unholy collage, lifting a hieroglyphic stone up to an image of Aleister Crowley. His part was credited as "Scapegoat."

Back at the Tower House, Page and Charlotte Martin were further troubled by uninvited residents who had moved in to the often-empty abode and had to be ejected, and by an undisclosed ailment Charlotte had come down with—serious enough for him to stay by her side despite their ongoing disengagement. "If you've been with someone for a long time and they get ill, then you immediately have that responsibility"[75] was all Page would say about his commitments.

The Song Remains the Same, both film and double album, were released in October 1976. Each version was popular with Zeppelin fans but neither were highly rated by the band themselves. The Madison Square Garden footage from 1973 depicted an imperfect gig (Jimmy Page notably fluffs the intro to "Moby Dick") and the twenty-seven-minute "Dazed and Confused" dragged on vinyl without any accompanying visuals of the bow or the Hermit. "It wasn't the best concert playing-wise at all," Page admitted, "but it was the only one with celluloid footage, so there it was. . . . It wasn't one of those real magic nights, but then again it wasn't a terrible night."[76] Today *Song* has been outdone as a live document by subsequent Led Zeppelin product, although it retains moments of you-are-there poignancy as John Bonham strolls arm-in-arm with his wife, Peter Grant profanely chews out a hapless Garden official for allowing the sale of contraband Zeppelin souvenirs, and as Robert Plant introduces "Stairway to Heaven" over a silhouetted New York skyline and its Twin Towers: "I think this is a song of hope. . . ."

Over the winter of 1976–1977, Page and his bandmates rehearsed for another tour of the U.S. Fifty-one gigs were planned for thirty cities around the nation. They now had seven albums' worth of songs to draw from, including a revival of the sit-down acoustic set (in which John Paul Jones would sing Sandy Denny's part from "The Battle of Evermore"), and they faced a challenge of fitting it all into a single show. Three-hour performances would just about do it. "Christ, when we did that first rehearsal we could have eased into it by playing familiar stuff," Jimmy Page reported, "but we went into the deep end by trying out 'Achilles Last Stand.' It just clicked all over again."[77] Other long pieces in the set list included "Ten Years Gone," "Nobody's Fault but Mine," "The Song Remains the Same," and Page's solo "Black Mountain Side," which was to jump a beat later into the Himalayan "Kashmir." Although Plant had recovered from his injuries of 1975, Page's health had become a matter of concern. "Every band was doing the drugs thing at the time . . . ," Jones would remember, "but by then it was getting a bit out of control."[78] Peter Grant agreed. "There were definite drug problems with one or two people, including myself,"[79] he revealed. "I remember the first time [promoter] Jerry Weintraub saw Jimmy Page on stage. He said to me, 'Is that guy gonna live?'"[80]

After waiting out Plant's bout of tonsillitis, Led Zeppelin flew *Caesar's Chariot* (another luxury jet they obtained when the *Starship* was unavailable) into Dallas, Texas, on April 1, 1977. Despite his shaky physique, Page was well armed with his '58 and '59 Les Pauls, the Gibson double-neck, a Telecaster, the Danelectro, a Martin acoustic, and a Gibson A-4 mandolin, playing through four Marshall cabinets (modified to blast 200 watts apiece), plus his wah-wah, theremin, MXR phaser, and Maestro Echoplex units. The electrics, as always, were strung with very light Ernie Ball Super-Slinky strings and hit with heavy-duty Herco picks. Page was also attired in a Coco-designed white silk "poppy" suit that matched the black dragon garb of previous outings.

His band was fronted by a battalion of roadies, security agents, and the tour's on-call physician, Dr. Larry Badgley. There was also John "Biffo" Bindon, a small-time actor and big-time London underworld figure who was on board as Led Zeppelin's personal protection, hired by Peter Grant and Richard Cole as they sunk deeper into cocaine-induced paranoia. Whereas Grant and Cole did have practical obligations as manager and road manager, Bindon was there purely as a hit man and intended to earn his pay. Badgley, Bindon, and the Zeppelin road crew became part of the havoc wrought by the '77 shows, crashing into pharmacies for prescriptions while pillaging the shelves for whatever they pleased and then throwing down ten hundred-dollar bills in their wake, and making a simple deal with the girls who milled around hoping to meet the headline act: "No head, no backstage pass."

At the center of the web was Jimmy Page. Throughout the spring, as *Caesar's Chariot* took him to Oklahoma City, Chicago, Minneapolis, St. Louis, Indianapolis, and beyond, his wolfish on-stage demeanor and spaced-out backstage condition became the stuff of rock mythology. He only made it through the initial songs of one Chicago gig after stomach cramps felled him and the concert was cancelled; "I'm not into solid foods very much. . . . I can't remember when I last had a steak,"[81] he apologized. At another Windy City performance he came out in jackboots, T-shirt, scarf, SS cap, and sunglasses, shading his vision from the lights and lasers and likely drugged to the eyeballs, an idol of heavy metal self-destruction. In Cleveland, he paid tribute to Jimi Hendrix with his own "Star-Spangled Banner," while elsewhere he was known to repair not to his dressing room but to his *hotel* during Bonham's "Moby Dick." His teeth showed the combined effects of Marlboros and Jack Daniel's. There were tales of Jimmy Page staggering out of his limo going the wrong way to wherever stage he was expected; Jimmy Page soloing to completely different numbers than the rest of the band; Jimmy Page so scrawny the pants of his poppy suit fell down in Los Angeles after doing "Sick Again"; Jimmy Page so stoned he collapsed mid-interview with New York DJ Scott Muni and resumed his talk from the studio floor; Jimmy Page being bodily lifted across the tarmac to his airplane for another flight. The good Dr. Badgley was said to have asked Page about Quaaludes missing from his medical valise—"Accusing me? Who the fuck does he think is paying his salary?"[82] the guitarist shot back. At Led Zep's stops, Page had found choice party companions with the best stocks of intoxicants, as related by Bonham's American mistress, Linda Aldretti: "We would lose him halfway through the night and find him in the women's bathroom, in the stall with three drag queens doing drugs."[83]

In May there was a mid-tour break, which Page used to fly

to Cairo, Egypt—in 1904, Aleister Crowley had been there with his wife and it was in the shadow of the pyramids that she had transcribed the spirit message that became *The Book of the Law,* his occult manifesto containing the adjuration "Do what thou wilt shall be the whole of law." Back in America for more recitals later in the month, the great scale of volume and light and ticket sales had become almost too much for the band to handle: a rained-out concert in Tampa, Florida, resulted in fifty arrests and nineteen injuries among 70,000 fans, and John Paul Jones would recall that playing gargantuan venues like Detroit's Pontiac Silverdome were like "a sound check in the dark."[84] Whiling away the hours in a Los Angeles hotel room with Angela Bowie, wife of David, the decadent glamour of their lifestyle went full circle into a kind of squalor, with John Bindon saying, "Fuck me, Hoover nose is here—hide the grams!"[85] at Page's arrival; after snorting up his rightful entitlement of cocaine, Page and a female visitor were handcuffed to a toilet for a half-hour by a smirking Richard Cole so the other revelers could make it through their blizzard in peace.

Reformed and reflective, Page would talk of his drug use in these years as an inexorable byproduct of the excitement and pure enjoyment he got from playing his music to hundreds of thousands of worshipful listeners. "We were doing three-and-a-half-hour concerts. . . . By the end of that, you come offstage and you're not going back to the hotel to have a cup of cocoa. *Of course* it was crazy; *of course* it was a mad life."[86] The risks? "It was totally reckless behavior. I mean, it's great that I'm still here to have a laugh about it, but it was totally irresponsible. I could've died and left a lot of people I love. I've seen so many casualties."[87] His example? "My lifestyle was just my lifestyle. I didn't feel the need to convert anyone; it was just the way that my life was taking me at that point. At the end of the day, from this vantage point, it can either be glorified or criticized."[88]

The '77 tour hit Oakland, California, on Friday, July 22, scheduled for two concerts at the Oakland Coliseum over the weekend where American rocker Rick Derringer and young British metalheads Judas Priest opened up. Local impresario Bill Graham was virtually a rock star himself, a mainstay of the psychedelic San Francisco era that had produced the Grateful Dead, the Jefferson Airplane, and Santana. Known to drive a hard bargain and not suffer slights of any kind—Robert Plant's first impression of him in 1969 was "Who *is* this asshole?"[89]—Graham was a West Coast equivalent of Peter Grant, and the irresistible force was about to ram into the unmovable object for the last time. To begin with, Richard Cole asked Graham for a $25,000 cash advance of the expected gate receipts of the shows, which was duly collected. "I went to the hotel where the band was staying," the promoter testified. "They announced me and I walked into this anteroom. There sat the dealer. Then it hit me for the first time. This is *drug* money."[90]

It got worse. During the Saturday gig one of Graham's team watched John Bindon ceremonially lick Jimmy Page's shoe during the performance, and another observed the ritual pulling of teenage girls by Led Zeppelin's road crew: "It was like these girls were going to be *sacrificed*. I wanted to go out and grab these girls and say, 'Don't do it, honey. Don't do it.'"[91] Then Jim Matzorkis of Graham's staff told a young boy he couldn't take down Led Zeppelin plaques off a dressing room trailer. "So I took the signs away from him. It wasn't a violent act of any kind."[92] But the boy was Peter Grant's son, Warren, and an enraged and coke-fired Grant became bent on vengeance. John Bonham kicked Matzorkis like a Ludwig bass drum, and John Bindon and Grant outmaneuvered the protective Graham out of the way while the two laid into Matzorkis. Richard Cole, whacked out of his mind himself, stood guard with a pipe. Savagely beaten, Jim Matzorkis barely escaped with his life.

The next day's concert went ahead only because Graham, fearing a riot by thousands of shut-out fans, signed a waiver absolving Led Zeppelin of any wrongdoing (a sickly Page was seated for most of the event), but the backstage mood was ugly, and before the weekend was over, John Bonham, Peter Grant, Richard Cole, and John Bindon were arrested and charged with assault. They got out on bail, pleaded nolo contendere, and settled for $50,000. "As far as I was concerned," said Graham's assistant Bill Barsotti, "every one of those guys in the band was absolutely one hundred percent accountable for that shit. . . . When we started looking into it, there were incidents like that all over the country on that tour. . . . The accountant would open up the valise as the guys were zooming off in their limousines and say, 'Okay, how much?'"[93] Jimmy Page, well sheltered from the security acting in his name, did not see any of the Oakland violence and prevaricated over its importance. "It was a very, very hairy scene. . . . Listen, if we'd *killed* anybody we'd be bloody in prison.[94] . . . I'm not saying that something didn't happen. But you know what it's like [in the U.S.]—if you sneeze on someone they sue you."[95]

But the tour had not yet reached its nadir. The next Zeppelin appearances were set for the cavernous New Orleans Superdome and the group arrived in Louisiana only slightly humbled. They were set to continue their spendthrift swath of destruction until, within a couple of hours and a phone call from his wife in England, Robert Plant was transformed from all-powerful rock god to grieving father of a little boy who had suddenly died of a viral infection. All of Led Zeppelin's remaining gigs were canceled.

Page did not attend the funeral for Karac Plant, which added to his partner's despondency. It fell to him to refute the stories of a "curse" over his band, which grew out of the urban legends around "Do what thou wilt," "Zoso," the dragon suit, and so on, and now took in the family accidents and tragedies that had struck Plant. Where once Page had spoken of his very guarded spiritual leanings ("I don't really want to go on about my personal beliefs or my involvement in magic")[96] and strange noises at the Boleskine House ("A man was beheaded there and sometimes you can hear his head rolling down"),[97] he now backed away from the subjects. "The whole concept of the band is *entertainment*," he insisted in an interview for the English paper

Melody Maker. "I don't see any link between that and 'karma,' and yet I've seen it written a few times about us, like 'Yet another incident in Zeppelin's karma.' . . . It's all crap. . . . It's a horrible, tasteless thing to say."[98] His feelings toward the press, already suspicious, became more irritable from this point.

With Led Zeppelin on hiatus while the Plant household mourned their son and brother, Jimmy Page grew restless again. He returned to Egypt briefly, then took his daughter and her mother to Guadeloupe in the Caribbean, inviting Richard Cole to tag along in hopes that the island's abundance of rum would help wean both of them off heroin. Page's former producer Mickie Most would also recall vacationing on a Bahamian island with the musician but "he never came out of his hotel room in two weeks."[99] In England there were also reports of his surprise stage jams with Ron Wood and Atlantic official Phil Carson, but months passed before Page, Plant, Jones, and Bonham were ready to play together again. In the spring of 1978, they assembled for tentative rehearsals at Clearwell Castle in Gloucester's Forest of Dean, near the Severn River on the Welsh border. "I didn't know whether it was worth it, to be honest,"[100] Robert Plant worried. "I've always believed in the strength of family. I don't think there's anything noble about that; I just think it's a better drug than anything you can buy around the corner."[101] "I remember asking, 'Why are we doing this?'" John Paul Jones looked back. "We were not in good shape mentally or health-wise. . . . It's not that we didn't have a laugh at Clearwell— it just wasn't going anywhere."[102]

It was going far enough, however, that by December the quartet had begun to record another album, returning to their first stomping grounds of Sweden to Stockholm's Polar Studios, home base of their musical antitheses Abba. As with *Presence,* the nocturnal sessions were affected by the heroin habits that had taken hold of the guitarist and, now, the drummer. "There were two distinct camps by then, and we were in the relatively clean one," Jones said of his and Plant's contributions. "We'd turn up first, Bonzo would turn up later and Page might turn up a couple of days later."[103] "There are people who say, 'Oh, Jimmy wasn't in very good shape,' or whatever," Page argued afterward, "but what I do know is that *Presence* was recorded and mixed in three weeks, and *In Through the Out Door* was done in a little over three weeks. So I couldn't have been in *that* bad a shape."[104] Although Jimmy Page did produce and master the Stockholm tapes (editing seven cuts from ten and mixing them down at home in Plumpton Place after being engineered by Leif Mases at Polar), it is true that they bear much more of Jones's influence than his own. On two songs he received no songwriting credit at all, unprecedented for Zeppelin originals.

Into 1979, Page prepared for the group's return to the stage after the devastations of the previous tour and the cultural upris-ing of punk rock, but he was still caught up in his own emotional dramas. During May's national election that brought Conserva-tive leader Margaret Thatcher to power the long-haired, strung-out rock star voted for the Tories. "I just couldn't vote Labour," he swore. "They actually stated that they wanted to nationalize the media, so what possible criticism of them would you be able to have?"[105] His own political instincts were for self-reliance, which he made clear when he stood to open a rebuilt harbor near the Boleskine House in Scotland. "My craft is music," he told the local fishermen and dock workers of Caithness who had done the heavy lifting, "and all the way along I've kept hammer-ing away at it to try and achieve excellence. You chaps involved in this project have also striven for excellence and have done a really worthwhile job."[106] Page also saw the down side of inde-pendence when he was forced to close down The Equinox book-store when its lease expired, as the boutique venture had been unable to turn a profit. "It obviously wasn't going to run the way it should without some drastic business changes and I didn't re-ally want to have to agree to all that,"[107] he admitted.

Led Zeppelin then announced a return to the British stage after more than four years, to be held in August at two succes-sive weekend spectaculars at Knebworth Park outside Stevenage in Hertfordshire. With another record in the can but not yet released, they played impromptu sets with Bad Company and conducted rehearsals of new and old material in Berkshire's Bray Studios while the supporting acts were slowly assembled. Page had hoped for personal favorites like Fairport Convention, Little Feat, latter-day progressive rockers Dire Straits, and his beloved Joni Mitchell, but in the end a modest lineup of performers were signed, among them Commander Cody and His Lost Planet Airmen, Todd Rundgren and Utopia, and the New Barbarians, a Rolling Stones spin-off featuring Page's friends Keith Richards and Ron Wood. By late July, the band were in Copenhagen, Denmark, for small and uncertain preparatory gigs. It had been a long time since they publicly rock 'n' rolled.

On the evening of August 2, Page, Plant, Jones, and Bonham arrived at Knebworth for a last-minute rehearsal, sound check, and photo call, and the cameras captured four different people than the smiling bearded young men who had been seen at the comparable Bath Festival in June 1970. Robert Plant's face was worn and lined beyond his thirty-one years, and Jimmy Page, gamely wearing a punkish blazer and skinny tie, was pale and thin beneath his tangle of dark locks that may have hidden the odd wisp of gray. Page had been driven to the spot by Richard Cole in a top-down car, and the Old Girl cursed out the road manager for letting the wind muss his hair. Later he repaired to the elegant Knebworth House of the locale's owner, David Lytton Cobbold, where he explored some of the curios of a previous resident, Victorian author and spiritualist Sir Edward Bulwer Lytton, and then with Peter Grant took in more immediate stimulations.

The performances themselves, on August 4 and 11, were uneven, and the British music papers, still attending to the orthodoxies of punk, were uncharitable. "Led Zeppelin did not do enough to live up to their legend," said one, while another damned with faint praise, "It's by no means all bad to be a living fossil."[108] Page especially was seen to be sweaty, haggard, and nervous, a perpetual Marlboro hanging from his lips, laboring his way through Zeppelin's history with "Whole Lotta Love," "Stairway to Heaven," "Kashmir," "Achilles Last Stand," "Nobody's Fault but Mine," and even "White Summer." Some witnessed him arrive to the first event by helicopter with Charlotte Martin, although American journalist Lisa Robinson saw him afterward with Krissie Wood, both looking "totally out of it."[109] Page's father, Jim, was also seen backstage at Knebworth, perhaps marveling that over 200,000 people had gathered to hear his son play guitar with his friends.

In Through the Out Door was released shortly after the Knebworth shows on August 20, 1979, and to the consternation of dinosaur-slaying music critics leapt to the top of the national sales charts throughout the Western world; fans had waited over three years for an all-new Led Zeppelin album. An outward wrap of plain brown paper covered a jacket photo of barroom blues incarnate (published in several different variations reflecting the points of view of its world-weary "characters"), in turn holding an inner sleeve black-and-white close-up of tequila, cigarettes, and a Dear John letter, the earliest issues of which could be moistened to produce a coloring effect that Jimmy Page first saw in one of his daughter's activity books. The package was designed by Hipgnosis's Aubrey Powell at Page's direction—Peter Grant, as always, was listed as "Executive Producer"—but on initial spin it was clear that John Paul Jones was the driving creative force behind the LP. He had recently acquired a factory-fresh Yamaha GX-1 synthesizer, and he and Plant had frequently been left alone in Polar Studios without their guitarist and drummer. "The thing is when that situation occurs you either sit down waiting or get down to some playing,"[110] he decided.

The last of Zeppelin's huge opening tracks, "In the Evening" found Page bowing his Lake Placid Blue Stratocaster for its Luciferian intro, augmented by an electronic device called a Gizmotron, then clanging into its metallic repeated progression. All the songs recorded in Stockholm ended up with a very "live" organic echo, and "In the Evening" shook with it. Then Jones and Plant went boogie-woogieing with "South Bound Suarez," Page taking a crisp electric solo, and held a samba siesta with "Fool in the Rain," the Yamaha to the fore. Page and Plant galloped to Texas for the comical "Hot Dog," a kind of thrash bluegrass outing where the Sorcerer played around on the quintessential country chords of G, C, and D7. The long and convoluted "Carouselambra" was another keyboard number that Page backed with his Gibson double-neck, unusual for studio work, and "All My Love" was a surprisingly sweet Jones-Plant piece adorned with one of the singer's most moving lyrical and vocal statements. Jimmy Page added tasty acoustic fills to the ballad, but was uncomfortable with its lilting choruses: "It sort of felt like the Rod Stewart sort of songs of the time with the scarf-waving.[111] ... And I thought, that's not us. ... In its place it was fine, but I wouldn't have wanted to pursue that direction in the future."[112] He was happier with "I'm Gonna Crawl," the third in the band's great trilogy of minor-key blues (after "Since I've Been Loving You" and "Tea for One"), laying down a slow roadhouse R&B rhythm and a haunted solo that closed on a sobbing, slowly released bend. It was the final performance of Led Zeppelin's career as recording artists.

By the end of 1979, *In Through the Out Door* was a major hit record and, along with Pink Floyd's *The Wall,* a major relief to an industry that had gambled and lost on the commercial viability of punk rock. Earlier Zeppelin albums also reentered the charts at this time, but while a gratified Plant, Jones, and Bonham went to receive readers' poll awards from *Melody Maker* in London, Jimmy Page was testifying in court at an inquest into the death of Phillip Hale, a young photographer and sometime member of the group's inner circle. He had passed out and choked on vomit in Page's home of Plumpton Place that October, with cocaine and alcohol detected in his system afterward. The death was ruled accidental and was never discussed again. "I knew a lot of people who used to [drink and pass out]," Page conceded eventually. "Maybe in this day and age it might ring alarm bells, but in those days it was the norm within the sort of people that you knew."[113] Hale was nineteen.

For musicians the best solution to personal problems is often to simply go out and play to an audience, and this was the option put before Page. "Looking back on that period," Jones spoke, "it did seem Robert and I were holding it together, while the others were dealing with other matters."[114] Sharpened up by the stripped-down ethos of punk, Plant added, "I was really keen to stop the self-importance and the guitar solos that lasted an hour."[115] For nonmusicians like road manager Richard Cole, personal problems like drug addiction only got him dismissed from the Swan Song operation.

As the '80s dawned, Led Zeppelin began to rehearse for a small-scale European tour as a warm-up for later trips to North America. Through April, May, and June, they went over an abbreviated set of tunes, including their new "In the Evening," "Hot Dog," and "All My Love," and reaching all the way back to "Train Kept A-Rollin'," the rockabilly chestnut they had first gelled around in 1968. Over June and July, they hit manageable indoor theaters in Denmark, the Netherlands, Belgium, Switzerland, Austria, and West Germany, sans lasers, drum solos, and dragon suits—Jimmy Page and Robert Plant now dressed in the New Wave fashion of tight T-shirts and jeans. They did bring other baggage, however: John Bonham collapsed early into a gig in Nuremberg, having gorged on twenty-odd bananas beforehand while still trapped in his heroin dependency ("We never had anybody checking us up saying, 'Oh, man, the test shows you're really low in minerals,'"[116] remarked Plant), while Page had taken to introducing "Black Dog" during concerts, in a voice observers heard as unsteady and disjointed. As well as the Les Pauls, the Stratocaster, the double-neck, and the Danelectro, he was also using Fender Telecasters again, among them an unusual chocolate-brown model that he fitted with the rosewood neck from his '58 Tele, after that instrument became unplayable following a friend's refinishing. "He thought he'd done me a favor!"[117] moaned Page (this Tele had also been seen on the '77 U.S. tour). In Vienna a firecracker thrown from the audience during his "White Summer" set piece almost took his eye out and he stood up and stormed offstage. On July 7, 1980, in West Berlin's Eissporthalle, the quartet played their last ever gig together.

In England, in August, Page moved into the Mill House in the village of Clewer in Berkshire, within walking distance of the British royal family's residence at Windsor. This was a grand red-brick Georgian structure on the banks of the Thames, named for its functional water mill; Page had purchased the Mill House from the actor Michael Caine for £900,000 after selling Plumpton Place, his not always happy home base throughout the '70s (his Sussex neighbor, the World War II singer Vera Lynn, had once complained Page was ruining the local peace and quiet). The response to the European tour had been encouraging, and Peter Grant had persuaded the reluctant Plant—who had since become father to a new baby boy—to make a tentative reentry into the North American circuit that fall. Page had already overseen designs of their projected stage rigs, and jam sessions and practices were planned for the many empty rooms of the Mill House.

John Bonham had his own misgivings about America. His Oakland arrest and civil suit of 1977 weighed on him, and another extended absence from his family was not what he wanted or needed. On Wednesday, September 24, he drove down from the Midlands to a Led Zeppelin studio rehearsal, then repaired back to the Mill House with the others and their team of roadies for informal run-throughs. He had been drinking vodka, lots of it, all day. At Jimmy Page's home, he was incapacitated enough that the exercises were put on hold and the work became just another rock 'n' roll party. Page's assistant Rick Hobbs hauled the burly drummer to an upstairs bedroom when he fell asleep late that night; sometime in the next several hours his heart stopped. Early the following afternoon, John Paul Jones and Plant's vocal technician Benji LeFevre looked in on Bonham and found they could not rouse him. "It was just so tragic," Jones recalled. "Jimmy and Robert were in the front room laughing about something. I had to go in and say, 'Hold it,' and tell them what happened."[118] Page, accustomed to his own and others' post-bender crashes, was shocked by the capriciousness of it all—only a year before another partier had died in one of his homes the same way. "So one day . . . he goes to sleep and he's had a lot to drink that day, and he's collapsed and goes to bed—and then he doesn't wake up. . . . It could have been any one of us that [was] lost, at that point."[119] John Bonham was thirty-two, with a wife, Pat, fourteen-year-old son, Jason, and five-year-old daughter, Zoë.

After an inquiry determined the fatality at Mill House was the result of "accidental suicide" brought on by pulmonary edema (swelling of blood vessels in the lungs) and having knocked back what amounted to an entire forty-ounce bottle of vodka in the previous hours, Robert Plant, John Paul Jones, and Jimmy Page conferred in Jersey and returned to tell Peter Grant they had no further interest in the active existence of Led Zeppelin. A public statement was issued from Swan Song on December 4, 1980, that officially shut down the group, and guitarist and producer Jimmy Page suddenly had no band, no purpose, and no idea what he would do with his music and his life.

Tea for One

1981–1990

I was not sufficiently enlightened to understand that the fame of the man had nothing to to with his real success, that the proof of his prowess lay in the invisible influence which he had had upon generations of men.

–ALEISTER CROWLEY,

CONFESSIONS

On January 9, 1981, Jimmy Page turned thirty-seven. His career as a musician had come to a shattering halt with the death of his friend and bandmate John Bonham, and the demise of Led Zeppelin, though mutually agreed among himself, Robert Plant, and John Paul Jones, left Page especially adrift. Plant had lost an old chum whose relationship predated their fame and fortune, and Jones had lost a respected musical partner, but the guitar player had lost his most sympathetic accompanists and his artistic drive. "I was constantly writing for the band, working on production, all the rest of it," he thought. "That was my life . . . [Bonham's] death just knocked me sideways."[1] Remembering the original Soho trial runs of "Train Kept A-Rollin'," he knew how unique the fusion had been. "When we finished it was scary. None of us had played with our musical equals until that point."[2] With rare exceptions, he never would again. During the winter of 1981, he had no desire to.

"I lived in a total vacuum. I didn't know what I was doing. In the end, I went to Bali and just thought about things."[3] Now a single man, he refused to pick up a guitar for several months, and one of his Les Pauls even went missing for a time. One story had him jamming at home with bassist Chris Squire and drummer Alan White of Yes in a half-hearted project designated XYZ (Ex-Yes, Zeppelin), but rough demo tapes were the only result. His opening public appearance as a solo act came in March at London's Odeon Hammersmith, where he guested with Jeff Beck on their familiar "I'm Goin' Down," after being introduced by Beck as "my old school pal."[4] He had also acquired his own recording space in Cookham, just ten minutes away from the Mill House—Sol Studios had been owned by Elton John's producer Gus Dudgeon—and Page liked it for its sound and its proximity to where he lived, and gradually he began to venture there more often to play and record.

Page's first official output of his post-Zeppelin life was a commission to write a film soundtrack. His Windsor neighbor Michael Winner was the director of the 1974 Charles Bronson shoot-out *Death Wish,* and with the production of a sequel, he invited the reclusive rock 'n' roller down the lane to come up with its music (they had more than residences in common—Winner had dated Miss Pamela of Los Angeles in the '70s). At first Page was uncertain about the job, mediated through Peter Grant in August in one of his last duties as a functioning manager. The first *Death Wish* had ended in Chicago, and Page imagined he would be composing in his known sphere of Chicago blues, only to see video rushes of *Death Wish II* set in Los Angeles. He went along with scoring the footage anyway, using Sol Studios and engineer Stuart Epps, and a selecting a variety of players to contribute, including singers Chris Farlowe (whose songs Page had played on for session gigs in the '60s) and Gordon Edwards (of Swan Song act the Pretty Things), plus drummer Dave Mattacks of Fairport Convention and bassist Dave Paton. Edwards, David Sinclair Whittaker, and Dave Lawson also added piano, and

strings were overdubbed by the Greater London Council Philharmonic Orchestra. "I wrote everything from scratch," Page
described his sound track. "There was actually one riff that I'd
had before but the rest of it was off the cuff. It was an absolutely
incredible exercise for discipline."[5]

The *Death Wish II* music is actually an impressive body of
tracks in a medium Page has never explored since. He deployed
his bow and theremin for some of the atmosphere on "Shadow
in the City" and played his Martin acoustic for the feminine
interludes of "Carole's Theme," but he had also begun to make
use of a Roland guitar synthesizer, a primitive six-string equivalent of the more common keyboard implements like John Paul
Jones's Yamaha. He had acquired the Roland back in 1977. "That
was the most I ever used it and then it just got more and more
annoying,"[6] he said in hindsight. "The Release" and "The Chase"
were natural evolutions of *Presence*-period Led Zeppelin, and
"Hotel Rats and Photostats" was a downright spooky mood-set-
ter that would not have been out of place on Kenneth Anger's
Lucifer Rising. "Prelude" was Page's most inventive appropriation of a classical theme, an electric blues version of Frédéric
Chopin's famous Prelude in E minor (Opus 28, Number 4), easily fitting alongside "I'm Gonna Crawl" and "Tea for One." An
album of the pieces was released in February 1982, and Michael
Winner reused some of them for a third Bronson sequel, *Death
Wish III*.

But Page's health was still precarious, and he remained enmeshed in a taste for hard drugs. In December 1981, he was in
Chelsea's King's Road in London, trying to cash traveler's checks
while shopping, and when he couldn't produce any identification, he flagged down a nearby policeman who somehow discovered a small packet of cocaine in his jacket pocket. He was
arrested. Some months later, a criminal proceeding dragged to
a close and he was given a twelve-month conditional discharge
and fined £100. He had been buying a gift for his mother's birthday. It was not his final brush with the law.

Meanwhile, Atlantic Records were owed a final Led Zeppelin album, and it fell to Page to deliver it. He felt the obligation of producing material for a band whose drummer was dead "disgusting," and considered assembling a collection of live tapes that would preempt the busy Zeppelin bootleg market. In what would become a long-running debate over the group's legacy, though, Robert Plant vetoed this plan, and so, said Page, "the donkey work on the *Coda* album began."[7] To his credit, Page (with Sol's Stuart Epps) did locate and sequence a solid set of outtakes and experiments that added up to a perfectly decent record. *Coda* (the title was John Paul Jones's) featured a chronological alternate history of Led Zeppelin, including a searing live "I Can't Quit You Baby" from a rehearsal at the Royal Albert Hall in 1970, the hard English folk of "Poor Tom" from the same year (Page once again on a C-tuned acoustic), and three numbers from the Polar Studios nights of 1978, "Ozone Baby," "Darlene," and "Wearing and Tearing," that showed the Johnny Rottens what fast and aggressive rock 'n' roll was all about. Most arresting was the planetary drum solo he had recorded in Switzerland during the tax exile period: "Bonzo's Montreux" was an awesome monument to his late percussionist that Page treated with electronic effects to illustrate the matchless talent of "The John Bonham Drum Orchestra."

By now Peter Grant was himself too caught up in cocaine and heroin to serve as Jimmy Page's manager, and so old crony Phil Carson of Atlantic took over. In any case, there was not much to manage. In 1982 and 1983, Page played to audiences on a handful of occasions, taking encores with Robert Plant and slick rockers Foreigner in Munich, and with Eric Clapton at Guildford Town Hall, playing "Further On up the Road" and (aptly) "Cocaine." Otherwise, he held private duets with his eleven-year-old daughter, Scarlet, while she tinkled the ivories. During these months the Sorcerer had very nearly become the Hermit.

But the Clapton connection led to a reunion of the Yardbirds' star guitarists later in 1983, with Page, Clapton, and Jeff Beck participating in charity shows to aid the British Action Research into Multiple Sclerosis (ARMS) cause. Multiple Sclerosis had struck the Small Faces' bassist Ronnie Lane, a well-liked veteran of the English rock scene whose mobile studio had been used in the making of *Physical Graffiti.* With Rolling Stones Bill Wyman, Charlie Watts, and Ian Stewart, plus ex-Traffic singer Steve Winwood and Who drummer Kenney Jones filling out the lineup, two ARMS concerts were held at the Royal Albert Hall on September 20 and 21. Page now favored the dark brown Telecaster he had brought on Zeppelin's 1977 North American and 1980 European tours, which was equipped with a "B-bender" device, a sort of string-specific tremolo unit that inflected pedal steel-like tones to ordinary electric guitars. At these events he performed "Who's to Blame," "City Sirens," and "Prelude" from *Death Wish II,* and satisfied fans of his old band with an instrumental "Stairway to Heaven" on the Gibson double-neck. At the end of the concerts, he, Beck, and Clapton took center stage before the happily married Prince and Princess of Wales to rock out on "Tulsa Time," "Goodnight Irene," and Clapton's classic "Layla." Still fragile, Page was nevertheless beginning to reemerge.

The goodwill and collective spirit of the ARMS affairs led the all-star ensemble to further charity drives in the United States later in 1983. (Sadly, Ronnie Lane succumbed to MS in 1997.) Page went along to Dallas, Los Angeles, San Francisco, and New York, and the response from the fans he received came as a strong reminder of how much Led Zeppelin were missed in North America, where they had last visited over six years previously. Throughout this mini-tour, he was spending most of his time withdrawn in his hotel room and came out for his solo spots looking vague and very thin (*Rolling Stone* reported him "the very picture of wrecked rock star elegance"),[8] but doing crowd-pleasing renditions of "Prelude" and "Stairway." "That Ronnie Lane thing did me a world of good," he intimated shortly afterward. "You can't *imagine.* It gave me so much confidence—I realized people did want to see me again.[9] . . . That was the thing that got me back, got my head into some sort of reasonable perspective."[10] It was around this period that he finally found the ability to clean himself of his heroin addiction. It was a start.

Jimmy Page was now in the position of numerous middle-aged ex-Beatles, surviving Doors, and original Pink Floydians, forties and beyond looming ahead while forever living up or down to the exploits of their twenties and early thirties. CSNY's underrated picker Stephen Stills, for instance, made a solo collection, *Right by You* at Sol Studios, and Page's guitar was heard on "Flaming Heart" and its title cut. John Paul Jones had left Zeppelin to pick up where he started in 1968 (though much richer)—an all-around musician for hire who could select an array of projects to occupy his time, e.g., a Michael Winner sound track for *Scream for Help* (to which Page added guitar on a couple of songs) and bass contributions to Paul McCartney's *Give My Regards to Broad Street* movie. Robert Plant, in the meantime, had intentionally distanced himself from his rock Viking mythos with sophisticated post–New Wave records like *Pictures at Eleven* and *The Principle of Moments*. His next project, begun in March 1984, was a nostalgic tribute to the R&B hits of his youth, and he asked Page to help out with his covers of "Sea of Love" and "I Get a Thrill," the latter getting a bluesy solo that might have been introduced at a Neil Christian appearance in 1961. The consequent extended-play disc, *The Honeydrippers Volume 1,* was an unexpected hit and boosted Plant's image as an artist with his heavy metal past long behind him. Not Jimmy Page's.

Apart from amusing himself with games of snooker and cricket (a photo of the guitarist dressed for some slow bowls was seen in the foldout of *Coda*), Page spent time with his friend and confidant Roy Harper, the funny folksinger he'd known and admired since 1970. The pair played some incognito gigs in Norfolk and at the Cambridge Folk Festival (Page using another Telecaster with a B-bender, this one a cream-colored '66), and joined forces for Harper's album, *Whatever Happened to Jugula?*

Jugula was a faintly Pythonesque offering typical of its author's eccentric outlook, but he did get some well-wrought acoustic guitar out of Page on "Elizabeth" and "Twentieth Century Man," that harked back to *Led Zeppelin III*. Die-hard Zeppelin fans still spoke reverently of Page's solo on Harper's 1971 song "Same Old Rock" and his spots on *Lifemask* from 1974, both of which found obscurity. "It seems a long time ago since I was on the inside," Harper laughed in retrospect. "Was I there? Am I here?"[11] Hats off to him.

All these walk-on parts had fired Page's enthusiasm for forming his own full-time band. "I really wanted to get out and play, but I couldn't find a vehicle to work with."[12] Another benefit concert with Ian Stewart on behalf of cancer-struck blues pioneer Alexis Korner bolstered him anew. "I heard people say, 'Oh, that guitarist wasn't bad,' and they didn't know who it was. Do you know that meant more to me than anything in the world?"[13] At the ARMS presentations in the U.S., he had done promising sets with Paul Rodgers of Bad Company, whose fortunes had faded with the slow demise of the Swan Song outfit in the aftermath of Bonham's death and Grant's incapacity. Rodgers's ties to his Bad Co. mates were strained, and thus he was cautiously receptive when approached by Page via Phil Carson. In the summer of 1984, they put together a four-piece ensemble after calling in Roy Harper's young fretless bass player Tony Franklin ("He'd been playing on Roy's album—maybe that's why he was on the dole,"[14] joked Page) and auditioning drummers from the Damned's Rat Scabies (Chris Miller) and King Crimson's Bill Bruford. Page got a kick out of Scabies's enthusiasm, and the compliments were returned: "Jimmy Page turned out to be a really nice geezer. . . . He looks half-Chinese up close, and a bottle of Grecian 2000 wouldn't go amiss."[15] Ultimately it was Chris Slade who got the drum stool after finishing a tour with Pink Floyd's David Gilmour; Slade had lost the studio job for Tom Jones's "It's Not Unusual" in Page's hired-gun days but had climbed back the ladder through Manfred Mann's Earth Band, and subsequently landed a stint with AC/DC. Page named this new quartet the Firm, and soon readied them for recording and live work. "We just wanted to have a go and play on stage,"[16] he said eagerly.

The Firm's debut was put off in September when Page was arrested for cocaine again, this time nabbed by a suspicious bobby at a London train station. In early November, he pleaded guilty to possession and was looking at jail time after his conditional sentence of 1982. Instead magistrate Brendan Mitchell dressed him down: "You must realize that to dabble with drugs of this nature is entirely wrong, especially when you are associating with other members of the music world, because it may well influence them to take drugs if you yourself use them." Perish the thought. "I take the view that if a prison sentence is passed, it may well prevent you from pursuing your chosen profession,"[17] he said before the gavel fell. Jimmy Page promised to be good and uneasily walked away minus a £450 fine. Phil Carson later made it known that he had tried to assist Page with his substance problems, and a magazine profile of Page from this time coyly mentioned his long right-hand pinkie fingernail, "shaped like a little dipper."

By November and December 1984, the Firm had begun to play live in Sweden, Denmark, Germany, and Britain. At first the reaction was supportive, despite Page and Rodgers' refusal to do any Led Zeppelin or Bad Company songs, and Page was certainly revitalized to be striding the stage once more. When the band's self-titled album was released in February 1985, however, coinciding with their opening American tour, an early rush of record and ticket sales tapered off. Expecting a combination of Bad Co.'s gutsy raunch and Led Zep's electric grooves, audiences got rather generic '80s rock like "Make or Break" and "Satisfaction Guaranteed." "Closer" and Rodgers's "Radioactive" had some funk to them, and the "Midnight Moonlight" opus Page and the vocalist had been constructing since the ARMS performances was ambitious, but Tony Franklin's fretless bass rendered the sound soggy and Page seemed unwilling or unable to lay down the devilish riffs that had made him famous—his guitar on *The Firm* was technically matured and musically subtler, maybe, just not very memorable.

They completed the U.S. run and returned to more dates in England, where their reception was tepid. For Jimmy Page, the real point of the project was to get back into gigging, and on those terms it succeeded. "The fact that people are willing to listen to what we're doing, and that they haven't gotten bored enough to yell for numbers from the past, makes me think I was right to do this,"[18] he summed up. With Rodgers and the others, Page also mimed "Radioactive" for the trendy new medium of rock videos—"I don't want to pretend to be an actor, because I'm not."[19] Outside the Firm, he found time to sit in with the Rolling Stones on their sessions for *Dirty Work*, playing a solo on "One Hit to the Body," and he got up in a New York club with the fated jazz bassist Jaco Pastorius, where witnesses said the two had "a cosmic jam."[20]

A slot in a very big gig opened up when the Live Aid shows were being put together in the summer of '85. With dozens of A-list pop musicians being signed on to Bob Geldof's transatlantic donation drives, the enormity of the proceedings induced Page, Plant, and Jones to reform for a short set in Philadelphia's JFK Stadium on July 13. Plant was touring the U.S. with his own act and inveigled drum duties out of both Tony Thompson, formerly of Chic (funk's nearest Led Zep equivalent) and Phil Collins, formerly of Genesis and occasional sitter-in with Plant. The well-intentioned gesture got the JFK crowd on their feet, and TV audiences turned up the volume and opened their wallets, but their spot was marred by Plant's vocal exhaustion, Thompson and Collins banging into each other rhythmically, and Jimmy Page's Les Paul being noticeably out of tune for "Whole Lotta Love" and "Rock and Roll," and having his Gibson EDS 1275 plugged into a too-short amplifier cable for "Stairway to Heaven." These were slight relative to the logistics of the whole day, but frustrating for the players. In the backstage chaos, the veterans were elbowed aside by Madonna's retinue, an affront to rock justice John Bonham would have quickly rectified. "Live Aid was such a fucking atrocity for us,"[21] Plant declared.

Jimmy Page went back to recording the next Firm album, but he did drop in on a Plant concert in New Jersey, and in January 1986, the guitarist, singer, and bass player of Led Zeppelin met up in Bath, England, again with Tony Thompson on the skins, for provisional jams. Thompson was soon injured in a car accident, though, and the ragged excitement they felt playing together for Live Aid quickly dissipated. Page was still remote, his wah-wah battery kept dying, and one of Plant's roadies served as stand-in drummer. "He'd just finished the second Firm album, and I think he was a bit confused about what he was doing," reflected Plant of his old foil. "Pagey wouldn't come out, which is hardly the way to get everything back together again."[22] Jones's version is more circumspect: "I don't know if Jimmy was quite into it, but it was good. . . . I suppose it came down to Robert wanting to pursue his solo career at the expense of anything else."[23] It was too soon for a reunion and Robert Plant could not abide Page's foibles as he had when he was twenty-one.

The Firm's *Mean Business* was shipped in January 1986 and another American jaunt began in March. The second disc was less popular than the first, and turnouts had slackened. "Jimmy had been off the road and was very keen to get back," Paul Rodgers described the band's course. "So we kind of compromised and said we'll make two albums and tour with them and see how we feel at the end of that time. . . . At the end of that two years, it was 'Okay, well, that was great, let's move on.'"[24] "I think at times it worked out all right," Page discussed in the end, "but it wasn't the sort of situation I wanted to get back into, and that's why we didn't do anything more after the second album.[25] . . . It wasn't the sort of vehicle that I wanted to be locked into.[26] . . . I was willing to go [Rodgers's] way to a degree—I just wondered if he could stretch into some more unusual stuff with that vocal quality."[27] Flexing his own talents, Page took an encore with unlikely comrades the Beach Boys in Washington, D.C., in July, sat in with Joan Jett and the Blackhearts, and paid homage to his longtime hero Les Paul (the man, not the guitar) in New York the same month.

As on *The Firm*, Page's guitar on *Mean Business* was somewhat obscured by the production (by Page, Rodgers, and Julian Mendelsohn) and anticipation of a new "Whole Lotta Love" was dampened by the heavily treated sounds of "Free to Live" and "Cadillac"—Page continued to toy with Roland guitar synthesizers, and was using more effects pedals like Chorus and Volume units. That Rodgers himself played occasional guitar also diluted his work. Happier news on the tour, however, was Jimmy Page's involvement with Patricia Ecker, a twenty-four-year-old Louisiana native (he was now forty-two) identified as an ex-waitress and model. Page brought Patricia Ecker back to the U.K. with him, and they were married in December.

Returned to matrimony and free of Firm commitments, Page settled back in Windsor and began putting together his first real solo album at Sol Studios. With Phil Carson's help, he found a broad assortment of backup players to record, like singers Chris Farlowe and John Miles, who he had first heard on the Spanish island of Ibiza, as well as bassists Tony Franklin, Felix Krish, and Durban Laverde. Barrymore Barlow contributed drums for a couple of songs, but out of familial loyalty and musical esteem, he tapped young Jason Bonham, who he had tried out over the years and whose band, Virginia Wolf, had been given billings underneath the Firm. "He's certainly got the power his father had; I would say his approach is similar,"[28] praised Page. The sessions, so near to Page's home at the Mill House, were leisurely through the spring and summer (Robert Plant came down to co-write and sing one number), and resulted in enough material for a double album before being reduced to a single record. With his wife's pregnancy, a genuine Jimmy Page resurrection seemed imminent, which he hastened by leaving Atlantic Records and signing with Geffen after relinquishing the services of a disappointed Carson. "Jimmy has to come to terms with the fact that he should act like a human being,"[29] his ex-manager grumbled.

During this hopeful time, Page gave guitar solos for "Tall Cool One" and "Heaven Knows" to Plant for his upcoming album *Now and Zen,* wherein the former Zeppelin front man began to warm to his own past, and boogied to "Trampled Underfoot" and "Rock and Roll" with Plant at one of the vocalist's London appearances. While Page finished mixing his album in April 1988, he became a father for a second time, naming his son James Patrick Page after himself and the baby's own grandpa. But the new parent's health was still uncertain. He took umbrage at a journalist's query about his association with heroin, asking, "Do I *look* as if I'm a smack addict? Well, I'm not. Thank you very much."[30] With Jason Bonham on drums, Page, Plant, and Jones had another Led Zeppelin revival at New York's Atlantic Records' fortieth-anniversary party, on May 14, at Madison Square Garden: after a long, agitating wait backstage while Atlantic acts from the Coasters and Wilson Pickett to Iron Butterfly and the Bee Gees took their bows, the foursome did iffy renderings of "Kashmir," "Heartbreaker," "Whole Lotta Love," and "Stairway to Heaven." Page's build, once the epitome of a lean 'n' mean rock gunslinger's, had become fleshier than fans recollected. "Jimmy had a bad day,"[31] surmised Phil Carson. "On the night, I remember coming off thinking it was *okay*,"[32] Jones skirted. "The performance, I thought, was diabolical,"[33] said Peter Grant. "I was always like, 'Fuck Led Zeppelin, I don't want to be that guy,'"[34] a firmly disillusioned Plant thought back on the reunion, while Page agreed, "The times we did come together only endorsed what you thought, as it did for me too.[35] . . . It's unfortunate to be measured by a one-off shot like that, when you haven't played for a while."[36] Pamela Des Barres accosted a distracted Page behind the scenes at Madison Square Garden. "Why, Pamela, dear. How are you?" he asked her coldly. "But his eyes weren't kind, and it was clear he didn't care how I was,"[37] the celebrated groupie lamented.

Outrider, Jimmy Page's first solo record since "She Just Satisfies," was in stores in June of '88. The cover was a blurry black-

and-white portrait of the artist, topped with a luxuriant '80s hairdo that didn't quite suit his forty-something face, holding a '70s Les Paul with a B-bender that he had brought out at the Atlantic anniversary event. Produced by Page and engineered by Leif Mases of *In Through the Out Door*, it showed off a confident return to heavy guitar playing little heard on the Firm's albums, and even boasted three instrumentals, "Writes of Winter," "Liquid Mercury," and "Emerald Eyes," that demonstrated Page's penchant for multiple guitar palettes. As well as the B-bender Les Paul, he also recorded his Stratocaster, Telecaster, '59 Les Paul, and the Roland guitar synthesizer, and his Martin and new Washburn acoustics, and had a Vox AC-30 amp doing duty alongside his regular Marshalls and Fenders. The publisher of Page's songs was listed as "Succubus Music."

On *Outrider*'s more commercial tracks like "Wanna Make Love" and "The Only One" (sung by Plant), Page's style had moved from the meaty single-note hooks of early Zeppelin and into a jagged, jangly treble reminiscent of "Wearing and Tearing" and "Ozone Baby" from *Coda*. But he was still at home with the blues: "Prison Blues," "Blues Anthem," and particularly the minor-key "Hummingbird" (covering a B. B. King song written by Leon Russell) had slow and thick pentatonic lines coasting securely on Jason Bonham's grooves, elegant and in control. On vocals, Page was slightly let down by John Miles, who sounded a bit like Van Halen's roaring Sammy Hagar, and by Chris Farlowe, owner of a juke-joint bluster so mannered it made Joe Cocker sound like Rex Harrison. Miles and Farlowe were also given free rein over the lyrics—"I was layering the textures of the guitars, and there was more time to put into that,"[38] said Page—and these too were clichéd. It was the voices and their words, not the guitars, which earned *Outrider* its dubious reviews and hesitant sales. "*Outrider* was made up in the studio, which was a bit foolhardy, really," he conceded, "but there we are taking risks."

Jimmy Page took his act on the road in September, first in

America and then winding up for gigs in the U.K. by year's end. There was no deluge of tickets purchased and the venues were modest, but the guitarist was in good musical form, along with Miles, Jason Bonham, and Durban Laverde, and like Robert Plant, Page was now willing to return to his roots, with versions of "White Summer/Black Mountain Side," "Kashmir," "Rock and Roll," "Train Kept A-Rollin'," "Custard Pie," "In My Time of Dying," and an instrumental "Stairway to Heaven," plus "Blues Anthem" and "Prison Blues." Attendees at the gigs came away more satisfied than the *Outrider* write-ups had led them to expect: "For two hours, at a wall-shaking volume, he played brilliantly,"[40] wrote one, while Robert Palmer in *Rolling Stone* lauded, "Rarely have precise, refined musicianship and a trash-the-classics attitude been so mutually, explosively reinforcing."[41] Page completed the tour gratified that the longest shadow over his name was not cast by young pretenders like Def Leppard or Kingdom Come, but by Led Zeppelin.

Indeed, by 1989 Zeppelin had risen above its detractors of twenty years before to become one of the most storied acts in rock. Even the 1984 satirical film *This Is Spinal Tap* contributed to the rehabilitation. Directed by Rob Reiner and played by actor-musicians Michael McKean, Christopher Guest, and Harry Shearer, "Spinal Tap" could have been any number of high-decibel British rock groups, but they did comprise an extroverted blond singer, moody lead guitarist, stoic bass player, and a drummer who had choked on vomit (though not his own), and their virtuoso, Les Paul–preferring axman Nigel Tufnel (Guest) took center stage when he scraped a violin back and forth across his guitar strings, pausing to carefully tune it before resuming his screeching solo. Jimmy Page later admitted he got the joke of *Spinal Tap* almost too well: "I definitely recognized the band politics—people getting puffed-up and self-important."[42] Nevertheless, *This Is Spinal Tap* was a hilarious and affectionate parody that enhanced Led Zep's currency.

The following year, the first unauthorized Zeppelin biography,

Hammer of the Gods, was published. Written by Stephen Davis in a tone more Bob Woodward than Boswell, the book's concentration on the sordid facts and rumors around the band—shark incidents and pacts with Lucifer—made it an unexpectedly big seller, finding an audience that had loved the music for more than a decade but had never known or guessed much about the men who performed it. Yet while fans lapped up all the salacious details, Jimmy Page and his surviving colleagues were dismayed to be remembered in such a light. "I couldn't bother to wade through that sort of stuff," Page sneered. "The whole humor of the band disappeared in the parts that I read, and it was just a sensationalist book.[43] . . . I read about four pages and I threw it away."[44] His years of ignoring the media had come back to haunt him. Page's and Led Zeppelin's reputation had taken on a life of their own.

Some of this was undoubtedly accidental. "I just know a lot of people have made a lot of money talking a lot of bullshit about an entity that never, ever stood up and said, 'You're wrong,'" dismissed Robert Plant. "Let it roll like crazy."[45] Very crazy were widely circulated news stories during these years contending hard rock groups had lured teenage listeners to the occult with hidden messages encrypted on the vinyl of their albums—inevitably, "Stairway to Heaven" came under scrutiny as one of the most popular and impenetrable anthems of a generation. Somehow the *Led Zeppelin IV* masterwork was interpreted as carrying *backward* lyrics that could only be heard by manually rotating turntables in reverse, from which then emerged muffled phrases like "Here's to my sweet Satan," "I will sing because I live with Satan," "There is no escaping," and "Whose path will make me sad, whose power is Satan." Thousands of otherwise functional phonograph needles were wrecked this way.

The "back masking" controversy spread to other acts like Judas Priest and Ozzy Osbourne, but Led Zeppelin's stonewalling made "Stairway" an ongoing source of speculation. Played counterclockwise, "Stairway to Heaven" *does* sound scary, but such is the power of suggestion. The origins of this fan fantasy lay in the earlier "Paul is dead" gossip around the Beatles' Paul Mc-Cartney, allegedly confirmed in backward snippets of *The White Album* and elsewhere, and "Rain," a 1966 Beatles B-side, did use real backward tracks of John Lennon's voice for one verse. Meanwhile, the blockbuster '70s novel and film *The Exorcist* did feature a key plot point of a disturbed child's gibberish discovered to be a demonic voice speaking inverted words and sentences, and it was held that some practices of Black Mass did blaspheme the Church by reciting prayers in reverse. Thus, in those pre-CD days, occult-obsessed audiences (and anti-rock religious zealots) spun their Zeppelin LPs the wrong way and put two and two together to come up with 666. There are no backward messages on any Led Zeppelin songs.

On the other hand, Jimmy Page's fascination with Aleister Crowley was genuine, and despite Plant's quip that "I think Page just collected the works of an English eccentric,"[46] the guitarist was no dilettante. The mystery arose less from Page than from Crowley himself, who rather enjoyed being the target of prigs and censors and who was happy to inflame the ire of his upright countrymen. "It's unfortunate that my studies of mysticism and Eastern and Western traditions of magick and tantricism have all come under the umbrella of Crowley,"[47] Page admitted to *Guitar World* magazine in 2003. Unfortunate, because at his most serious, Crowley was a thoughtful student of yoga, meditation, and other spiritual and intellectual disciplines, and might today be considered a New Age trailblazer—unfortunate, because at his least serious, Crowley encouraged his public image as "The Wickedest Man in the World," and this was how most rock 'n' roll listeners connected him with Page. Neither Aleister Crowley nor Jimmy Page were Satanists, a largely imaginary category of cultists who merely negated Christian ritual and belief, but in both men's worlds anyone who practiced a pre-Christian or non-Christian faith (while recasting Biblical figures like the Serpent, the Great Beast, and Babylon) was assumed to be a devil worshipper. The view was mistaken, but not as self-delusional as backmasking.

Just how much tangible results Page got out of his research into Crowley is impossible to know. When asked about Led Zeppelin's soul-selling legend and his supposed refusal to join in the deal, John Paul Jones deadpanned, "I'd run out of ink or blood or something. My old dad said, 'Never sign anything without first talking to a lawyer.'"[48] "Well, I don't pass any comment on them,"[49] Page brushed off backmasking allegations and the other folktales surrounding Zeppelin. "I don't want to get into too many backlashes from Christian fundamentalist groups. . . . I've given those people too much mileage already."[50] That said, Crowley did personally observe and transcribe many complex rites and sacraments connected with magick, and it would have been easy enough for Page to follow them himself in private or in the discreet company of other practitioners. Probably none of these would have pertained to music, money, or fame—Page could see to those in other ways.

More realistically, "Do what thou wilt shall be the whole of law" seems to have been closely observed by Page, not in the indulgent Me Generation sense of "If it feels good, do it," but as a doctrine of diligence and ambition. "What I can relate to is Crowley's system of self-liberation in which repression is the greatest work of sin," he acknowledged in 1977. "It's like being in a job when you want to be doing something else. . . . And when you've discovered your true will you should just forge ahead like a steam train. If you put all your energies into it there's no doubt you'll succeed because *that's* your true will."[51] The attainment of personal goals via focus and effort was something Page had experienced firsthand, and he credited Crowley with showing him the way: "Because his whole thing was liberation of the person . . . and that restriction would foul you up, lead to frustration which leads to violence, crime, mental breakdown, depending on what sort of makeup you have on underneath. The further this age we're in gets into technology and alienation, a lot of the points he's made seem to manifest themselves all down the line."[52] Page may not have signed anything in blood, but he gave up a great deal of his sweat. Aleister Crowley would have called it magick.

Si monumentum requiris, audio—If you seek a monument, listen. By the late '80s Jimmy Page was the most venerated living rock guitarist, and his influence over countless other musicians was enormous. Led Zeppelin's success—and that of other artists whose work Page had shaped, like the Yardbirds, Them, the Who, the Kinks, and Joe Cocker—had become so broad and so established that even players who had never consciously emulated his techniques had been affected by them. Distorted humbucking Gibsons, low-slung guitars, long unaccompanied solos, and the stardom of non-singing sidemen could all be traced back to Jimmy Page, and six-stringers from Ted Nugent, Rick Nielsen of Cheap Trick and ZZ Top's Billy Gibbons to Carlos Santana, Billy Duffy of the Cult and Nancy Wilson of Heart were all in his musical and visual debt.

Among all of Page's now-classic songs, "Stairway to Heaven" had been copied the most. Its light-and-shade template that he had so carefully constructed was the ultimate expression of rock 'n' roll as serious music: something that began with a slow, soft, and pretty prelude that then very gradually became harder and faster before exposing itself as heavy rock at its most mindblowing. Though this model was prefigured by the Beatles' "A Day in the Life," Procol Harum's "A Whiter Shade of Pale," and the Moody Blues' "Nights in White Satin," Page had perfected it with that pastoral A minor introduction—an intricate, gentle progression that could lull parents into thinking their sons and daughters had finally taken to "decent music"—which subtly mutated into blistering electric blues with no audible join. "Stairway to Heaven" confirmed to listeners pro and con that rock had a sensitivity and connection to older modes that had up to then been undetected, and in its train came copious rock cuts with similar layouts, many of which turned into beloved standards themselves. Sometimes called "power ballads," their best-known examples include Lynyrd Skynyrd's "Freebird" and their great "Simple Man," Aerosmith's "Dream On," Boston's "More Than a Feeling," Kiss's "Black Diamond," Blue Öyster Cult's "(Don't Fear) The Reaper," the Eagles' acme "Hotel California," Queen's "Bohemian Rhapsody," Journey's "Wheel in the Sky," and Styx's "Come Sail Away." Their melodies and lyrics were that of their composers and performers, but their light and shade was Jimmy Page's.

During the '70s and after, Page was not without competition as a guitar hero. Led Zep's two closest rivals in British hard rock both boasted talented soloists whose skills compared favorably to his: Black Sabbath's Tony Iommi and Deep Purple's Ritchie Blackmore. Iommi, a left-hander who had lost the tips of his two middle chording fingers in an industrial accident, took the dissonance implicit in early Zeppelin numbers like "Dazed and Confused" and created an entire new strain of amplified riffs using the *Diabolus in Musica* interval of the flattened fifth, resulting in the peerless cathedral doom of Sabbath signatures like "Black Sabbath," "War Pigs," "Iron Man," "Children of the Grave," "Sweet Leaf," and "Sabbath Bloody Sabbath." Many critics trace the true origins of heavy metal music to Iommi rather than Page, since Page tended to keep his electric work tied to blues scales, played on a conventionally tuned instrument, while Iommi often lowered the pitch of his Gibson SGs by several steps when hitting the sludgy power chords that defined Black Sabbath and their host of apocalyptic imitators.

Like Robert Plant and John Bonham, Tony Iommi and the other members of Black Sabbath were from around Birmingham in the English Midlands, and crossed paths with Led Zeppelin on friendly terms—Bonham had even briefly invested in a local record shop with Iommi and vocalist Ozzy Osbourne. Page and his bandmates were privately less than enthused with Sabbath's repertoire, however. "The heavy bands that instantly come to mind, the riff kings, didn't always employ that [light and shade quality]," he chided in a 1976 interview. "They more or less just keep going on one level, whereas we'd be shooting off in all directions."[53] Robert Plant added, "Not naming names, there are a lot of groups in England who still rely on riff after riff after riff,"[54] while John Paul Jones distanced his group from "all this glowering, Satanic crap."[55] Apart from occasional acoustic interludes (e.g., "Laguna Sunrise" or "Orchid"), Iommi's range of influences was indeed less eclectic than Page's, his soundscapes were usually smaller, and Black Sabbath's reputation suffered through a revolving door of members after Osbourne was fired in 1979. In many ways, Sabbath were the nastier, dirtier Rolling Stones to Zeppelin's classy Beatles: sometimes more appealing for just that reason, but often limited by their own reactionary formula.

Much the same could be said of Ritchie Blackmore. The Deep Purple leader had actually followed in some of Jimmy Page's footsteps, from a season with Neil Christian's Crusaders to session work in the thriving London studios of the '60s, and he had the chops to show for it. With the gradual formation of Purple into its classic lineup of the albums *In Rock, Machine Head,* and *Made in Japan,* Blackmore revealed himself as a technician whose fluency with Baroque lines exceeded Page's on his sometimes labored pentatonic licks. His Stratocaster solo on "Highway Star" is directly shaped by Antonio Vivaldi and J. S. Bach, and other Purple hits like "Space Truckin'" and the elemental "Smoke on the Water" also have a melodic precision that pointed the way to out-and-out "neoclassical" rock guitar sounds as demonstrated by Swedish master Yngwie Malmsteen in the '80s. "Jimmy Page says he listens to piano solos," Blackmore challenged, "but I don't see how that helps, because a pianist can play about ten times the speed of a guitarist. . . . Singers, violinists and organists are generally the musicians I enjoy listening to most of all. I can't stand guitarists!"[56] Measured strictly by formal ability, Ritchie Blackmore may be Page's superior. But Deep Purple also went through a series of debilitating personnel changes, and the temperamental Blackmore himself split the band to form Rainbow in 1975, (replaced by soon-to-be casualty Tommy Bolin) before rejoining and leaving through the next decade. Like Tony Iommi, his standing was compromised by expending his dexterity on too much stale songwriting and by the volatility of his partnership with his colleagues.

More elevated were Brian May of Queen and David Gilmour of Pink Floyd. From the mid-'70s onward, Queen were a commercial success and popular attraction to rival Led Zeppelin, especially in Britain, and the quartet racked up a potent library of hits: "Killer Queen," "We Will Rock You / We Are the Champions," "Crazy Little Thing Called Love," "Another One Bites the Dust," and many others. The stupendous vocal prowess and gaudy showmanship of vocalist Freddie Mercury was Queen's most obvious asset, but May's guitar was not far behind. Playing a unique home-built ax he had constructed with his father, the university-educated physics graduate had an instantly identifiable liquid note to his leads and a likewise exceptional "dry" bite to his riffs—"Stone Cold Crazy" and "Tie Your Mother Down" are as fast and as furious as Page's "Heartbreaker" or "Communication Breakdown." Queen carried on until Mercury's death from AIDS in 1993, but despite their increasing direction into lavishly operatic work May's gifts were never unheard. (A latter-day model of Queen, coincidentally, recruited Paul Rodgers to take Mercury's place.) In the arena of '70s English guitar gods, Brian May has almost as many followers as Jimmy Page, and the two stood together when they met the real queen herself.

David Gilmour, in contrast, does not have Page's inseparable association with instrumental wizardry, but he, too, helped create a serious challenger for Led Zeppelin's dominance of the touring circuit and album chart. Pink Floyd were the ultimate purveyors of "head music," built on Rick Wright's spacey keyboard effects, bassist Roger Waters's melancholic introspective lyrics, and Floyd's shattering live concerts, no less than Gilmour's slow, melodic Strat bursts. And for someone not readily remembered as a guitar prodigy (he also shared Floyd's vocal duties with Waters), Gilmour actually can cite authorship of three of the music's most famous solos, in "Time," "Money" (both from *Dark Side of the Moon*), and "Comfortably Numb" (*The Wall*). Unlike Page, whose fingers could really fly on a good night, Gilmour took his time when soloing, giving him a distinctive soaring tone—graceful, sustained, and as perfectly suited to the bright Fender sound as Jimi Hendrix's and Eric Clapton's. Page himself respected both the band (who occasionally enlisted the contributions of his friend Roy Harper) and Gilmour's unfortunate predecessor, Syd Barrett: "It was an absolute tragedy that that chap fell apart because in the nine month period of the early Pink Floyd all that writing that came out of him was absolutely brilliant and inspirational. . . . People tend to say Pink Floyd are still just a 1967 'Flower Power' group but they are not. They sound fresh and beautiful."[57]

Page's impact spread around the world. In the United States, Joe Perry was a devotee from his Yardbirds period, and after forming Aerosmith with Steve Tyler, Brad Whitford, Tom Hamilton, and Joey Kramer, the group covered no less than three Yardbirds gems: "Train Kept A-Rollin'," "I Ain't Got You," and "Think About It." Perry even became Aerosmith's amalgam of Jimmy Page and Keith Richards, the slouchy accomplice of Tyler's Jaggeresque front man, and his long dark hair and expressive blend of pout and sneer were a fair approximation of Page's own demeanor. He also studied Page's approach to heavy blues, adapting Zeppelin's rhythmic whiplash to Aerosmith on their favorites like "Sweet Emotion," "Nobody's Fault," and "Round and Round." "People who saw [Zeppelin] before their first album even came out were blown away by what this incredibly dynamic band could do onstage,"[58] he commented; though he would eventually strike up a friendship with Page and share gigs together, he still confesses, "I'm a fan—always will be."[59]

Another American admirer was Ace Frehley of Kiss. Known as much for their greasepainted comic book personas and platform boots as their arena-glam music, Frehley was probably the best player of the act, marshalling a straightforward but effective use of repeated pentatonic licks, unison bends, and vibrato—e.g., "Strutter," "She," "C'mon and Love Me"—that might have come straight from Page's fiery breaks on "Moby Dick" or "Whole Lotta Love." Not coincidentally, some Kiss cuts were produced by Eddie Kramer of *Led Zeppelin II* fame, who coaxed Frehley into channeling his limited but well-honed phrasings into tight and very dramatic solos. "I steal a little from Page, a little from Hendrix and some from Beck," said the Spaceman, "but it all comes out sounding like Ace Frehley."[60]

From Australia came the monolithic stomp of AC/DC, led by Angus Young and his Gibson SGs. While other guitarists paid homage to Jimmy Page's ominous onstage aspect, it was Angus who created one of the most unforgettable rock 'n' roll images after Page himself, in his impish schoolboy costume that dared fans to deny the full-grown scale of his riffs. Young peeled off very strong yet supple bluesy solos where not a note was out of place, and he paid credit to his roots on behalf of all his cohort: "I have great respect for Muddy Waters, B. B. King, Chuck Berry, Willie Dixon—if those people weren't there, you wouldn't have your Stones, your Zeppelins, your Who . . . all the big blues-based bands."[61] In "Whole Lotta Rosie," "Hell's Bells," and "Live Wire," Young demonstrated a massive hold on long bends and rapid trills, sounding like B. B. King on steroids, that easily matched Page's fluency on "Since I've Been Loving You" and "You Shook Me." Unlike Page, of course, Young and AC/DC never did acoustic material and became legendary for the predictability of their output. Angus Young was also accompanied by his big brother Malcolm on rhythm guitar, whose ball-breaking open chords on a Gretsch were the real source of AC/DC's brawn, and the sleazy-yet-sincere double entendres of original singer and wordsmith Bon Scott gave the group the proletarian authenticity they have never surpassed after his death in 1980. A superb guitar player by any measure, the schoolboy could still take a lesson or two from the Sorcerer.

"Page was probably my greatest influence early on," affirmed

Alex Lifeson of the durable Canadian trio Rush. "Rush started just a little before the time Led Zeppelin came out, and when I heard the first album, I thought, 'They're doing just the things we want to do; they have the sound we want to have.' And if we were that good, we would have played like that too, if you know what I mean."[62] In fact radio stations playing tracks off of Rush's eponymous debut in 1974 were often phoned by curious listeners asking if "Working Man" and "In the Mood" were new Zeppelin tunes. Lifeson's guitar glossary was reminiscent of Jimmy Page's in his effortless jumps from proficient classical acoustic ("The Trees," "A Farewell to Kings") to full-on electric rock ("Anthem," "The Temples of Syrinx," "Subdivisions") that won kudos from Page around the time of the Firm: "I *do* like the new heavy bands, because they're not polite! I used to go to a club in town called the Funny Farm and they played heavy metal all the time like Rush, who are extremely good."[63] Rush also expanded on Zeppelin's mystical themes with the runic verses of "The Necromancer," "Xanadu," and the album *2112*. "I wanted to look like him, and play like him, and be just like him," Lifeson remembered his youthful infatuation with Page, which came full circle when they came face to face backstage many years later. "You meet your hero, and he's a hero! He was everything I hoped he would be—I'll never ever forget that."[64]

As the '80s progressed, a new breed of hard rock hotshots looked to share space with Page at the peak of the guitar Olympus, foremost among them the brilliant Eddie Van Halen. Transplanted to Southern California from their native Holland, Eddie and drummer brother, Alex, built a self-titled band and debut album in which the guitarist's jaw-dropping fretboard sound and speed soon had fans comparing his innovations with those of Jimi Hendrix. Eddie Van Halen was among the first rock musicians to popularize the use of artificial harmonics, in which both hands "tapped" the strings across the neck of the guitar to achieve a very swift and fluid stream of notes, octaves higher than the instrument's natural range, sounding not unlike an electrified violin. He also customized his gear with heavy-duty tremolo arms which permitted the strings to be violently slackened and tautened without (as on the conventional Fender Stratocaster units) putting them completely out of tune. The LP *Van Halen* and its successors were replete with these intense and very fresh advances—notably "Eruption," the Kinks cover "You Really Got Me," "Mean Streets," and "Unchained"—and Eddie Van Halen was vaulted to the front ranks of guitar heroism.

Jimmy Page took a while to notice the newcomer. "An English radio interviewer asked me once about Van Halen and I didn't know if it was a group or what," he revealed. "Mind you, the guy did say, 'Do yourself a favor and go buy his album.'"[65] He quickly recognized the flashy young American's virtuosity. "I am *extremely* aware of him, actually, and I take my hat off to him for working out that technique. You know, you talk about what I've done on the guitar and that's what *he's* done on guitar. I must say that I can't do it.[66] . . . For my money, he was the first significant new kid on the block. . . . And I think he played a vital role in keeping kids interested, because they could look up to this cheeky little guy with the big smile. He flew the flag well, I think."[67]

At first Eddie Van Halen did not repay the flattery. "As a player [Page] is very good in the studio. I never saw him play well live—he's sloppy. He plays like he's got a broken hand and he's two years old." Mellowing through the years, he came around, and even saluted Page for inspiring him to develop his tapping tricks: "I got the idea a long time ago when I saw Led Zeppelin, back in '71 or something. Page was doing 'Heartbreaker' [the a cappella solo], standing there going, open string, pull off. I'm going 'Wait a minute—I can do that! Use that finger up here, and use this as the nut and move it around.' That's how I first thought of it."[68] Artificial harmonics, he discovered, are much more audible and musically effective when played through a high-gain amp as Jimmy Page did. Ultimately, and notwithstanding his own giant stature as a rock 'n' roller, Van Halen gave Page his due: "He's a genius. . . . Put it this way, he might not be the greatest *executor* of whatever, but when you hear a Page solo, he speaks. I've always said Clapton was my main influence, but Page was actually more the way I am, in a reckless abandon kind of way."[69]

Credit must also be given to Van Halen's fellow Californian, the short-lived but progressive Randy Rhoads, hired into Ozzy Osbourne's group in the early '80s. Rhoads, too, made harmonics a part of his arsenal, but he also incorporated the long rolling scales of such classical composers as Vivaldi and Johann Pachelbel. In this respect he was more reminiscent of Ritchie Blackmore than Jimmy Page, but Rhoads's formal training in more prescribed genres than rock (he had been a guitar instructor) allowed him to follow Page's example in layering several duplicate takes of precisely the same bars on record. On Osbourne's "Crazy Train," "Flying High Again," and "Suicide Solution," Rhoads's solos were given a thicker, deeper timbre through multiple overdubs à la Page. As well, he showed off his wide range of guitar know-how with the very pretty, classical acoustic snippet of "Dee," almost certainly an emulation of Led Zep's "Black Mountain Side" and "Bron-yr-Aur," and he also co-wrote Ozzy's Gothic threnody "Mr. Crowley," a more explicit (if sensationalized) tribute to the Wickedest Man in the World than Page had ever committed to tape. Killed in a wretched airplane stunt at the age of twenty-six while on tour in 1982, Randy Rhoads was just beginning to understand the obstacles faced by Page during the same time: "The main thing I'm going through is how to get more back to being a musician than being in a big band."[70]

By the end of the decade, the Van Halen and Rhoads field of heavy metal shred superstars had become a crowded one, and it was left to a group of Californian decadents to bring back some of the blues feel of '70s rock 'n' roll. Unlike their big-haired Hollywood contemporaries, Guns N' Roses wore denim, didn't shy away from acoustic guitars, and looked not to the latest Mötley Crüe or Metallica album for inspiration but to early Aerosmith, Ted Nugent, the Rolling Stones, and Led Zeppelin. The Gunners' lead guitarist was born Saul Hudson in England but became Slash in Los Angeles, where between sex, drugs, booze, and other assorted debaucheries, he acquired some of the soulful lead mannerisms and prolific riff production of Jimmy Page. Slash looked the part, too: he puffed on a succession of Marlboros as he played, strummed a one-of-a-kind electric-acoustic Guild double-neck, kept the Jack Daniel's close by, and hid his face under a thick mass of dark curls. On his Les Pauls—a retro selection in the years of Van Halen–copped "superStrats," with their double cutaways and industrial-strength whammy bars—Slash had a vicious picking attack and went over nasty pentatonic licks in GNR cuts like "Nighttrain," "Paradise City," "November Rain," "Civil War," and the lethal "You Could Be Mine." Wah-wah pedals ("Sweet Child o' Mine") and slide solos ("The Garden") were other throwbacks he reintroduced. If the Jimmy Page of *Led Zeppelin II* and *III* had been reincarnated into 1990, the Slash of "Parental Advisory—Explicit Lyrics" would have been him.

The common thread running between Page and all these illustrious rock guitarists of his own and following generations was that all of them were members of *bands*, joining forces with two or three or four other talents in what were ostensibly democratic partnerships. In many cases, lead guitar players were set off to far better effect by the musicians alongside them—Slash, Eddie Van Halen, Brian May, or Tony Iommi by outrageous mike-wielders Axl Rose, David Lee Roth, Freddie Mercury, or Ozzy Osbourne, say, or Ritchie Blackmore by organist Jon Lord, and Alex Lifeson by world-class drummer and bassist Neil Peart and Geddy Lee. Had 1968 seen the formation of the Jimmy Page Experience or the Jimmy Page Group rather than Led Zeppelin (a realistic proposal given Page's curriculum vitae next to that of Robert Plant, John Paul Jones, and John Bonham), his own attributes would have had to carry the whole show. They may not have been able to. Page wisely spread out the artistic work, and the public attention, more evenly, and his legions of competitors and disciples learned from Zeppelin's international success.

Alone among them all, Jimmy Page became known as a musical chameleon. Owing to his variety of session gigs in the '60s, Page came naturally to the different genres essayed by Led Zeppelin in a way that born rock 'n' rollers like Angus Young and Ace Frehley did not. He had the broadest diversity of guitar techniques of all the rock legends, including Jimi Hendrix and Eric Clapton, and if he did not have the phenomenal speed of Randy Rhoads or the polish of David Gilmour, he could always pull out a surprise—raga rock, twanging rockabilly, or Celtic drones—that no one else had in their stash. Page's guitar eminence rests on his being very good at a multiplicity of styles rather than being extremely good at one.

In November 1989, one of the happier Zeppelin reunions took place at the twenty-first birthday celebrations of Plant's daughter, Carmen. A spontaneous and unpretentious jam where members of Plant's own touring group sat in, the occasion had none of the pressures or pitfalls of the Live Aid or Atlantic spotlights. "Pagey was playing so good—I had a big lump in my throat," the birthday girl's father confessed, after running through "Trampled Underfoot," "Misty Mountain Hop," and "Rock and Roll." "That little time of playing with him gave me something I hadn't had for a long time."[71] On April 28 the following year, another fun impromptu session occurred at Jason Bonham's wedding, when Page, Plant, Jones, and the groom picked up instruments lying around at the reception and entertained the guests with the traditional bridal songs "Bring It on Home," "Rock and Roll," "Sick Again," "Custard Pie," and a Jerry Lee Lewis nugget, "It'll Be Me." Jimmy Page arrived at the ceremonies looking very dapper in a suit and tie, accompanied by his wife, Patricia, and two-year-old son. Peter Grant, resurfacing after years of drug-related illnesses, observed that Page "looked fantastic. . . . We spent a lot of time together at the wedding—we even had breakfast the following morning at 9:00 AM, which is unheard of for us."[72]

With the worst of his own drug problems behind him, and his confidence buoyed by the *Outrider* tour (whatever the disappointments of the record itself), Page was stepping out for bigger public performances. The day after he turned forty-six, on January 10, 1990, he joined American jock rockers Bon Jovi onstage at London's Hammersmith Odeon, doing "Train Kept A-Rollin'" and "With a Little Help from My Friends" in the Joe Cocker arrangement he had constructed in 1968. In August, he played with longtime fans Aerosmith twice, first at the huge outdoor "Monsters of Rock" festival at Donington in Leicestershire, England, then a couple of days later in his teenage haunt of the Marquee nightclub in Soho. The members of Aerosmith, themselves cleaned up after almost two decades of very heavy partying, were thrilled to have Page as their guest. "I'm dreaming," thought guitarist Brad Whitford at Donington. "Some people can take this in their stride. I still have to pinch myself."[73] At the Marquee, Steve Tyler brought Page out as "the man who set us on the path."[74] Page joined in with his crimson B-bender Les Paul on the Yardbirds' "I Ain't Got You" and "Think About It," plus some of the Hendrix blues "Red House," then finished with a triple-guitar "Immigrant Song" and "Train," with Tyler urging on his solo—"Stroll on, Jimmy!"

The most portentous of Jimmy Page's appearances in 1990 took place at Knebworth at the end of June. Robert Plant's band was launching another tour in support of his new record *Manic Nirvana,* and shared the bill with Paul McCartney, Elton John, and Pink Floyd at an all-day show there, amid much speculation of a Led Zeppelin reunion at the site of their last concerts in England. There was no reformation of Page, Plant, and Jones, but the crowd went wild when Plant, finishing his set, invited "my good friend"[75] Jimmy Page onto the boards with him. They did "Misty Mountain Hop" and then a surprise version of *Coda*'s brutal rocker "Wearing and Tearing," one of Zeppelin's lesser known but heaviest tracks, and closed with "Rock and Roll." It was the most exciting and triumphant of the pair's get-togethers yet, and fueled more public expectations of an official relaunch of their old outfit.

The late '80s had seen the real or recorded revival of many acts from the '60s and '70s, in response to the deluge of synthesized video pap (Culture Club, Cyndi Lauper, Billy Idol, the Go-Gos, ad nauseum) that had swamped the previous years. The Who, the Rolling Stones, Aerosmith, the Grateful Dead, and Pink Floyd had all enjoyed lucrative touring demands during this time, and retrospectives of the Doors and Jimi Hendrix were also affording the departed stars new acclaim. North American FM radio stations, in particular, had shifted from the free-form broadcasts of their early years to carefully plotted "classic rock" formats that sanctified the back catalogues of Pink Floyd, AC/DC, Queen, the Eagles, Creedence Clearwater Revival, Neil Young, Janis Joplin, and their peers. Not terribly adventurous or imaginative, the programming nevertheless turned on a new generation to the glories of rock 'n' roll's peak artistic and commercial era.

In the vanguard of these rehabilitated reputations was Led Zeppelin's. A staple of classic rock networks—most of them featured a daily "Get the Led Out" segment, and some even flirted with "All-Zeppelin" playlists—Led Zeppelin had taken on a cultural import the sneering reviewers of 1969 would have been loath to predict. The revolutionary ambitions of punk rock had died out with the demise of so many amateurish Mohawk-and-safety-pins acts, and only U2, the Police, the Pretenders, and R.E.M. had really scored major popular success with anything like a punk spirit. On the street level of high school and college campuses, Led Zeppelin were cool again. Even '80s tyros like White Lion and Kingdom Come had surfaced as veritable Led Zep tributes, doing close-but-no-cigar covers of "Since I've Been Loving You" and "Immigrant Song" as well as nominally original light-and-shade pastiches. Jimmy Page called Kingdom Come "Kingdom Clone" and was baffled by the guitarist's claim never to have heard Page play. "A rock 'n' roll guitarist who's never heard any Led Zeppelin music—that's quite amazing," he snorted. "It must be that I visit him as a vampire and leave my mark psychically."[76] New technology enabled dance-oriented Frankie Goes to Hollywood and white rappers the Beastie Boys to digitally sample John Bonham's skins and cymbals (as recorded by Page) for their own material. Dread Zeppelin had an Elvis Presley impersonator singing good-hearted reggae spoofs of "Heartbreaker," "Black Dog," and other *I, II, III,* and *IV* highlights.

For many listeners in their teens and twenties, Led Zeppelin represented a kind of ideal rock band: long-haired, musically sophisticated stoners who had lived through both the hippie heyday of the '60s and the dissolute splendor of the '70s. Since disbanding after Bonham's death, their status was as preserved as Mozart's or Robert Johnson's, forever fixed in an ageless paradigm of youth and power. Unlike the Beatles, Zeppelin did not have a faintly twee teenybopper past to embarrass them, nor were they weathering a continued slide into irrelevance like the Stones and the Who. With the debatable exception of *The Song Remains the Same,* all of their albums were highly venerated and lasting works, showing a scope and profundity that still rewarded close attention and repeated play. But it was here where Jimmy Page decided to step in and ensure that Led Zeppelin's legacy was not tarnished.

Another reason for the '80s resurgence of interest in '60s and '70s rock 'n' rollers, of course, was the development of the compact disc. The record industry was able to reissue hoards of forgotten or neglected material at great profit and little investment by transferring the music to CD, which all agreed was a sturdier and sharper medium for recorded sound. However, older music made with analog equipment (electronic impulses set to tape or even wax cylinder) did not always make a quality jump to digital (sonic information transposed to a series of ones and zeroes): despite the standard provisos that "the Compact Disc can reveal limitations of the source tape" some of the first CDs of predigital performers suffered in translation. Led Zeppelin's were among them.

Simply, the initial CD issues of the oeuvre were put to disc without Jimmy Page's supervision, and consequently much of the producer's clarity and ambience were lost. "They hadn't put any effort into it at all," he recognized. "They'd just run the tapes and that was it—no EQing [equalizing]."[77] On *Physical Graffiti*, for example, "In My Time of Dying" was left completely without the closing studio patter ("That's gonna be the one!" "Can we have a listen, then?") heard on vinyl. "In the past I've always been in charge of mastering the records," Page said, "and some of the CDs didn't sound at all up to scratch to me.[78] . . . I knew, right from the kickoff, that a far better job could have been done. . . . I was keen to get a better sound quality for the CDs."[79] By 1989, then, he gladly accepted Atlantic's invitation to remaster the original Led Zeppelin tapes for CD, and took on what would become a regular role as curator of the Zeppelin heritage.

Page spent May 1990 in New York's Sterling Sound with George Marino and his staff, going over the reels of source tapes from all nine Led Zeppelin studio albums (including the posthumous *Coda*) to assemble a four-CD box set that would be available for the fall and the valuable Christmas market. Robert Plant and John Paul Jones willingly contributed their ideas of what songs did and didn't belong on the package, which had room for most but not all of the canon, while Page and Marino used state-of-the-art technology to punch up the original tracks. They were not going to remix anything—that is, change the relative balance of instruments and voices on each piece—but they were able to clean up individual takes to achieve a sparkling new volume and crispness. "It was quite satisfying that the original tapes held up pretty well,"[80] Page remarked on the labor of love and archival quest. "The ones that I handled personally were where they ought to be, so that was fortunate."[81]

Aside from the dry process of moving from analog to digital, Page also got to sequence eleven years' worth of songs into the running order of a single collection, much the way he had with the original albums. In loose chronological succession, they now resounded with the unexpected juxtapositions and segues which were among his trademark devices as a producer—so "Heart-breaker" now cut not to "Living Loving Maid" but "Commu-nication Breakdown," the peaceful coda of "Over the Hills and Far Away" was broken by the ferocious overdrive of "Immigrant Song," and the long fade of "In the Light" was similarly jarred by "The Wanton Song." There was also space for a few obscuri-ties, like BBC radio archives of Led Zeppelin's electric version of Robert Johnson's "Travelling Riverside Blues" and Page's Dan-electro solo "White Summer / Black Mountain Side," and the rare "Hey Hey What Can I Do" that had hitherto only been found on the 1970 B-side of "Immigrant Song." Jimmy Page thought the digitalized "Achilles Last Stand" "sounds absolutely fantastic,"[82] but he was especially pleased with his weaving of John Bonham's "Moby Dick" and "Bonzo's Montreux" together into one colos-sal drum solo via a Synclavier editing program. "I didn't have any proper recording equipment at home," he explained, "but armed with a metronome I checked out the two things; the tem-pos seemed pretty similar.[83] . . . I think John Bonham would be happy with it, which is the main thing."[84]

The box set came evocatively designed by the graphic artists of Mission Control and featured a colorful booklet of essays by longtime Zeppelin friends Cameron Crowe, Robert Palmer, and Kurt Loder. The four members' "symbols" from *Led Zeppelin IV* were on prominent display (one for each CD or cassette), and the slick visual look and detailed production notes of the package set the standard for other rock group's retrospectives to come. Though the CD trend had begat much selling of old wine in new bottles, the fifty-four-track *Led Zeppelin* collection was more than a cynical cash-in. Along with a two-CD compilation, titled *Remasters*, the updated Led Zeppelin took to the air in Oc-tober 1990 with an amount of media hoopla the group would have never received, or expected or wanted, during their existence. They got a *Rolling Stone* cover story and interviews, and "Travelling Riverside Blues" and "Over the Hills and Far Away" were even adapted to video by Hipgnosis's Aubrey Powell, and were frequently shown on European and North American cable channels. Considering the size and price of the box set, sales were high, and unexpectedly hit the platinum mark (over one million copies sold), making it the most popular such anthology ever released.

Most satisfying of all for Jimmy Page was the critical respect he and his band were now given. "That seemed weird after all those years of getting nothing but bad reviews. It was really quite strange,"[85] he felt. "*I* thought I was in the greatest band in the world.[86] . . . Every musician hopes that their music will hold up, and that, along with having been part of a fabulous band in the bargain, is wonderful."[87] The only catch was that no one, not even its proud founder, could ever be able to top Led Zeppelin.

All My Love
1991-2006

It was a strange dream that these wizards cherished. They sought to make themselves beloved of those they cared for and to revenge themselves upon those they hated; but, above all, they sought to become greater than the common run of men and to wield the power of the gods. They hesitated at nothing to gain their ends.

—SOMERSET MAUGHAM,
THE MAGICIAN

The critical and commercial triumph of the *Led Zeppelin* box set was a great vindication for Jimmy Page, and his returns to the stage with other acts big and small had fired his enthusiasm for taking his own show on the road again. Audiences were clearly receptive to the idea, and he made optimistic noises in the press about what they could expect. "I love playing that stuff," he said after one of his Aerosmith gigs. "It's part of me and I love playing it."[1] To another interviewer he suggested, "Obviously there's been such a following for all these years that it'd be great to do it."[2] Reasonably healthy, and very confident of his repertoire, in early 1991, Page discussed a reunion project with Robert Plant and John Paul Jones. "I think I had always hoped we could work together again in some capacity because basically there was such a wonderful songwriting collaboration. The important thing was that we all had the time to do something together again. I had free time and John Paul Jones basically had an empty year and Robert Plant was taking a year off."³

At first it seemed like a real possibility. In search of an appropriate drummer to round out the lineup—the unwillingness to play Zeppelin numbers without John Bonham had diminished with time—Page wavered between Jason Bonham and Mike Bordin, a solid percussionist with the eclectic American rockers Faith No More. Videos of Bordin at work (Faith No More did a superhuman version of Black Sabbath's "War Pigs") were brought to the attention of Jones and Plant, but soon enough Plant backed out. The singer had built a more than viable solo career, for one thing, but perhaps more importantly he was uneasy with any attempt to repeat his own past, as other bands of his vintage had. "I saw the Who trundled around the stadiums of America, and I found it so dull, obvious and sad," he said. "I don't want to be a part of that aspect of entertainment. I've played Vegas already."⁴

Disappointed by Plant's rejection, Jimmy Page considered his prospects. At this point in his professional life he did not need to be managed so much as maintained; currently Brian Goode was answering the phones and fielding offers on his behalf. Page was now in the midst of a transformation from guitar hero to rock legend, comfortably wealthy and assured of deferential treatment everywhere he went, with nothing to prove for the balance of his working days. In the music business he was a "prestige property," an artist with widespread name recognition sitting on a very profitable stock of hit records and steady royalties, whose every outing was guaranteed substantial media exposure and support from thousands of loyal fans. How to find a contemporary vehicle for this potential, besides unplanned guest sets, was the issue worrying him. "I think everyone goes through a period where you have a fear of losing . . . that spark," he knew. Reflecting on the frustrations of the Firm and his *Outrider* effort, he admitted, "I was fully aware the work that I did during

Preceding page: Page with his iconic dragon suit, "Zoso" emblem, and Gibson EDS 1275 double-neck guitar.

Photo by Graham Wiltshire / Redferns.

Above: With John Bonha[m] on the infamous 1977 tou[r].

Photo by Rick Gould / ICP.

Left: "White Summer/ Kashmir" on the Danelec[tro] at Knebworth, 1979.

Photo by Fin Costello / Redferns.

Top: Page (far left), Eric Clapton, bassist Bill Wyman, and Jeff Beck perform together for ARMS in 1983. *Photo by Ilpo Musto / Redferns.*

Middle: At Live Aid, 1985. "An atrocity," declared Robert Plant. *Photo by Ebet Roberts / Redferns.*

Bottom: A frail Page on his Telecaster at an ARMS gig, early '80s. *Photo by Andy Sopczyk / ICP.*

Above: With Paul Rodgers in the Firm, 1985. Note Page's blue Stratocaster. *Photo by Rick Gould / ICP.*

Left: During the "Outrider" solo tou 1988, with Jason Bonham on drums Note "B-bender" device on Page's L Paul. *Photo by Rick Gould / ICP.*

Above: Reunited with Robert Plant, 1995. *Photo by Rick Gould / ICP.*

Left: Page and his eternal foil Robert Plant, around the time of *Walking Into Clarksdale*. *Photo by Mick Hutson / Redferns.*

Above: John Paul Jones, Robert Plant, and Jimmy Page in New York, May 2003. *Photo by Gary Gershoff / Retna*

Left: With Chris Robinson of the Black Crowes, 1999 *Photo by Rick Gould / ICP.*

bove: The Sorcerer hale and hearty in the new century. Page receives an OBE for his work ith disadvantaged children in Brazil, December 2005. *Photo James Veysey/ROTA/Camera Press/Retna.*

elow: With wife Jimena Page at Action for Brazil's Children (ABC) party. *Photo by Danny Clifford/Retna.*

ollowing page: Jimmy Page—Magus, Musician, Man. *Photo by Rb/Redferns.*

the Eighties certainly wasn't of the quality of Zeppelin, but that wasn't necessarily my own fault. The other components weren't there."[5] Unsure, Page started to sift through the innumerable audition cassettes directed his way over the years as he tentatively planned another solo album. Nothing grabbed him. "I was getting quite depressed. I certainly didn't want to do an instrumental album."[6]

It was Brian Goode who mentioned David Coverdale. A journeyman English vocalist, Coverdale had first found success replacing Deep Purple's Ian Gillan in 1973, a spot which lasted until 1976, when he quit the ever-fragmenting DP to form Whitesnake (ironically, Terry Reid had turned down Deep Purple's microphone back in 1968, the same year he turned down Led Zeppelin's). Under the names David Coverdale's Whitesnake and the David Coverdale Band, he slogged through the late '70s and early '80s with a succession of guitarists until the advents of the rock video and post–Van Halen eras propelled him to the top of the charts, on the strength of pop-metal hits like "Here I Go Again" and "Fool for Your Loving," and TV promos that featured his sexy wife, thespian Tawny Kitaen. There was no question that Coverdale had been around and knew his craft.

In March 1991, Jimmy Page and David Coverdale met in New York, where Page had been seen sitting in with a small-time band called the Reputations and also jamming with the great Les Paul. Page had heard Coverdale's voice but didn't know the man—"So we had a meet just to see how it went socially. We thought we'd give it a couple of weeks, and if it didn't work out we'd shake hands."[7] The two struck a rapport and agreed to collaborate, a decision made smoother by the fact of their both being signed to the Geffen label; it was Geffen's A&R man John Kalodner (who had also engineered Aerosmith's rise from the ashes) who steered the pair into a formal working relationship. Page and Coverdale went to the vocalist's Nevada home to develop material, and then sketched further ideas in Barbados. In Reno, Nevada, in May, they appeared together on stage at a concert by the hair-metal band Poison, where one report had Page stumbling off the boards and being helped to his feet by a roadie, while Coverdale tried out his imperfect memory of Led Zeppelin lyrics from "The Rover" and "Stairway to Heaven."

"It was suddenly right back to that original spark of creativity," Page claimed of these initial rehearsals. "I feel I have it in my heart again."[8] Others weren't so sure. The tall and blond David Coverdale had acquired a reputation as an obvious Robert Plant knockoff in a field where such figures where common—Plant himself derided him as "David Coverversion"—and both his stage poses and vocal inflections had long been suspect for their derivativeness. Few took Whitesnake seriously; guitarist Adrian Vandenburg had even brandished a violin bow in one video. "I literally fell out my bed laughing," Page had cracked about the clip in 1988. "I couldn't believe anyone could be so cheap."[9] When word of his alliance with Coverdale came out in 1991, many thought it was either Jimmy Page's elaborate retaliation against Plant for his reunion snub, or only a cheesy effort to fabricate Led Zeppelin with a second-rate substitute. Said Phil Carson, by then an independent record executive, "I don't think Jimmy would have chosen to do anything with David Coverdale if he thought there was even a prayer of doing something with Robert Plant."[10] Plant, for his part, was diplomatic. "Jimmy's always had a bleak sense of humor. . . . I wish the best for Jimmy, and however he gets the best is entirely up to him."[11]

By the fall of 1991, Page and Coverdale had formed a package deal with Geffen Records and John Kalodner, and backup musicians were assembled: Denny Carmassi, late of Sammy Hagar's Montrose and '80s-era Heart, was to drum, while bass duties were assigned to Ricky Phillips of Bad English, although studio musician Jorge Casas would wind up with most of the credits on the resultant disc. Along with the other mostly anonymous players recruited for the venture, they may have been Jimmy Page himself, playing for Burt Bacharach in 1965. Recording began in the rainy Canadian metropolis of Vancouver in November, at the popular Little Mountain Studios that had been used by everyone from native son Brian Adams to Metallica, with Mike Fraser at the mixing deck. While there, Page was able to fit in spots at the local Yale Club and even a jam with expatriate Long John Baldry, with whom he had last played at Cyril Davies's Marquee a lifetime before.

Over a fitful schedule in 1992, Page and Coverdale produced their album in Vancouver, Nevada, Miami, and completed the tracks at London's Abbey Road. Page dictated that the production be made in analog for its "warmer" ambience, as against the sometimes sterile atmospherics of digital records. While Coverdale dealt with the terminal illness of his mother in England, Page found time to attend the induction of the Yardbirds into the Rock and Roll Hall of Fame in New York, prepare a follow-up Led Zep box set consisting of the songs left off the original (including the previously unreleased "Baby Come on Home"), and even play some blues with the young jazz crooner Harry Connick Jr., in Florida. The constant travel that was so much a part of Page's occupation may have strained his marriage, but when the album *Coverdale-Page* was released in March 1993 its liner notes gave special thanks to Patricia and "Li'l James."

Despite its dubious provenance, *Coverdale-Page* contained some unexpectedly credible rock music and Jimmy Page's most aggressive guitar playing since 1980. The opening cut, "Shake My Tree," sounded like a revamped "Nobody's Fault but Mine," with its hammer-ons, pull-offs, and herky-jerky rhythmic breaks, while "Absolution Blues" faded in with electric lead that sounded like a long call from the minarets before uncoiling a heavy spiral-time riff, and "Feeling Hot" gave current headbanging bands like Guns N' Roses and Skid Row an incendiary run for their money. Slower numbers "Take Me for a Little While" and "Easy Does It" had chorused six- and twelve-string acoustics painstakingly layered underneath electric solos, and Page even strummed a dulcimer on "Pride and Joy." For "Absolution Blues," he used a Les Paul specially modified with a TransPerformance tuning system, an ingenious computer-controlled motor attachment that allowed him to change tunings at the touch of a button even while playing—the perfect gift for a guitarist with his love of deviations from EADGBE. All the songs were co-written with Coverdale (Page still named his publisher Succubus Music) and the CD cover used a motif of a "merge" highway sign to signify the joint venture. Coverdale, of course, brought some of his own compositional and vocal melodramatics to the material, and there was a lot of banshee wailing about his being a lonely man, baby, who was gonna make you feel all right, etc. The album and singles "Take Me for a Little While" and "Take a Look at Yourself" peaked at the middle levels of the sales charts.

Page hoped to promote the disc touring the U.S. in the fall, and a forty-five-date itinerary was drawn up, but weak ticket bookings could not justify the undertaking to his and Coverdale's management teams. "It's got nothing to do with me," he shrugged to *Rolling Stone*. "All I know is what's recommended to me at the end of the day."[12] He may have been a legend, but his association with David Coverdale revealed Page was still mortal. In the end, a Coverdale-Page band (with Denny Carmassi on drums, versatile English vet Guy Pratt on bass, and Brett Tuggle on keyboards) was put together for seven shows in Tokyo, Osaka, and Nagoya, Japan, in December, performing both Zeppelin classics such as "Kashmir" and "In My Time of Dying," as well as some Whitesnake hits. "I'm enjoying doing those Whitesnake songs,"[13] Page claimed, though many of his fans would have felt them beneath him. After their skeptical public response, the partnership was quietly dissolved. "David was really good to work with," he remembered. "It was very short-lived, but I enjoyed working with him, believe it or not."[14] *Coverdale-Page* was better for Jimmy Page the musician than Jimmy Page the rock star.

Before flying to Los Angeles to rehearse for concerts in Japan, Page had already met up with Robert Plant in Boston before one of Plant's shows there, supporting his most recent collection, *Fate of Nations*. Plant had been asked to do a spot on the MTV cable music network's *Unplugged* show, where popular acts performed in an intimate and mostly acoustic setting, and he decided that this would at last be the occasion to team up with Page once more. "The offer from MTV really was so fortuitous," he believed, coming at a time when he was returning to some of his own geographic and artistic roots. "I'd started going to the Welsh mountains again, and reading the old books about mythology and Celtic history. . . . I missed the kind of thing that Jimmy and I had."[15] Page, whose post-Zeppelin directions had never found the modernist poise of Plant's, was only too pleased to link up. "The MTV thing really was a catalyst. . . . It was really the first time we had a chance to think about the future constructively—to kick it around, see how to do it, how not to do it."[16]

As early as 1973, Page had told Lisa Robinson, "My dream is to go around like some sort of motorized caravan, with a small unit—just to go to Morocco and record musicians, go through the East recording."[17] Twenty years later, he and Plant agreed that their *Unplugged* would not try to replicate Led Zeppelin numbers but to reshape them under the influence of their continued fascination with Middle Eastern music; they would use the bassist Charlie Jones and drummer Michael Lee from Plant's solo band and call in a variety of Egyptian, Moroccan, and English players to accompany them. This mooted the participation of John Paul Jones, as much as anything else to avoid leaving the impression that they were staging a Led Zeppelin reunion without John Bonham, the one member who could definitely not make the gig. Sensible in theory, they did not inform Jones of their plans, which soon led to some awkwardness and hurt feelings.

In March 1994, Jimmy Page and Robert Plant initiated runthroughs in King's Cross in London, first with tape loops, then gradually with other ensembles, including the London Metropolitan Orchestra. "Robert and I went into a real dark, dank rehearsal studio in the north part of London and we just had the tape machine, some North African rhythm loops and my guitar and it was, 'Let's see what you can do,'"[18] Page described the trials. The two were now being jointly managed by Bill Curbishley at Trinifold Management: together again, Page and Plant were a very hot client to represent, and the record of their performance would be released by their former label Atlantic. By April, they played a tribute show for Alexis Korner in Buxton, England (doing "Baby Please Don't Go" and "I Can't Quit You Baby," among other tunes), and in August, they visited Marrakech to have loose jams with local street musicians, recorded and videotaped on the spot. Back in Britain, they went to Snowdonia in Wales, with Charlie Jones, Michael Lee, and Porl Thompson on guitar, Jim Sutherland on mandolin and bodhran, and Nigel Eaton on hurdy-gurdy, for more audio and visual documents. Thompson, once of Goth pioneers the Cure ("Killing an Arab"), had been tapped to augment Page's sound with his six-string and banjo expertise—clearly, Page and Plant were serious about not turning themselves into a Led Zeppelin tribute act. Finally, in London, they taped two nights of sets before a select audience, backed by Jones, Lee, Thompson, Eaton, Sutherland, and the London Metropolitan and an eleven-piece Egyptian group, as well as Plant's current partner, Najma Akhtar, on vocals.

Onstage in London, the cameras captured a fifty-year-old Jimmy Page visibly worn by the years. Stout under loose clothing, he was seated for several songs (which suited the mellow *Unplugged* format), and his circa 1975 curls hung in contrast to his jowly 1995 face. Even his guitars had matured: although he picked Les Pauls for some numbers (including the TransPerformance custom), he also used a unique double-neck Ovation acoustic, a twelve- and six-string model of the beautiful Roundback line, and a fantastic *triple*-necked mandolin, twelve- and six-string acoustic custom-made by British luthier Andy Manson. With so many other musicians alongside him, it took a while for him to warm up to his parts, but when he did, he was in good form, both quiet and cranked. Edited and mixed by Mike Gregovich over the next two months, the MTV *Unplugged* program was aired in October and November in North America and the U.K., and the corresponding album, *No Quarter*, was released at the same time.

Also known as *Jimmy Page and Robert Plant Unledded*, the pictures and music came as pleasant surprises to a public used to big-ticket superstar outings that heeled closely to the winning formulae of yesteryear. Instead they saw and heard a tasteful, even classy, extension of Led Zeppelin's folk and Arabic leanings ably assisted by real folk and Arabic artists. "Yallah," "City Don't Cry," and "Wonderful One" had the dusty sound and feel of Marrakech, with indigenous players adding the beats and backings of *G'naoua*, the healing and spiritual tradition of black Moroccan slaves and their descendants. Brian Jones of the Stones had attempted to capture pure *G'naoua* rhythms in 1968, but these were original merges of English lyrics and structures with desert modes. "Nobody's Fault but Mine," "The Battle of Evermore" (Najma Akhtar as an Egyptian Sandy Denny), "No Quarter," "That's the Way," and "Gallows Pole" emphasized their latent Celtic aspect, while the Nile flowed through new readings of "Kashmir" and *Led Zeppelin IV*'s dark horse, "Four Sticks." The heavy electric version of "Thank You" came across with undimmed ardor. "Since I've Been Loving You," backed with violins, violas, and celli, took on an apt soul dimension reminiscent of B. B. King's "The Thrill Is Gone" and the Temptations' "Papa Was a Rollin' Stone," with Page's blues bends and Plant's tortured screams bearing the scars of two decades since they first performed the song as young men.

Throughout *No Quarter*, Jimmy Page's guitar was restrained and dignified, especially on acoustic: other than "Since" and "Thank You," he took no long Les Paul solos, seeming more at home strumming the Andy Manson and the Ovation with his idiosyncratic tunings and timings. He was careful to downplay his guitar heroics while reveling in the accompaniment of classical and African instruments, saying, "We already knew that we wanted to be totally enveloped, Western orchestra this side, Egyptians this side, feel this whole force that was going on, this joy and jubilation—it was wonderful."[19] Critics and audiences agreed, making *Unledded* one of the rock highlights of 1994, and a Page-Plant tour was slated for the following year. Demand for tickets would be high. After the compromises of Paul Rodgers and David Coverdale, Jimmy Page had returned to his most successful partnership.

Promoting their latest work and the upcoming gigs around the world, the guitarist and vocalist journeyed to South America in November for radio and TV spots and interviews. From his hotel suite in Rio de Janeiro, Brazil, Page was disturbed to see what amounted to an urban civil war taking place in the city's *favelas*, or shantytown districts. Long troubled by poverty, drugs, violence, and criminal gangs, units of the Brazilian military had been called in to quell unrest on the streets and found themselves facing armed resistance; tanks and other heavy firepower were deployed to put down the uprisings. Page, who had experienced fan rampages at Zeppelin concerts (like the 1971 Milan riot), had never witnessed anything of this scale before and was taken aback. While in Rio he also met a pretty native named Jimena Gomez-Paratcha, who explained the severity of the conditions in the *favelas* to him. Some thirty years his junior (Page was almost fifty-one), Jimena had the wide eyes and smile of a Latin Lori Mattix. Back in London in January 1995, his wife, Patricia Ecker, filed for divorce, with the tabloid press speculating on her settlement of $6 million (U.S.) and their custody battle over James Patrick, now almost seven.

Before the Page-Plant shows began, the surviving members of Led Zeppelin were formally inducted into the Rock and Roll Hall of Fame in New York on January 12. John Paul Jones drew laughter in his acceptance speech, saying, "Thank you, my friends, for remembering my phone number,"[20] and the three closed the occasion with an all-star jam on "When the Levee Breaks," with fellow honoree Neil Young. Jason Bonham sat in the drum stool for the show while his sister, Zoë, looked on, although Plant had wanted Michael Lee to pound the skins. Introduced by Aerosmith's Steve Tyler and Joe Perry, Led Zeppelin's Hall of Fame ceremony generated timely publicity buzz for the imminent world tour of its two stars.

Jimmy Page and Robert Plant played 115 shows in nineteen countries over 1995 and 1996. They were joined by their lineup from the *Unplugged* program, with Hossam Ramzy directing the Egyptians and Ed Shearmur conducting local orchestras who learned the *No Quarter* scores on short notice. Second guitarist Porl Thompson came along for the first European and North American rounds as well, and some concerts featured a version of the Cure's "Lullaby" in acknowledgment; even more unexpected were the Page-Plant renditions of "Shake My Tree" from *Coverdale-Page*. What the fans really wanted, of course, were Led Zeppelin tunes, and they heard many, including "Achilles Last Stand," "Since I've Been Loving You," "Whole Lotta Love," "Thank You," "Going to California," "Rock and Roll," and even rarely showcased pieces like "Tea for One" and "Tangerine." Other than a genuinely unplugged promotional platform on Japanese TV, Plant had put the deathless "Stairway to Heaven" off-limits, saying, "There's only so many times you can sing it and mean it."[21] The generous mix of old favorites with foreign interpretations garnered strong public and critical endorsement. Rock legends though they were, in contrast to other '60s and '70s groups (the Rolling Stones or the reformed Eagles, for instance), no one thought Page and Plant were resting on their laurels.

There was no attempt to disguise what those laurels were, however. Both Jimmy Page and Robert Plant displayed their "Zoso" and "Feather" symbols as part of their stage set (Nigel Eaton reportedly asked Page what "Zoso" really meant and got a cold stare in return), and advertising posters proclaimed, "The Evolution of Led Zeppelin Continues." Page's theremin was sounded during the gigs, and he took long electric solos to the roar of the crowd. A cache of Page's guitars were exhibited, among them his rarely seen sunburst '50s Stratocaster. He took the acoustic segments as a chance to unload his heavy Gibsons and rest sitting down with an Ovation, amplified by better equipment than the primitive rigs with which Led Zeppelin circa 1975 had had to make do (he had Vox and Fenders on board, as well as his faithful Marshalls). At an appearance in Michigan, an unbalanced young attendee ran toward Page in a bid to stab him, but was wrestled to the ground before getting too close—demons told him to do it, he said, since the guitarist was making "Satanic music." Page himself may have been reliving some of those dangerous glory days, as when he was caught smoking in the washroom of a commercial flight between San Francisco and Portland, Oregon. "Visibly intoxicated,"[22] he dared police to arrest him and faced a $1,000 fine.

In Europe for the summer, the band played grand assemblies and seasonal festivals across the continent. By now the title card seemed to be firmly carrying on the tradition of English performers like Laurence Olivier or Alec Guinness: dedicated, lifelong show people who were as happy to recite Shakespeare in a provincial theater as earn a million dollars in a Hollywood film. Substitute rock 'n' roll for Shakespeare and Wembley Stadium for Hollywood, and that was Page and Plant in 1995. In England, Page and Plant were humbly introduced to Bert Jansch after years of lauding the folk virtuoso from afar. "Every song, with an audience made up of people all my age—the whole place was singing along," Jansch witnessed. "It was my first time meeting up with Jimmy and it was really quite nice."[23]

At Wembley on July 26, Plant delivered a special thank-you to Peter Grant in the audience, overseeing his charges at work one last time. Though slimmed down and cleaned up, Grant collapsed and died of a heart attack later that year at the age of sixty. Page and Plant attended his funeral in Hellingly, East Sussex, along with other rockers like Jeff Beck, Paul Rodgers, and ex-Yardbirds Chris Dreja and Jim McCarty. Jimmy Page issued a terse farewell to the man who had helped make his career: "Peter was a tower of strength as a business partner and a friend. I will miss him and my heart goes out to his family."[24]

After the celebratory conclusion of the tour in March 1996, with concerts in South America, Japan, and Australia winding up, Page went to Mexico and Brazil with his new love, Jimena, then returned to London. Fatherhood was again on his agenda since Jimena had given birth to a daughter, Jana, the previous year, but plans were also afoot to write and record new material with Robert Plant. Another project was the compilation of Led Zeppelin's live BBC radio broadcasts of 1969 and 1971. Heavily bootlegged in their day, Page heard the recordings as more valuable rarities that would appeal to a broad fan base (a comparable two-CD Beatles package, *Live at the BBC*, had been a success in 1994) without an undue amount of production overhauls. As with Zeppelin's *Coda* and box sets, Page was the driving force behind the assembly. "It didn't require us to dig through our archives, and it didn't involve the complication of extensive remixing,"[25] he knew. In April 1997, he and engineer Jon Astley edited several hours of tapes into a marketable album.

On sale by November, Led Zeppelin's *BBC Sessions* satisfied listeners who had long regretted that *The Song Remains the Same* was the only "official" testament of the band's stage presence. Here was the document of a rock group still on their way up, hungry and loose, dropping breaks of James Brown into "Communication Breakdown," doing a rollicking Eddie Cochran cover with "Somethin' Else," and previewing a variant of the "Moby Dick" riff with "The Girl I Love She Got Long Black Wavy Hair," a Sleepy John Estes blues rendered unrecognizable under Page's Les Paul and John Bonham's Ludwigs. Small audiences in the studios and larger ones tuned to their radios were also treated with debuts of "Stairway to Heaven," "Black Dog," and "Going to California" before *Led Zeppelin IV* was pressed—on *BBC Sessions* they had a vividly precarious quality, the infant masterpieces of musicians at the dawn of realizing what they had together. "We were becoming tighter and tighter," Page pointed out, "to the point of telepathy. . . . Led Zeppelin were really moving the music all the time."[26]

It was also noteworthy that songwriting credits for the 1997 CDs listed Willie Dixon as co-author of "Whole Lotta Love" and Chester Burnett (Howlin' Wolf) as the source of "The Lemon Song." Dixon had filed a suit against Led Zeppelin in 1985 and settled out of court two years later—"I wasn't sure I was going to have any justice pertaining to it,"[27] the heavyweight bluesman thought. Jimmy Page, meanwhile, though agreeing to the earlier copyright resolution, continued to argue that there was nothing underhanded about the original use of Dixon's or Wolf's blueprints. "We got into some trouble because people felt we lifted ["Whole Lotta Love"] from Willie Dixon, but if you took the lyric out and listened to the track instrumentally, it's clearly something new and different.[28] . . . Robert may have wanted to go for the original blues lyrics, but everything else was a totally different kettle of fish."[29]

BBC Sessions did deservedly decent business, but aside from such strolls down memory lane, in 1997 Jimmy Page was more excited to compose and record fresh numbers with Robert Plant. Even during the tour of '95 and '96, the duo had considered their follow-up. "The most obvious thing for us to do," Page believed, "was to go back to the four-piece unit that we knew best and that has always worked best for us. A lot of people thought we were going to carry on with that big extravaganza from the last tour, but for us it was important to come to terms with the songs.[30] . . . Scaled down to just the rhythm section, guitar, and singer, it's the lineup I've been used to since I was a teenager."[31] Page and Plant would retain the engine room of the *No Quarter* sets, drummer Michael Lee and bassist Charlie Jones (who had become Plant's son-in-law upon his marriage to his daughter, Carmen). As they had never before, they now brought in an outside producer, Steve Albini, a young master of the alternative scene, with albums by Nirvana, the Pixies, and P. J. Harvey to his name. Page detected in Albini's work something of his own organic recording techniques—capturing as much of the band's live sound as possible—that didn't rely on console trickery to balance the tracks. "Steve

EQs using microphones, and that's what the science of making a record is all about," he complimented. "That's exactly the science that was developed in the early days and it's been forgotten, to tally forgotten in the Eighties. . . . Steve's job was just getting this stuff down on tape and he's a wonderful man to do that."[32]

Page, Plant, Lee, Jones, and Albini cut an album of songs in London's Abbey Road Studios in August and September. Page had played in the hallowed halls of Abbey Road as a session man, but never as a signed artist. "I'd never had the freedom to turn up an amp in there before," he laughed. "This time I had the freedom in their huge room, and I just took full advantage of it."[33] Thus liberated, he and his guitar tech "Binky" brought in many of the soldiers from his guitar army, including the 1958 Les Paul, his Gibson double-neck, a 1966 cream Telecaster first acquired as a Yardbird, his Martin acoustic, and even a Gretsch Country Gentleman like he had owned back when he was Crusading with Neil Christian. The instruments were amplified through Fender Tonemaster amps at the recommendation of Joe Perry, although he still went back to his Vox AC-30 for its inimitable brightness. Thinking of the sessions' good spirits and productivity, he admitted, "A lot of this record was written on the spot. . . . Ideas are coming out fast and furious. . . . If I have an idea, [Plant] knows exactly where I'm coming from."[34]

What emerged from Jimmy Page and Robert Plant's few weeks at Abbey Road was a complex sequence of words and melodies that continued the exoticism of *No Quarter* without the baggage, or the cushion, of numerous "ethnic" players. Titled *Walking Into Clarksdale* and given a cover by photographer Anton Corbijn (depicting two young boys no one would mistake for the teenage Page and Plant), the album was an electric quartet's travelogue from Arabia ("Most High," "Shining in the Light") to Mississippi (the title track) to the tranced-out nightclubs of contemporary London ("Heart in Your Hands," "Sons of Freedom"). To the extent that there were any vestiges of Led Zeppelin in the disc, it was the experiments of *Houses of the Holy* or the eclecticism of *Physical Graffiti* audible this time out, with both vocalist and guitarist curiously laid back on "When I Was a Child" and "Upon a Golden Horse." Page played his now-familiar strummy style, with arpeggios and skipped or extra beats abounding, perhaps under the influence of the Brazilian tribal drumming he had taken in on travels with his new family. "Brazil was the last country to abolish slavery," he pointed out, "and so you've still got this very strong African element to the music.[35] . . . Music is everywhere there; you can't escape it.[36] . . . I guess it depends whether you think of a song as being an excuse to play a solo at some point or as a journey which you just travel on the guitar."[37] Plant, too, had outgrown his youthful Delta mannerisms to accentuate his whispery Moroccan breaths and Mecca-directed moans. *Clarksdale* was neither blues nor blues-rock, but a sort of international folk carried home by nomadic English adventurers. It was a daring but difficult record.

Critiques and sales confirmed this. In stores in April 1998, *Walking Into Clarksdale* met with a cautious response that credited Jimmy Page and Robert Plant for taking their music further than their comfortable reps required, while conceding they may have gone too far for most fans' tastes. "A few songs work well on their own," said one report, "but on the whole the collection sounds forced and self-conscious."[38] No matter—a second Page-Plant world tour was scheduled for the rest of the year, across Europe, North America, and as far east as Turkey. Though their album was far from a nostalgia fest, the two rock stars in their fifties were discovering, as the Rolling Stones, Pink Floyd, Kiss, the Who, and others already had, that the public wanted to hear the hits. Where once Led Zeppelin had given concerts to promote their latest LP, now classic rock acts released a CD to promote their latest concerts. And where once Page and Plant had blown minds at the Fillmore, the Kinetic Circus, the Tea Party, and the Bath Festival, now they were filling seats at General Motors Place, the Continental Airlines Arena and the Molson Ampitheatre. One of *Clarksdale's* more effective songs was "When the

World Was Young," which took on a poignant resonance as the shows drew near.

In February 1998, Jimmy Page confounded his public again when he collaborated with the American hip-hop star Sean "Puff Daddy" Combs on the latter's "Come with Me," which was to be used on the sound track of a multimillion-dollar remake of *Godzilla*. Puff Daddy was a typically flamboyant producer and mogul whose first big hit, "I'll Be Missing You," was a tribute to his murdered partner and friend, the Notorious B.I.G. ("Biggie" Smalls), rapped over a sample of the Police's 1983 smash "Every Breath You Take." "Come with Me" took the mountainous Page-Bonham "Kashmir" progression to achieve the same urban swagger, but this time an original musician was to join in. Led Zeppelin's hooks had been taken this way in the past, to their authors' displeasure: "They steal your riffs and then shout at you,"[39] Page sneered at the genre, and in 1994, he and Plant, as the surviving writers of "Kashmir," had sued the Home Box Office network to remove Schooly D's "Kashmir"-based "Signifying Rapper" from the sound track of the violent film *Bad Lieutenant*.

Page now praised Puff Daddy for his inventiveness. "It was a real privilege working with him,"[40] he smiled, although the recording was actually made via satellite links between London and Combs's base in Los Angeles. "I explained to him that because the guitar is in an open tuning, I prefer to play it in D, and then I suggested that we modulate to E. He paused for a moment and said, 'I don't know nothing about no D's and E's,' which I thought was a great answer."[41] "Come with Me" became a successful single—Jimmy Page's first-ever appearance in the *Billboard* Top 10—and it tickled him to think his ten-year-old son, James, who lived in New Orleans with his mother Patricia Ecker, could now connect his dad with someone as current as Puff Daddy. "When parents say to their children, 'You go to school with Jimmy Page's son,' that doesn't mean anything to most kids. But they understand if something's in a *Godzilla* film."[42] Page met up with

Puff Daddy to do "Come with Me" on the U.S. TV program *Saturday Night Live* (he appeared as a towering cameo in the video release), and again commended the rapper for his musicianship, such as it was. "He kept changing the arrangement all through the soundcheck and dress rehearsals. . . . I thought, 'He's never going to remember all these changes, he'll never get this right.' But he was right on the nail every time. So you've got to give him his due for that."[43]

The Page-Plant tour commenced shortly after the *SNL* gig, in Pensacola, Florida, on May 19, and would continue for another eighty-eight shows until December. Page, definitely shorter and wider than in 1975 or 1988, nevertheless looked hale and happy under a tidy, almost conservative head of black hair. He even managed a few low-altitude stage jumps. His conventional, B-bender and TransPerformance Les Pauls were unleashed, as well as the double-neck Ovation, Yamaha acoustic and a new Paul Reed Smith electric with a vibrato arm; his theremin and his violin bow were given solo spots. Songs from *Walking Into Clarksdale* were duly aired, with "Most High," "Shining in the Light," and the hypnotic "Heart in Your Hand" taking on a crowd-pleasing luster the album takes hadn't quite manifested, but as Bert Jansch had testified, the Led Zep catalog really got the arms in the air and the lighters sparking. "The Wanton Song," "Bring It on Home," "In the Light," "Trampled Underfoot," "Babe I'm Gonna Leave You," "Rock and Roll," "Going to California," "Tangerine" (keyboardist Phil Andrews helping out on mandolin), and "Whole Lotta Love," as well as flashbacks like "Crossroads," "Train Kept A-Rollin'," and "Baby Please Don't Go," dominated the sets. Such concerts took in an estimated £15 million, but money had never been the point.

"Everything had become remote,"[44] Robert Plant concluded before the act was to travel to Japan and Australia. "I began to feel intimidated committing myself to large parts of touring."[45] Long leery of becoming an oldies purveyor, and not as deeply infected with the travel bug as Jimmy Page, the preponderance of Zeppelin classics in the gigs weighed uneasily on him and the singer bowed out of further Page-Plant performances in 1999. By then some of the popular interest in the reunion had waned, with latter recitals failing to sell out, which may have also dampened Plant's commitment. Page hoped to tempt Plant back into the fold with wordless demo tapes he put down with Michael Lee, but, he related, "I presented scenario after scenario to Robert,"[46] all in vain. "We seem to draw out the best in each other, but unless I'm working with someone who's really passionate, I don't see it as positive."[47] Let down but not out of options, Page had been rejuvenated enough by the two global circuits to resume performing on his own.

In June 1999, Jimmy Page did the odd charity gig in London, with Lee drumming and Guy Pratt playing bass. He then appeared on the same bill with American rockers the Black Crowes, who were playing in Britain with Aerosmith, and their onstage jams of blues chestnuts like Fleetwood Mac's "Oh Well," B. B. King's "Woke Up This Morning," and Willie Dixon's "You Shook Me" were particularly satisfying. Based in Atlanta, Georgia, and fronted by brothers Chris Robinson on vocals and Rich Robinson on guitar, the Crowes were known for their Southern-fried roots rock, sounding like a '90s cross between the Rolling Stones of *Exile on Main Street* and the Allman Brothers. They had previously scored with albums *Shake Your Money Maker* and *Southern Music and Harmony Companion*, with bluesy singles "Hard to Handle," "She Talks to Angels," and "Remedy," although by the decade's end their retro novelty had worn off somewhat. They had already opened for Page and Plant back in '95 and, reintroduced by Page's favorite portraitist, rock photographer Ross Halfin, the combination of the veteran English guitar hero and the strutting Dixie boogiemen sounded like an excellent match. "It felt really, really good,"[48] Page said of guesting with the Crowes at London's Café de Paris. "We had such a good time doing what we had done."[49]

The next move came from the Black Crowes' manager, Pete Angelus, who asked Page to join the group for several midsized dates in the U.S. The shared spots would both highlight the Crowes' visibility and let Jimmy Page blow off the rock 'n' roll steam *No Quarter* and *Walking Into Clarksdale* hadn't vented. Page's manager, Bill Curbishley, himself stymied by Robert Plant's departure, was fully behind the deal: "Jimmy came to me and asked me what I thought of the idea. So I said, 'Well, it's all about enjoyment.' That's the most important aspect at this stage of Jimmy's life and career."[50] Six shows were arranged for the autumn, with two at New York's Roseland Ballroom, one at Boston's Worcester Center, and two at the Greek Theater in Los Angeles. In October, Page played with Puff Daddy at the Net Aid (an Internet-based antipoverty organization) concert in New York's Giants Stadium. After doing "Come with Me," he teamed with Guy Pratt and Michael Lee to do an instrumental "Dazed and Confused," and an elaborate unfinished piece called "Domino." Page was seen and heard picking a one-of-a-kind double-neck Jerry Jones model (resembling a Danelectro) along with his TransPerformance Les Paul at the event; his set closed with Chris and Rich Robinson taking the stage for versions of "In My Time of Dying" and "Whole Lotta Love."

Jimmy Page and the Black Crowes pulled good box office at their American blasts. Heavy with Led Zeppelin titles, they also fit righteous renderings of Crowes staples "Remedy," "No Speak No Slave," and "Shake Your Money Maker" into the act, on top of the Yardbirds' peak "Shapes of Things" and "Oh Well" (a one-time model for "Black Dog"). In artist- and audience-friendly venues, they all found a friendly and scrappy rapport with each other that left plenty of room for improvisation, as explained by the easygoing Chris Robinson: "We always like to keep things a bit spontaneous in the Black Crowes. . . . You get out there and see what the vibe is."[51] For Page, hearing three guitarists (himself, Rich Robinson, and Crowe rhythm man Audley Freed) go over the epic Zeppelin songs he had once had to play alone was a special reward. "When we did 'Ten Years Gone' with Led Zeppelin, there's all these guitars on the record, and I used to do my best to try to get through it with just one guitar. The thing is, when we did 'Ten Years Gone' with the Crowes it was quite fantastic—they had obviously done their homework. I was in the middle of this guitar orchestra and it was quite stunning. It was a real treat for me."[52] To mark the personal and musical gratification of the whole outing, Jimmy Page quit smoking.

So pleased were all the participants, in fact, that a bigger Page–Black Crowes tour was planned for 2000. In the meantime, managers Angelus and Curbishley wanted to release a live accounting of the L.A. shows, but decided on the (for the time) unprecedented innovation of selling it via the Internet through *musicmaker.com*. By cutting out the middlemen of marketers and distributors, songs from the Greek Theater could be purchased and downloaded in any number or running order by fans at home with their computers, something many were already doing with pirated music files anyway. However briefly this moment of online idealism was to last, it made commercial sense in the first months of the new millennium. "The one person who's disappeared out of the business is the A&R man," Page said, extolling the new format. "Because the listener at home *becomes* the A&R man. He's the one who chooses what tracks he wants on the album, and that's cool."[53] Once thrilled to put out a 45-rpm single in 1965, Jimmy Page was now breaking ground in the Information Age. "It's wonderful to be at the forefront of this,"[54] he spoke to the press. One cut from the *musicmaker. com* selections, the Page-Crowes update of *Led Zeppelin II*'s "What Is and What Should Never Be," actually made the Top 15 of *Billboard*'s mainstream rock chart, as no prior Internet-only offering ever had.

Eventually, *Live at the Greek* came out as a "traditional" CD retailed in stores, bearing record of a fine night for lovers of classic rock 'n' roll. The cover illustration pasted the "Zoso" icon over an emblem of two crows. Chris Robinson had a relaxed, raspy singing voice not *too* derivative of Rod Stewart or Otis Redding, and Jimmy Page was in his prime element with

"Heartbreaker," "The Lemon Song," and "Custard Pie." Indian and Arabic tones were all very well for his bolder excursions, but here, backed with two other like-minded guitarists, he was back where he started, when he first met the blues. Through June and July 2000, Page and the Black Crowes made gigs in the Midwest United States, alternating with the latest incarnation of the Who, who were also managed by Bill Curbishley at Trinifold. Playing their best Zeppelin, Crowes and covers from *Live at the Greek*, and appearing on U.S. TV shows *Late Night with Conan O'Brien* and *The Tonight Show with Jay Leno* (where they did a diamond-hard "The Wanton Song"), Page could solo to his heart's content as he never could with his four-piece groups, knowing he had a flesh-and-blood guitar army behind him.

His own flesh and blood failed him, however, when a persistent back problem forced the cancellation of several concerts in August and, it turned out, the rest of the tour, as well as anticipated forays into Europe and the Far East. At age fifty-six, there could have been any number of explanations, but it was likely that decades of lugging weighty solid-body guitars around his knees for hours on end (he'd even stood up to play while recording in studios) was the prime culprit. On doctor's orders, Page took a break from sustained stage performances which, as of 2006, have not been resumed. He did make one-time shows with Robert Plant in Montreux in July 2001, an MTV-Europe awards gala in Frankfurt in November of the same year ("Thank You," with nu-metaler Fred Durst of Limp Bizkit), and a charity affair in London in 2002 (he played an instrumental "Dazed and Confused," backed up by members of former Jam leader Paul Weller's band). Sidelined, he began to put together an ultimate Led Zeppelin compilation.

Two of them, in fact. Although *BBC Sessions* had gone some way to demonstrating Zeppelin's live chops the way previous discs had not, neither it nor *The Song Remains the Same* represented the scope of the band's existing permanent record. Page knew there was a fair amount of raw tape and video footage from the years 1969 to 1979, but no formal release of either had ever been prepared. "I've always wanted to put out a chronological live album of Zeppelin stuff . . . but I can't get the others to agree, so I've stopped trying,"[55] he muttered in 2000. As joint owners and authors of the material, Page, Plant, and John Paul Jones had only occasionally sat down to discuss their legacy, and neither Plant nor Jones were as motivated as Page to screen or listen to the treasures from the vault. Two "greatest hits" CDs, *Early Days* and *Latter Days,* had been shipped in 1999 and 2000, but these contained nothing hitherto undiscovered (and came in somewhat tacky covers to boot, of the four musicians' heads stuck into astronaut suits). By 2002, though, the three survivors came together to initiate the digital exhumation of Led Zeppelin. Jimmy Page, as always, was to produce.

The first task was to gather the video, celluloid, and audiotape. Led Zeppelin had deliberately eschewed most television offers, but a clutch of early tunes had been previewed on the tube, and they had been filmed at the Royal Albert Hall on Page's twenty-sixth birthday in 1970, and the rear projection screenings of their shows at the Earl's Court in 1975 and Knebworth in 1979 had been preserved as well. Many Zeppelin gigs—most, some would say—had been bootlegged by audiences across Europe and North America with varying results, yet there were some good recordings directly from the soundboard (the mixing deck used at concerts and operated by the road crew) from two American gigs in 1972. Page hired engineer Kevin "Caveman" Shirley, whose engineering job on *Live at the Greek* had impressed him, to punch up the sonic archive, while Dick Carruthers, who had worked on analogous video features for the Rolling Stones, the Who, and Oasis, was responsible for editing the images. Half the task entailed restoring the master copies to conform to the specifications of modern technology and scouring the world for appropriate equipment with which to make accurate transfers and even for the masters themselves. Page had some of these in his possession, but others had been lifted from his home at the Mill

House in the '8os: "Someone who was pretending to be a friend stole the tapes. . . . They were staying at my house comforting my ex-wife."[56] He even secured some contraband cine reels shot from the stands for a fuller perspective.

Once the pictures and music had been put in place, Page found there was enough for a triple-disc CD and a two-disc DVD, together making up over eight hours of Led Zeppelin in action at their pinnacle. They were to be both dynamite and gold in a market starved for virgin Zeppelin; like the box sets of 1990 and 1993, they were sure to create a new awareness of the group for the children and perhaps even grandchildren of their original fans. Both Jimmy Page's management at Trinifold and his distributors at Atlantic eagerly supported the productions. As overseer, Page was especially occupied with cleaning up the sound for maximum impact, which had always been his specialty. "In terms of overall consistency," Kevin Shirley put it, "we simply tried to make the band sound like itself," filtering the analog '70s sources through high-tech digital programs like Peavey's Kosmos and the pervasive ProTools. Shirley got to know Page while huddled together in the control booths: "There are lots of stories I can't tell you," he chuckled, "and most of them revolve around what the band was doing while they were backstage during Bonham's drum solo on 'Moby Dick.'"[57] Never partial to digital as a basis for recording, Page himself was pleased with the results of his and Shirley's cleanup. "There's so much you can do with ProTools, although you can't play CDs backwards and hear messages from Satan,"[58] he revealed, probably in jest.

For all the careful, frame-by-frame and bit-by-bit restoration, when the *Led Zeppelin* DVD and CD *How the West Was Won* collections came out in May 2003, the performances alone had stood the test of time—big time. Both opened at the number-one tier of the music and video *Billboard* charts, setting sales records and winning rhapsodic reviews from industry professionals and ordinary consumers. Rock legends of years' standing, Led Zeppelin now could be considered one of the best live rock 'n' roll shows ever staged and unassailable pop icons. "Reunion?" asked an overwhelmed Dave Lewis, speaking for the Led Zep fan community through his publication *Tight but Loose.* "Who really needs it now?"[59]

The DVD was loaded with stunning front-row revelations of Page, Plant, Jones, and John Bonham, doing awesome bare-bones English blues at the Royal Albert Hall, glorious acoustic numbers at Earl's Court, and an almost elegiac "Whole Lotta Love" at Knebworth. Bonham could now claim his due as the most powerful rock drummer ever, with the clips of his muscular propulsion of "Trampled Underfoot," "Rock and Roll," "Black Dog," and "The Ocean" (the last two revived from outtakes of Madison Square Garden in '73) properly stealing the show. Non-musical insert segments portrayed a very civilized Bonham answering queries from journalist Germaine Greer in Australia, and a bearded and subdued Jimmy Page and Robert Plant sitting down for baffled reporters in New York in 1970. Asked if they expected to win "the order of the garter," Page, his mind evidently on French showgirls, nudges his mate and giggles, "Is that the can-can?"

How the West Was Won blew *The Song Remains the Same* off the boards, blending a pair of heroic concerts in Los Angeles and Long Beach the year Led Zeppelin were overshadowed by the Rolling Stones for mainstream coverage—Truman Capote and Terry Southern would have barely survived the onslaughts of those nights. Sprawling jams on "Whole Lotta Love" and "Dazed and Confused" joined with the Valhallan "Immigrant Song" and "Stairway to Heaven" as the hammer of the gods came down on teenage California, no harder than on the seventeen-year-old Edward Van Halen in the bleachers, cracking the secrets of six-string sorcery from "Heartbreaker," and on fourteen-year-old Lori Mattix, watching from the wings as her black-suited new boyfriend showed her what is and what should never be. "Each member of the band was playing at their best during those performances and giving like 150 percent," said Jimmy Page of his refurbished masterpieces. "And when the four of us were playing like that, we combined to make a fifth element. That was the magic, the intangible."[60]

The unanimously favorable reaction to the DVD and CD premieres of 2003 clinched Jimmy Page's passage from controversy-dogged heavy metal guitarist to permanent member of the entertainment aristocracy. With no great recording or touring obligations on his horizon, he was easing into a contented semi-retirement where the desperate pace of making, say, *Presence* was not something he wanted to recapture: "It required a sort of keen energy that I'm not sure I have anymore,"[61] he was quoted in *Guitar World*. Instead he was free to collect both the riches and acclaim now directed his way. Had he been born twenty years earlier, he may have taken on the persona of an old soldier, posing with his medals and ribbons beside his trusty Spitfire—as it was, he could pose with his gold and platinum records while cradling his trusty Les Paul.

At a London service in July 1999, Page presented Elvis Presley's guitarist Scotty Moore with a custom-built Gibson guitar, one of the manufacturer's line of instruments that replicated the preferred dimensions of legendary pickers. It was only fitting, since Moore himself had twanged the rockabilly chords to "Baby Let's Play House" while an adolescent James Patrick Page sat openmouthed by his radio on Miles Road. Page, probably the most visible exponent of Gibsons with his iconic Les Pauls and the EDS 1275, has had a continued relationship with the American firm, and in 2004, the Gibson Custom Shop issued a limited-edition Les Paul that was a minute replication of his 1959 ax, down to neck measurements, fret radii, pickup output, and even the wear and tear of its inevitable scratches, dings, and cigarette burns. Twenty-five of these were retailed for $23,000 apiece (personally inspected and signed by Page), while 150 more went on sale at a mere $16,400. "It's a really great guitar," Page's guitar handler "Binky" told it, "but ultimately it's like trying to recreate a Stradivarius."[62]

Other honors have come Page's way. He has been a celebrity judge at the annual "Riffathon" contest in the United Kingdom, with talented amateurs and wannabes wailing out their best guitar heroics. Led Zeppelin were given a Lifetime Achievement Grammy Award in 2005 (they had never come near one when they were a functioning rock band), which Page, John Paul Jones, and John Bonham's children, Jason and Zoë, accepted in Los Angeles on February 12. Also in 2005, Led Zeppelin received the annual Polar Music Prize from the Royal Swedish Academy of Music, a tribute administered by former ABBA manager Stig Anderson (*In Through the Out Door* had been recorded in Abba's home base of Polar Studios in Stockholm); previous winners included Bob Dylan, Quincy Jones, Joni Mitchell, Ray Charles, and B. B. King (to whom Page bestowed the trophy the year before).

In the United States on May 11, 2005, Page appeared at the New York Stock Exchange to ring the opening "bell" of the venerable trading institution—the occasion was the initial public offering of shares in Warner Music, the parent company of Atlantic, which Page's skills had helped make a billion-dollar enterprise. While the graying VIPs of Warner Music Group (including chairman and CEO Edgar Bronfman Jr.) waited for the stock to go on sale, Page stood with a Les Paul and a Marshall stack and chugged out the riff of "Whole Lotta Love" plus some stray power chords to the delight of the floor. Despite this fanfare, the Warner shares took an immediate tumble, with traditional music businesses losing clout in the age of downloading and file-sharing. On August 23, Jimmy Page was commemorated with the first star on the London Walk of Fame in Piccadilly Circus, casting his hand prints in cement while a crowd cheered. "It's a real privilege and a great honor to be the first," he said. "I'm really chuffed. . . . If you started putting in all the people I think are deserving, you could cover the whole of London."[63] And in 2006, the U.S. toy company Wizard Universe announced it was taking advance orders (at $15.99) for the collectible Jimmy Page action figure, a small-scale version of the guitarist circa 1973, decked out in the dragon suit and raising his double-neck beside his Marshalls. "Immortalized in plastic for the first time!" crowed the ads.

Whether tasteful or tacky, all such flatteries meant less to Page than his quite serious charity endeavors. Although Led Zeppelin had done some benefit shows and donated free records or guitars to worthy causes, it was only after his marriage to Jimena Gomez-Paratcha that he took an active role in an aid organization. Since getting an unintentional firsthand look at the Rio de Janeiro riots of 1994, he, at the Brazilian Jimena's encouragement, began to donate significant sums to alleviate the chronic poverty and social ills afflicting urban areas in the giant South American state. Perceived by outsiders to be a surf-and-samba tropical paradise, in reality Brazil has suffered from decades of government inefficiency and corruption, pressures of competing in a free-trading global marketplace, ugly economic stratification, and truly frightening levels of street crime and violence. In 1996 and 1997, Page contributed to the British trust TASK (To Abandoned Street Kids) Brasil, which led to the construction of "Casa Jimmy," a safe house for homeless children and teens, including single mothers, in Rio's Santa Teresa area. Rescuing kids out of the surrounding shantytowns, many of whom had been reduced to drug addiction or forced into prostitution, Casa Jimmy and its staff of teachers and social workers give comfort and education to youngsters who have received almost none of either in their lives. After receiving shelter, medical treatment, and schooling— and affection—the residents can go on to healthier homes and employment away from the brutal realities of the *favelas*.

Allied with TASK Brasil is the charity Jimmy and Jimena Page established themselves in 1998, the ABC (Action for Brazil's Children) Trust. This, too, uses Page's name, as well as those of celebrity patrons like actor Jeremy Irons, Brazilian singer Bebel Gilberto, and Page's friend Brian May of Queen, to raise funds for poor and disadvantaged Brazilian boys and girls. A full calendar of donation drives and media contacts occupy the Trust, along with the hands-on efforts to instruct, house, protect and care for literally millions of at-risk children living in Brazilian cities and the countryside. Gibson Guitars and the Sanctuary Group, under whose umbrella Trinifold Management operates, are among the corporate sponsors. In 2002, Page returned to his home neighborhood, raising over £10,000 for ABC from students and faculty of Epsom College while he took questions, signed autographs, and sat in with the school band on Bob Dylan's "Subterranean Homesick Blues." The College's Senior Chaplain found Page "a lovely, generous, and kind-hearted man who has a great passion not only for his music but for his charity."[64] As ABC's spokeswoman, Jimena put their challenge into perspective in 2002, noting, "Fifteen hundred children have been murdered in Salvador alone in the past ten years. Six hundred were killed in Rio in 1998 alone. . . . Between 1987 and 2001, eight times as many children were killed as a result of gunfire in Rio than died in the bloody Israel-Palestinian conflict." She also paused to recognize ABC's deepest well of income: "From myself and the charities, thanks go to my wonderful, supportive, and ever-patient husband, Jimmy Page."[65]

Page, indeed, has money. In 2006, the London *Times* estimated his personal fortune at £70 million, most of it from the continued sales of Led Zeppelin issues—today estimated to number between 250 and 300 million units worldwide in all formats since 1969—as well as from the more recent Page-Plant tours. Zeppelin's rank of commercial achievement hovers just underneath the Beatles' and Elvis Presley's, though the Fabs and the King had head starts and released many more records in the cheaper 45-rpm medium. Some Zep cuts have been used in films (notably those connected with their longtime American booster Cameron Crowe, like 1982's *Fast Times at Ridgemont High* and 2000's *Almost Famous*), and in 2002, snatches of "Rock and Roll" were licensed for use in a Cadillac TV commercial, to the letdown of many fans. The important point is that, thanks to his and Peter Grant's business acumen, and determination not to be victimized by promoters and record companies as had other acts like the Yardbirds, Jimmy Page has made a very good living from his own music.

With his expenses thus no object, Page is able to live and go wherever he chooses. He still owns the Tower House in the Kensington district of London, and in 2004, allowed the residence's richly ornamented interiors to be photographed for a book on its architect William Burges—the Tower House is the only of its designer's works privately owned and not open to the public. "If you have the privilege of living in a house like this and find someone else who is just as passionate," Page was quoted, "of course you want to help."[66] The Mill House, where John Bonham died, was sold in the early 2000s, and Page relinquished the nearby Sol Studios around the same time ("It was ten minutes down the road, and when I moved there was no point in keeping it").[67] In 1999, Page had won a court battle with the owner of the home next door to the Mill House, Dudley Burnside, a *real* old warrior with whom he had fought over tall trees that had intruded on the RAF veteran's property. The Boleskine House, where Aleister Crowley lived, was sold in 1992. While there Page had commissioned roof repairs and retained a caretaker (who he eventually dismissed on bad terms), but he had never stayed for any extended periods and the building had been empty for some time when purchased. The redecorations Page had requested of Charles Matthew Pace, a Scottish mystic who called himself "the Jackal of Egypt," were nowhere to be seen. Today an exclusive bed-and-breakfast that attracts the more reverent Crowley and Page aficionados, its owner reported in 2005 that mail addressed to Led Zeppelin's guitarist still trickles in, much of it from young women.

His wealth and schedule enable Page to keep homes around the world where he may visit at different times throughout the year, including in Windsor, and in Lencois, Brazil, in the country's northeastern mining region of Bahia. "It's just stunning, rugged nature, with waterfalls and rivers and caves," he has said of the former colonial outpost. "It's really beautiful there and there's a river that intersects the town. I'm on one side of it and you can hear the drums coming from the other side where people are having their candle and bride ceremonies."[68] While there he has also been introduced to the Brazilian tradition of capoeira, a mixture of dance and martial arts once practiced by slaves and accompanied by its own musical idiom. "It's very, very fast," Page reported, "and the music that goes along with it is wonderful: chanting and a *berimbau*—a one-string instrument that's played with a stone and also has this gourd that you move in and out to give this phasing sound. It's so African, similar to stuff I've heard before in Mauritania, places like that."[69] Page has also been speculatively linked with houses in Florida, France, and California, although it may be truer to repeat that he can simply afford to travel anywhere and be confident of finding private lodgings for himself and his family.

Jimmy Page has five children: Scarlet, James, and, with Jimena Gomez-Paratcha, daughters Jana (born in 1995), Zofia Jade (June 1997), and a son, Ashen Josan (January 1999). Like many celebrity parents, he is discreet about the younger ones' appearances and rarely if ever puts them on public display. As a father, he helps ready them for school and handles other domestic routines, and in 2003 took time out from the Led Zeppelin CD and DVD production to attend James's high school graduation in Florida. His kids and their mothers are annually gathered during the holidays, he told the *Independent* newspaper in 2004. "Every Christmas we are all together, all the mums and all the children. . . . We are a close-knit family."[70]

Page's eldest daughter, Scarlet, is the only one to have lived through his dissipated period of leading Zeppelin and its aftermath. "In those early years of my daughter's life I was not physically there for her," he has admitted. "I missed all those precious moments in a child's life—getting their first teeth, taking their first steps and all that."[71] Her own memories of the era are cheerful enough. "There were musicians coming in and out of the house," she spoke in 2001, "but it wasn't all parties and orgies. . . . The really great thing was that I'd meet people like Donny Osmond."[72] Under the tutelage of Ross Halfin, Scarlet studied at the University of Westminster and is today a professional photographer, with a specialty in contemporary rock 'n' rollers like the Darkness, the Smashing Pumpkins, and the Foo Fighters. Though certainly advantaged by her father, Scarlet's last name does not have the instant identification as, for instance, Stella McCartney or Elizabeth Jagger, and many of her riff-happy subjects have been taken aback after they casually inquire of her, "No relation to Jimmy, I suppose?"[73] A pretty, willowy blonde like her mother but with her dad's pursed pout, Scarlet has sometimes been seen escorting Jimmy Page to public functions.

Offstage, Page remains as private as he was during the '70s and '80s, though without the attendant menace of occultism and self-destruction that eddied around him in those days. His personal manager is Allan Callan, who had worked for Peter Grant at Swan Song and who has known Page since 1968; Page is also often accompanied by his friend and sidekick, lensman Ross Halfin, while on business journeys. He did put his foot down in March 2000, when *Ministry,* a London magazine published by the Ministry of Sound nightclub, alleged the year before that he had "selfishly and stupidly"[74] stood by while John Bonham died, throwing Satanic spells and being more worried about the drummer's vomit ruining his furniture than the drummer's survival. Challenged by his lawyer Norman Chapman, the publication apologized for the story, denied its veracity, and paid Page undisclosed but "substantial" damages, which were donated to his Brazilian charities. In 2001, Page purchased a rarely available box at the Royal Albert Hall for £300,000, and he is known to keep collections of old cars, antique art, and furniture (among them items by William Burges and Aleister Crowley), and of course guitars of all years and makes. His musical tastes are kept up to date—probably more so than most of his own Baby Boomer constituency—with everyone from the Red Hot Chili

Peppers, Prodigy, and Korn to the White Stripes, the late Jeff
Buckley and Canadian neo-psychedelicists the Tea Party rating
his good mentions.

Although he sometimes wears glasses, Page has made no
mention of hearing loss, a common problem among rock musicians of his era (e.g., Pete Townshend and Roger Daltrey) who
played before the development of onstage ear monitors. At many
a Led Zeppelin show, the band was listening to the same massive speaker systems as the audience, only from a much closer
distance. Edging toward retirement age (he turned sixty-three
on January 9, 2007), he has creased, natural features that bear
the faint Asiatic aspect Rat Scabies once detected. Though an
inconspicuous force of bodyguards are on hand at charity events
and premieres (like the 2003 gatherings that heralded the Led
Zeppelin DVD), fans and well-wishers tell of Page being soft-
spoken, courteous, and even a little shy when approached. Security is a justifiable concern for him, given his fame and his
peculiar association (real or fantasized) with the occult, which
continues to excite the unstable minds of some Zeppelin freaks.
Such individuals may be disillusioned to find that, in interviews,
the Sorcerer of "Stairway to Heaven" and the Equinox bookshop
uses expressions like "crikey" and "my goodness gracious," and
leaves with a pleasant "God bless."

In 2005, Page won two of his highest honors to date: an honorary citizenship of Rio de Janeiro bequeathed by Paulo Meno,
house leader of the Brazilian Democracy Party in appreciation
of his charity work; and for the same reason he was made an
Officer in the Order of the British Empire (OBE). This title is
above the Member of the British Empire's (MBE) but lower than
a Commander (CBE), typically given to British subjects for at-
tainments in industry, philanthropy, or public service. "I'm never going to be offered [a knighthood],"[75] he had once dismissed.
"Put it this way, I'm not chasing one. . . . But I would think long
and hard about it."[76] The OBE announcement was made around
the time Page, along with Jeff Beck, Eric Clapton, and Brian May

met Queen Elizabeth II in Buckingham Palace at a party for the British music industry. Though the clueless sovereign was heard to ask, "And what do you do?" and "Are you a guitarist too?"[77] the three lads from Surrey may have glanced at each other as they thought about how the blues had taken them further than in their wildest dreams. On December 14, 2005, Jimmy Page was formally invested with his OBE at the palace and afterward posed with the medal for a gaggle of photographers in his tie and tails, and his bottle-black hair. Led Wallet and Hoover Nose were long gone, but a bit of the Old Girl remained.

Page's status as a musician and creator of mass entertainment are assured. As with all the classic rock groups of the '60s and '70s, Led Zeppelin are now audible as a *historically* significant representation of a time when there was still an overlap between pop culture and folk art, a primitive but evolving cottage craft practiced on an international assembly line. For all the millions of dollars washed over Jimmy Page and his friends and rivals, the industry they helped turn into a global giant had yet to attract the retinues of pundits, technicians, PR gurus, media buyers, professional spectators, and other specialists that massage it today—rock 'n' roll music, in its heyday, was still largely a conversation between performer and audience unmediated by insiders and trend-spotters. At the same time, rock stars did not merely provide streams of electronic "content" to fill up the empty space of shopping malls, waiting rooms, and personal listening devices. "I don't think that rock 'n' roll can be enjoyed for twenty-four hours a day," Page's pal Jeff Beck has opined. "When we were young, there was so precious little of it, but when we got it, the fix lasted at least a week. Now rock music has become too *available* and somewhat mundane."[78] Not only were the players themselves screened by higher standards of craftsmanship than apply today, but they had to regularly prove their ability with live concerts and records they wrote, performed, and, in Jimmy Page's case, recorded themselves. The social and almost mystical importance fans placed on Zeppelin songs and their authors (as well as that of the Beatles, the Rolling Stones, Bob Dylan, Jimi Hendrix, Neil Young, Janis Joplin, Bob Marley, David Bowie, Pink Floyd, et al) has come to seem redundant when the sheer amount and accessibility of leisure product has become more valuable than the matter of who makes it, what it says, or how widely or narrowly it is received.

Page's specific talents bear some scrutiny. He is unlikely to make it to the Songwriters' Hall of Fame: not known for his lyrics or song structures, he tends more to hit on memorable riffs or progressions and then build from there with others' help. Many of Led Zeppelin's best tracks bear the stamp of his bandmates as much as his own, with "Since I've Been Loving You," "Celebration Day," "Black Dog," "No Quarter," and "Trampled Underfoot" owing heavily to John Paul Jones, likewise "Good Times Bad Times," "Out on the Tiles," "When the Levee Breaks," and "Kashmir" to John Bonham, and certainly with Robert Plant's words enhancing the band's entire catalog. "You can always tell my riffs from Page's because mine have got lots of notes and are linear," Jones has reminded. "His are chunkier and chordier."[79] With lesser comrades, like David Coverdale or Paul Rodgers, his work has declined accordingly.

As a guitarist, on the other hand, Jimmy Page is undoubtedly one of the greatest in rock. "His playing lacks the lyricism of Eric Clapton's, the funk of Jimi Hendrix's, or the rhythmic flair of Peter Townshend's," wrote Jim Miller of *Rolling Stone*, "but of all the virtuoso guitarists of the Sixties, Page, along with Hendrix, has most expanded the instrument's sonic vocabulary."[80] True enough. His distorted pentatonic riffs from the first four Zeppelin albums became the fodder for other players' entire careers, with "Dazed and Confused," "Communication Breakdown," "Whole Lotta Love," "Heartbreaker," "Immigrant Song," "Celebration Day," "Black Dog," and "Rock and Roll" serving as the fuzz-boxed templates for thousands of other hard rock and heavy metal lines. When average listeners think of him, it will be his slouchy Les Paul postures, walls of Marshalls, and these overdriven sounds that first come to mind.

Yet there is more to Page's guitar than this. "Many people think of me as just a riff guitarist, but I think of myself in broader terms," he has asserted. "As a musician I think my greatest achievement has been to create unexpected melodies and harmonies within a rock 'n' roll framework."[81] He seldom played at maximum distortion: there was always more to his electric control settings than turning everything up to ten and switching to the rear (more trebly) pickup of his Fender or Gibson. "I turn up pretty high, but I vary my pick attack—I don't play hard all the time," he clarified. "I find that this approach helps me get more tonal or dynamic variation, especially when I'm playing close to the bridge or close to the neck. . . . If you go hard all the time, you just won't get the difference in tone."[82] In Led Zeppelin and later partnerships Page often let the bass and drums supply the music's weight while he spun thinner or more syncopated licks and chord fragments over and around the bottom. While he has put his hand to some grinding rock passages like "The Rover," "Achilles Last Stand," and "Feeling Hot" from *Coverdale-Page,* he deployed them only sparingly throughout his records. His stage and studio use of the theremin and violin bow, limited in themselves, confirm he was always seeking a wider array of tones than just the volume or gain that make electric guitars distort; the fact that he also owned and played semi-acoustic or synthesizer instruments (a hollow-body Gibson ES5 Switchmaster and a Roland GR 300 were used for *Death Wish II*) again points to a subtler approach.

Page was certainly an expert boogie guitarist, but here too he soon moved beyond the genre. After making Them's "Baby Please Don't Go," the Yardbirds' "Think About It," and then Led Zep's "I Can't Quit You Baby" or "The Lemon Song," he pretty much said all he needed to with urban blues or blues-based scales. An underappreciated skill was his *minor* blues assurance, as in "Tea for One," "Prelude," "Hummingbird," and "Take Me for a Little While," where his guitars have an almost human depth of phrasing. Although he would always be drawn to the Chicago styles of Otis Rush or Hubert Sumlin, he was not as faithful to them as other rockers ("Once that happens it becomes boring—you might as well listen to the originals"),[83] and nor was he driven to compete with the shred kings who followed him. "When it comes to other techniques, like tapping, that's not my bag and I don't listen to it for hours on end because I'm not going to get that much from it," he explained in 1998. "But if there's a street musician from Morocco or a country blues player, I'm going to get far more exhilaration out of that because that's where I'm coming from."[84] When presenting him with a star on the Hollywood "Rock Walk," in 1993, Eddie Van Halen gushed, "What I respect the most is that Led Zeppelin is known as one of the heaviest metal bands of all time, and ninety percent of their music is acoustic, which I think is great."[85] Van Halen exaggerates the figure, but his message is valid.

Indeed, through much of his electric repertoire Jimmy Page sounds like a frustrated acoustic guitarist, tickling little hammer-ons and ringing open strings like a man with a Martin rather than a Marshall. On his actual acoustic music, which does comprise a good chunk (if not 90 percent) of Led Zeppelin cuts, he has always acknowledged his use of "CIA tuning" (Celtic, Indian, Arabic) to get the droning sustains of "Friends," "Gallows Pole," "Going to California," "Poor Tom," and others. This derives from his investigations of British folk music in the '60s and his attempts at the formal modes of the sitar over the same years. While other rock guitarists like Keith Richards and George Harrison used alternate tunings, Page (following his beloved Joni Mitchell's example) was unusual in inventing his own variations as he found them: "I just moved the strings around [changed their tension] until it sounded right."[86]

"I got fascinated with the whole science of [Indian music]," Page divulged later. "It eventually became too complicated because of the divisions between a semitone. . . . But the main thing that I did get from the ragas was the timings—they do things in sort of sevens and elevens."[87] Both the harmonies and the beats of North Africa and the subcontinent became key elements of his technique, yet he has always denied any conscious attempts to only imitate "foreign" motifs. "I don't like all those categories myself, putting things in pigeonholes—it's all music to me,"[88] he complained around the releases of *No Quarter* and *Walking Into Clarksdale*. "Today everybody keeps going on about bloody 'world music.' It isn't new music at all. . . . I was listening to that music [as a student], and I've listened to it all the way through my life."[89]

Other than his proficiency on one instrument, Jimmy Page must also be revered for his advances as a producer. His recording instincts illustrated by Led Zeppelin's *I* through *IV* were groundbreaking developments of microphone placement, ambient sound, and plain loudness, imparting the basic audio texts of a rock 'n' roll quartet with the presence of a symphony orchestra. Though less reliant on the multiple overdubs of his guitar armies as commonly supposed, he did saturate the tapes of "Black Dog," "Ten Years Gone," and "Achilles Last Stand" for extreme punch, and he displayed a sure ear for conducting a wide sweep of instruments, caught on separate takes, into unified arrangements. But Page's dynamic sequencing of songs and silences, together with his captures of John Bonham's drums, are the facets of his studio magic that most reverberate today. Pop music now depends almost completely on an emphasis of machined rhythms and climaxes anticipated by the cut-to-the-chase tensions of "Whole Lotta Love," the speed of "Immigrant Song," Bonham's entry in "Stairway to Heaven," and the inescapable groove of "Kashmir." Even other mediums like film and video rely on the high-powered explosions of image and edit, drama and catharsis, scale and space, light and shade, that were Page's secret recipes in the mixing room. For better or worse, the big-budget stimulations of pure visceral excitement thrust upon the modern public stage are at least partly his responsibility.

"I would like to be remembered as someone who was able

to sustain a band of unquestionable individual talent and push it to the forefront during its working career,"[90] Page summed up in 1998. The kind of autonomy assured for him by Peter Grant and used to its fullest extent was exceptional in the '70s and almost nonexistent now. Page not only ran the recording rooms but commissioned album cover art and approved stage layouts; he consented to touring schedules and got the master bedroom on board the *Starship*. When John Bonham died, Page, Grant, Robert Plant, and John Paul Jones publicly disbanded, and Led Zeppelin, under Page's authority, has put out only the most conscientious posthumous material since. Again, this kind of creative control—whereby the players credited with a given work (and paid for it) are in fact the ones who made it—is a touchstone of a lost cultural age. Discussing his art school term, he has remembered how "most of the abstract painters that I admired were also very good technical draftsmen. Each had spent long periods of time being an apprentice and learning the fundamentals of classical composition and painting before they went off to do their own thing."[91] A cerebral man who studied the field before rushing into it, Page likewise took care to capitalize on others' innovations and to not repeat others' mistakes.

Rock stars like Page and his bandmates in Led Zeppelin earned the adulation of their public with an artistic independence and musical competence that subsequently became more and more discounted: the "irony" of punk rock and the "meanings" of Madonna were in many ways critical rationalizations that glossed over the performers' technical mediocrity and their managers' and record companies' media manipulations. Page's Wagnerian gestures with his guitars and bows and his epic solo spots were of a time before pop culture became the echo chamber of self-consciousness it is today. No one can pull off that kind of grandiloquence anymore.

Jimmy Page himself is almost a living embodiment of rock's golden eras. The boy whose life was transformed by Elvis and

the blues; the teenager living out of vans while delivering rockabilly to the provincial towns of England; the studio tyro caught
up in the lucrative backstage business of British Invasion pop;
the young guitar hero trekking the world; the rock architect
building his own group, member by indispensable member; the
debauched millionaire feeding his most illicit appetites; the sur-
vivor picking up the pieces; the elder statesman looking back on
it all while still carrying the flag—the story reads like a one-man
history of rock 'n' roll.

Page's most unique contribution to the narrative is his legendary secretiveness. From him comes the archetype of the rock
celebrity as Renaissance man—privy to scholarship and wisdom
well outside the fields of guitars and groupies and limousines, the
introverted, preoccupied waif of a character elevated to mythical status no human can long or safely uphold. Other rockers
became famously diverted or reinvented after they had already
become successful, like Bob Dylan or John Lennon or Pete Townshend, but Page is the rarity whose eccentricity and complexity
preceded his fame. Later personalities like Trent Reznor, Glenn
Danzig, and Marilyn Manson claimed their own arcane beliefs,
Prince briefly adopted a Zosoesque glyph as a pseudonym, and
a few fringe death-metal bands boasted of their full-on Satan-
ism, but Page set the standards. Shedding many of his shadowy
passions and pretenses as he has gotten older, there will, even so,
always be a penumbra of mystery over his renown.

One of the many variants of the Faust fable is of the mortal
signatory who comes to regret his deal and spends the rest of his
earthly days doing good works in order to cheat the Devil out
of a satisfyingly corrupted soul. This hardly sounds like Jimmy
Page. He has in his own fashion been just as indulgent as millions
in his own and younger generations, in his lust for travel and
escape, in his embrace of drugs and alcohol and serial, heedless
sex, in his temptation toward unknown spiritualities, and in his
all-consuming loyalty to the singular demographic flashpoint of
rock 'n' roll. He has also lived through an indulgence fewer than

two hundred or so persons on the planet have experienced: the vertiginous rush of taking the stage under the simultaneous effects of premium whiskey, uncut cocaine, post-coital bliss, and the psyche-blasting awareness that you are the receptacle for an ocean of humanity's collective emotional energy. But because the energy that zeroed in on him during his life has been fired with admiration and joy and a sort of fearful reverence—reverence for the overpowering music and the cagey, charismatic genius who generated it—then in his time of dying Jimmy Page may well find himself climbing the stairway to heaven after all.

Epilogue:
Writes of Winter
2006-2008

What an exquisite life you have had! You have drunk deeply of everything. You have crushed the grapes against your palate. Nothing has been hidden from you. And it has all been to you no more than the sound of music.

—OSCAR WILDE,
THE PICTURE OF DORIAN GRAY

Since the release in hardcover of this first full-length biography in early 2007, Jimmy Page has been more active—and visible—than ever after Zeppelin's demise, his elder statesmanship giving him a newfound openness to interviews, photo sittings, and other public appearances. While he still maintains a phalanx of managers and assistants who prevent unwanted intrusion into his private sphere, he did allow unusual degrees of press access when promoting his latest ventures, the biggest of which would make international headlines and draw phenomenal popular attention.

By the 2000s Led Zeppelin itself was now practically a worldwide brand, the name, insignia, and music standing for an apogee of rock 'n' roll artistry and excess in its most artistic and excessive years. Not only were the surviving members—the dignitary Page, the modest Jones, and the reluctant Plant—inescapably tied to their roles in the group, but the Swan Song and *Hindenburg* logos, the four symbols from *LZ IV*, and Zeppelin's precious few hours of original tunes were recognized and valued around the world. It was odd to think that this work, the bulk and best of which was accomplished between 1968 and 1974, had endured for almost four decades and only rose in prominence after the act's official disbandment in 1980. The licensing of Led Zep product extended from the usual T-shirts, posters, and decals to 3-D reproductions of the *Led Zeppelin* album cover, Zeppelin baby clothes, sexy underwear, wall hangings, a collection of Zeppelin songs adapted as children's lullabies, and tribute anthologies of Zep covers by lower-level performers. The strangest yet may have been "Led Zeppelin—The Ride," a roller coaster that opened in 2007 at the Hard Rock theme park in Myrtle Beach, South Carolina, where the adventurous could climb aboard a zeppelin-style miniature train that looped and plummeted fifteen stories to the cardiac strains of "Whole Lotta Love." Fun for the whole family.

In his early sixties Jimmy Page had made tantalizing references to solo projects he was planning, perhaps along the lines of Carlos Santana's 1999 hit *Supernatural*, where the master brought a number of younger singers and accompanists to join him on new material. "It's time to do something which is entirely new and radical," Page said to rock writer Charles Shaar Murray in 2004. "As far as Jimmy Page goes, it's time to do something new and unexpected." He later revealed on BBC radio, "I'd been hoping earlier on this year to be recording some music that I've already got together, but I had a few things that got in the way of it. . . . It's an album that I really need to get out of my system." Page was heard joining forces with Jerry Lee "the Killer" Lewis on a piano-heavy "Rock and Roll," included on Lewis's 2006 disc *Last Man Standing*, where Keith Richards, Ringo Starr, Willie Nelson, Little Richard, George Jones, and Eric Clapton also made appearances, but this was the only fresh music from Page since his truncated Black Crowes performances. His retirement looked to be a leisurely one.

Page's firmest commitment remained Led Zeppelin. In Glasgow, Scotland, in July 2007, he testified at the trial of Robert Langley, charged with pirating and selling unauthorized CDs and DVDs, including some of Zeppelin gigs and soundchecks at Knebworth and elsewhere. While there had always been bootlegs taped at concerts and exchanged between collectors, Page was incensed that substandard recordings might be passed off as official releases. "The legitimate part is where fans trade music, but once you start packaging up and you do not know what you are getting, you are breaking the rules legally and morally," he told the court. "There are some of these recordings where it is just a whirring and you cannot hear the music." Bootlegging had been a sticky subject among Zeppelin aficionados, given Page's (and before, Peter Grant's) strong opposition to the underground market. Didn't the illicit merchandise only enhance the artists' stature for listeners, and could the rock stars really resent the modest revenue being generated? "If it's someone with a microphone at a gig, that's one thing," Page said in 1998. "They paid for a ticket, so it's fair game. But things that are stolen out of the studio—works in progress, rehearsal tapes and things like that—are quite another. . . . It's theft. It's like someone stealing your personal journal and printing it." Page's testimony at Langley's copyright infringement case was sober as he arrived with bodyguards, signed a few autographs, and—for the first time—was seen with a natural head of wispy gray hair.

As with Page's music, his Zeppelin-era guitars were themselves widely sought and imitated. Two more pricey Gibson reissues were sold in limited quantities in 2007 and 2008, the first being remakes of his EDS-1275 (of which fewer than two hundred had been built originally), followed by reproductions of his ebony Les Paul Custom, used from his session years and stolen while traveling with a North American Led Zep tour in 1970. Page had been impressed with the Gibson team's work on duplicating his 1959 Les Paul and was equally pleased with their latest achievements. When trying out the first line of sample double-

necks and exercising his *droit de seigneur* to keep a favorite for himself, Page immediately knew which one he wanted. "He just strummed one chord on it and said, 'That's it! This is my number one right there,'" noted Gibson's Pat Foley. "I was floored. I know that Jimmy can be very sensitive and intuitive when it comes to guitars, but I didn't know he was *that* intuitive." Just 275 of the Page-model EDS 1275s were produced, twenty-five of them with Page's personal seal of approval and ticketed at about $30,000; the Page Customs underwent a similar inspection process but, owing to the disappearance of his original, were not crafted to its exact specifications.

Live recitals from Jimmy Page kept falling through. In August 2006 he was billed to join his old pal Roy Harper at the Rhythm Festival near Bedford, England, but bowed out, citing his recovery from arthroscopic surgery on his knee. "Although surgery was completely successful," it was posted on Harper's website, "Jimmy is still in the midst of ongoing physical therapy sessions to complete the treatment and his doctors have advised against playing until recovery is complete." This came shortly after he withdrew from a scheduled June performance at the Montreux Jazz Festival with Robert Plant in a tribute to Atlantic Records' Ahmet Ertegun, again pleading recuperation from surgery. Some prospective attendees grumbled. Why publicize bookings knowing that they might clash with elective medical care? Had the announcements been mere teases?

It was Ahmet Ertegun's death on December 14, 2006 (following his collapse at an October Rolling Stones show given in honor of former U.S. president Bill Clinton), that set in motion the long-awaited return of Jimmy Page to the concert hall—and the longer-awaited return of Led Zeppelin. As the head of the label that signed Zeppelin, the Rolling Stones, Iron Butterfly, and before them a Who's Who of R&B greats like Ray Charles, Aretha Franklin, and the Drifters, Ertegun was widely respected in the industry by musicians and listeners alike, and Zeppelin's resident blues connoisseur Robert Plant had formed a lasting friendship with him. The popularity of its '60s and '70s rock groups made Atlantic a multimillion-dollar corporation (sold to Warner Brothers in 1967, it remained independently operated), although the refined and cosmopolitan Ertegun, some twenty years older than members of Led Zeppelin and the Stones, invested in the acts more for business than pleasure. He was said to have nodded off during a presentation of *The Song Remains the Same* (he wasn't the only one) and to have returned home after a Zeppelin stadium gig to relax with several hours of Billie Holiday. Yet Plant, John Paul Jones, and Jimmy Page retained great respect and affection for Ertegun: "I've stayed with him in his home in Barbados and hung out with him," Page remembered, "holding court in these really seedy clubs, getting more and more tipsy as the night went on. . . . At his memorial service you were hard pressed to spot pop musicians. Henry Kissinger gave an address."

The reunion rumors began to fly after Page, Plant, and Jones were seen at an invitation-only memorial for Ertegun in April 2007. Plant had already been approached by Ertegun's widow, Mica, to ask if he would play a charity performance for the Ahmet Ertegun Education Fund, raising money for the Atlantic boss's old school of St. John's College outside Washington, D.C., in Annapolis, Maryland (Ertegun was the son of a Turkish diplomat), and other academies in Britain and Turkey. Gradually a succession of meetings and negotiations transpired to corral the players into the affair, mediated through managers (Page's was now Peter Mensch) and lawyers. While the trio of shareholders had met annually to discuss the continued maintenance of the band's catalog and investments, the three ex-Zeppelins had always respected each other's musical talent more than they enjoyed each other's company, and, as with other separated superstars, regrouping in public was for them and their assistants a Very Big Deal. Absolute secrecy was maintained and for some time none would admit any Zeppelin activity was afoot. On June 10, 2007, they held their first rehearsal at a guarded English location, with the now matured and sober Jason Bonham again contributing drum work. At forty-one he had outlived his father by nine years. "Jason knows the numbers," Page said. "But not only that, he understands them. . . . We're taking it very, very seriously, and I know it will be good."

The four carried on practicing through the summer and fall of '07, until a formal declaration of the reunion was made in September. Slated for November 26, Page, Plant, Jones, and Bonham would play the Ahmet Ertegun benefit at London's mammoth O2 Arena (formerly the Millennium Dome), organized by promoter Harvey Goldsmith and with tickets available through an Internet lottery. The numbers quickly grew staggering: for no more than eighteen thousand available seats untold millions of people around the world applied, crashing the lottery's online application and raising caveats of fraudulent ticket sales. For its historic magnitude and huge draw the concert became a legitimate news item and cover story even non-fans couldn't miss, and more than two million dollars was raised for Ertegun's school charities. Though other performers like Pete Townshend, Bill Wyman, Paul Rodgers, and Foreigner were on the bill (all of them colleagues and friends of Page as well as former Atlantic talent) the real reason for the demand was the headline artist— not Page, not Page and Plant, but Led Zeppelin.

This coincided well with a duo release of more retouched material from the band, a two-CD package of twenty-four songs titled *Mothership* put out in early November 2007, and a few weeks later an updated DVD of *The Song Remains the Same*. Again the product of Page's careful technological modernization, this time in the latest sonic enhancement of 5.1 audio, both were instant best sellers, although critical response suggested an acoustic law of diminishing returns might eventually kick in. "Should loyal Zep fans rush out and buy a bunch of songs they already own?" asked one reviewer. "They'll certainly get a different take on them, albeit one that, after a while, they'll struggle to differentiate from the last one. . . . [I]f you miss *Mothership*, don't fret. There'll be another one along in a couple of decades." Another remarked on Page's established role as caretaker rather than innovator: "While Robert Plant's solo career flourishes, it's tempting to see Jimmy Page as a figure stuck in the past. With the band's reunion show looming, *Mothership* provides a timely corrective: why bother with new songs, when your old ones are this potent?" Perhaps Led Zeppelin's ultimate step into the present came on November 13, when its entire canon was at last made available via Internet download, making the band one of the very last major acts to have resisted the online evolution (or revolution, or devolution) in pop music; the songs were also re-tailed as ringtones and other handheld accoutrements for the Gen @ set.

With all this publicity, the suspense was heightened with the surprise postponement of the O2 concert in early November, ow-ing to Page's fracturing of his left little finger, apparently after an evening fall in his garden. The injury was such that a fortnight's healing was required, putting off the reunion until December 10. After the letdowns of Page's no-shows at Montreux and with Roy Harper, fans feared the worst—another cancellation on eva-sive medical grounds—but the guitarist assured the public that he would pull through. Acknowledging that many concertgoers had booked travel and accommodation for a November date, Page apologized and said, "Led Zeppelin have always set very high standards for ourselves, and we feel that this postponement will enable my injury to properly heal, and permit us to perform at the level that both the band and our fans have always been accustomed to." He stayed away from his guitars for two weeks while the world, at least the headbanging portion of it, held its breath.

At last the night arrived. All four musicians knew that previ-ous reunions had been disappointments—the chaos of Live Aid in '85 and the stiffness of Atlantic in '88—and they were deter-mined not to fumble this one. "We had one shot at it," Page real-ized. "There was no warm-up gig." The instrument that had least weathered the years was not any guitar, bass, keyboard or drum, or even Page's recovered finger, but Plant's voice, and consequently some of the numbers were played in a lower key than the originals to correspond with the singer's stretched pipes. Page came equipped with his Number One and Number Two Les Pauls, the Transperformance Les Paul, a new "Black Beauty" Les Paul Custom, the B-bender Les Paul, and the EDS-1275, changing axes (and their variety of tunings) every few songs. Marshalls and an Orange amplifier (for the theremin spot) were in his backline. A Gibson ES-350 was also spotted in Page's hands, a semi-acoustic instrument said to have once belonged to Chuck Berry. Originally invited by Mica Ertegun to do no more than forty minutes, for December 10 Page, Plant, Jones and Bonham readied an almost two-hour recital to accommodate their best-known pieces. "There's no way I can take on playing three-and-a-half-hour sets now," Page admitted, "because I just don't have that energy any more."

It was, nevertheless, a fantastic gig. The immediate reaction was delirious plaudits from all corners: "Old Boys Rock Heaven and Hell for the Mothership of All Reunions," ran one headline, while another proclaimed, "ZEPPELIN STORMS LONDON," and a third said the performance "ranks as one of the great rock comebacks of modern times." Opening with the rarely essayed first song of their first album, "Good Times Bad Times," the quartet drove through a run of classics, including "Ramble On," "Since I've Been Loving You," "In My Time of Dying," "Trampled Underfoot," "No Quarter," and a surprising choice of *Presence*'s cocaine crash, "For Your Life." Wearing shades for the early part of the show and dressed in a neat dark blazer and dress shirt, the grizzled Jimmy Page looked and sounded like the veteran bluesmen who'd inspired him—old, wise, worldly, and investing his licks and riffs with thirty-odd years of guitar heroism. There was a near train wreck in "Dazed and Confused" where Bonham, Page, and Jones didn't quite come in off the solo together, and the much-anticipated "Stairway to Heaven" had perhaps worn out its welcome to the audience and players alike, but "Kashmir" now came forward as the definitive Led Zeppelin epic, John Bonham and Page's original DADGAD plod having accrued into a thing of unyielding, elephantine power. They closed with "Whole Lotta Love" and encored with "Rock and Roll" to a vast roar of applause, the foursome stepping forward to take their laurels while Jason Bonham briefly turned to genuflect before his dad's old mates. Backstage, families and intimates gathered to congratulate the undisputed emperors of hard rock as they sipped tea and bottled water. Jimmy Page later said it was the first time he'd performed sober.

What now? "It's a bit selfish to do just one show," suggested Page with all the politeness he could muster. "If that's it, we probably shouldn't have taken the genie out of the bottle." Both the Cult and Velvet Revolver were said to be in negotiations as possible Zeppelin opening acts. But while Jason Bonham sounded acquiescent and John Paul Jones noncommittal, Page tried manfully to downplay his own or anyone else's optimism about a reunion tour. "[A]t this point in time, Robert is continuing his duet, or solo career, or however you want to put it. . . . So it's not really on the cards, is it? For the moment." As insider speculation regarding a full-scale Led Zeppelin outing mounted, Robert Plant continued to deny any such plans. "The conveyor belt of expectation is bullshit," he told *Rolling Stone*. "The more people talk, the more pressure it puts on everybody." Throughout his post-Zeppelin career, Plant had created new music and a new public image with no little success, and, enjoying a new collaborative album and tour with retro-country singer Alison Krauss (which featured a cover of his *Walking into Clarksdale*'s "Please Read the Letter"), he seemed, as always, disinclined to resurrect his past for profit. Some in the Zeppelin camp begrudged him as a holdout, while others admired his integrity and unwillingness to demean a legacy by letting it age before the eyes of the world. In late September 2008 the vocalist expressly told the media he had no future performances to do after completing his work with Krauss: "It's both frustrating and ridiculous for this story to rear its head when all the musicians that surround the story are keen to get on with their individual projects and move forward." Thus the saga had closed, for the moment.

His appetite for live playing whetted, again Jimmy Page searched for fresh opportunities. One came on June 7 at London's Wembley Stadium, where Page and John Paul Jones— playing together for the first time sans Plant or Bonham since Jones's *Scream for Help* soundtrack of the early '80s—joined ex-Nirvana drummer Dave Grohl's the Foo Fighters. "Playing here at Wembley Stadium is the fuckin' . . . the greatest fuckin' night in our band's lives. . . . And if we'd didn't take this opportunity to do something special for you motherfuckers . . . " exulted Grohl by way of introduction, showing all the professionalism and stagecraft that made Nirvana famous. The two ex-Zeppelins did "Ramble On" and "Rock and Roll" with the Foos while eighty-six thousand punters went wild. Then that was all.

With the prospects of a long-term Led Zeppelin reunion apparently downed for good, Page resumed his role as rock aristocrat. From October 2007 he has been pleased with his expanding family legacy, since his daughter Scarlet and her partner Tom Brown presented him with his first grandchild, Martha Alice. He was awarded an honorary doctorate from the University of Surrey in June 2008 for his "services to the music industry," and posed for photos while he signed a guitar and wore the formal scholar's cap and gown; he was also featured in a documentary film on the art and history of the electric guitar, *It Might Get Loud*, with U2's the Edge and the White Stripes' Jack White. Outside the music scene, a lavish pre-Raphaelite tapestry from Page's Tower House was put up for auction by Sotheby's, offering a glimpse into the extravagance of his inner domain; the item failed to sell, however.

The most unusual, and certainly the biggest, event in which he participated was the closing ceremony of the Beijing 2008 Olympic Games, where the proceedings included the "handover" ritual from Beijing to the next Olympic city of London. As Mayor Boris Johnson accepted the official flag from Beijing's Guo Jinlong, an elaborate parade of English athletes and artists entered the gigantic "Bird's Nest." Troupes of dancers popped umbrellas, football star and husband of "Posh Spice" David Beckham delivered a kick into the eager crowd, and then a red double-decker bus opened its roof and London pop sensation Leona Lewis, winner of the national *X Factor* talent search TV show, rose out of the vehicle followed by a gnomish, gray-haired, ponytailed figure wielding a Les Paul electric guitar. Lewis and Jimmy Page—for it was, indeed, the leader of Led Zeppelin— did a semi-mimed version of 1969's nuclear aphrodisiac "Whole Lotta Love" for tens of thousands of Olympic spectators in Beijing and millions more around the planet. It was a surreal moment, somehow imposing, trivial, tacky, and thrilling all at once, but for Jimmy Page, OBE, it showed beyond doubt that the old groupie heartbreaker, alleged Satan worshipper, Jack Daniel's chugger, two-time drug criminal, heavy metal idol, and hard-rockin' grandpa had been deemed worthy of taking his person and his music to represent his city and his country to the globe. Few could say he hadn't earned the right.

Do what thou wilt shall be the whole of the Law.

The study of this Book is forbidden. It is wise to destroy this copy after the first reading.

Whosoever disregards this does so at his own risk and peril. These are most dire.

Those who discuss the contents of this book are to be shunned by all, as centers of pestilence . . .

There is no law beyond Do what thou wilt.

Love is the law, love under will.

—THE BOOK OF THE LAW

Outrider: Interpreting the Rune of Zoso

For almost forty years, the term "rock star" has conjured up an iconic gallery of images and ideas: Guitar heroes. Millionaire gypsies. Technical troubadours of the dawning information age. Shrewd and sensitive professionals, yet self-destructive artists trapped in a cocoon of indulgence and excess; adult tastemakers in a lucrative and coldly competitive industry, living out juvenile fantasies for an obsessive following. Legendary compositions, classic albums, and anthems for an entire culture. Thunderous concerts given in gigantic stadiums; the envy of and examples to whole generations. Emperors. Eccentrics. Addicts. Enigmas.

More than any other figure of his time, Jimmy Page embodies these archetypes of rock stardom. As the originator, guitarist, and producer of Led Zeppelin, he created one of the most commercially successful and critically acclaimed bands of the classic rock era, rivaled only by the Beatles and the Rolling Stones in power and popularity. Zeppelin's artistic reach across a diversity of styles, from supercharged blues to haunting ballads to impenetrable Asian and Middle Eastern meters and sonorities, forms one of rock 'n' roll's greatest catalogs, the bulk of which Jimmy Page wrote, arranged, played, and recorded. Page himself has come to exemplify a range of the genre's enduring personas—the brilliant, emotionally fragile recluse (like Brian Wilson, Bob Dylan, or Syd Barrett), the business mastermind (like Mick Jagger or David Bowie), the virtuoso instrumentalist (like Jimi Hendrix, Eric Clapton, Jeff Beck, or Eddie Van Halen), and the reckless hedonist (like Keith Richards, Keith Moon, or Jim Morrison)—and most notoriously founded a reputation of the rock 'n' roll performer as practitioner and proselytizer of the occult. To know the life and work of Jimmy Page is to comprehend the singular phenomenon of rock music's ascendancy to the top of the entertainment world in the 1960s and '70s and the peculiar style of celebrity lived by artists like Led Zeppelin and their compatriots.

There is another story here. Apart from addressing both the public records and long-standing speculation surrounding Page, and acknowledging the dark whispers about his backstage habits alongside more sober analyses of his musical method, there is also a study of how one human being can survive the passage to and from a kind of pagan divinity. In this is the risky biographical venture of rescuing the subject from his admirers. Many accounts of popular entertainers' careers tend to drift toward fandom, awash with unreferenced superlatives and unverified feats of publicity ("broke all records," "everyone owned a copy," "sales were through the roof," "one of the top agents in the business," "all Hollywood was at his feet," etc.) and never quite coming to terms with the imperfect, even ordinary, individuals at their center. Here, Jimmy Page—to whom some quite objective superlatives certainly apply—is considered as just such an individual: striking and original in some ways but rather typical in others, a demigod of myth, but a son, father, friend, bandmate, husband, and lover of reality. And for all the timeless appeal of Led Zeppelin's music and image, it is important to place Page and his peers in the temporal context of their period and recall the paisley shirts, flared bell-bottoms, and Dickensian sideburns worn by the musicians and their followers, as well as the chart competition they faced in (say) Humble Pie, Spooky Tooth, and Blodwyn Pig. Regarded as influenced and influential artist of a particular age first, and legendary rock star second, the truer and more valuable Jimmy Page begins to emerge.

Of course, it was as a rock star that I first knew him. Long before becoming a Jimmy Page biographer, I was a Jimmy Page fan, an awestruck we're-not-worthy teenager to whom the head Zep was an unapproachable epitome of cool. I had already been deeply impressed by the Beatles, the Rolling Stones, and the Who, and had a healthy and growing respect for Elvis Presley, Bob Dylan, the Doors, Eric Clapton, Creedence Clearwater Revival, and Neil Young, when I was ushered into the time-honored shrine of a friend's basement stereo room, rock iconography from floor to ceiling, and after an appropriate ministration of cannabis resin, heard the album *Led Zeppelin,* open-eared and open-mouthed. Struck first by Robert Plant's impeccable blues style—like a male Janis Joplin's, it occurred to me—I then felt the seismic rumble underneath the vocals, the huge stereophonic breadth between the speakers, the absolute precision of the sound. Though the guitar itself was strong and clearly the handiwork of an expert, it wasn't a record of solos. It was Led Zeppelin, hard rock 'n' roll distilled down to an irreducible sonic monolith. On the back of the sleeve was the explanation for all that was before and all that was to come: "Jimmy Page: Electric Guitar, Acoustic Guitar, Pedal Steel Guitar, Backing Vocals . . . Produced by Jimmy Page."

This happened to me not in 1970 but in 1985, when I was seventeen. In those days Led Zeppelin, though never completely neglected or forgotten, had not assumed the classic rock status the band would later attain. They were a dinosaur act then, faceless English hippies who paled next to the telegenic glamour of Madonna and Michael Jackson, and stoner heavy metal long since outmoded by the socio-political relevance of punk and New Wave. Getting into Led Zeppelin in the mid-1980s meant taking a stand against rock videos and synthesizers, and against the burgeoning media-cultural colossus that was foisting the likes of Cyndi Lauper and Quiet Riot on the high school demographic of North America. At their lowest critical ebb, Led Zeppelin represented for me a substance and permanence that would endure long after the music my generation was being goaded into consuming had passed.

Eventually Jimmy Page was to become one of the brightest stars of my personal rock 'n' roll firmament. It mattered that I was already a guitarist, playing acoustic and electric instruments since I was fourteen, and on a ready lookout for new inspirations. For a shy, smart, skinny kid feeling his way over barre chords and blues scales, Page was an ideal example of how far you could go with the guitar—the delicate, introverted boy from the London suburbs who had gone on to become rich and famous and dangerous, all on the strength of his versatile musical ability and intimidating intellectual depth. During my youth I was taught, or taught myself, how to play passable approximations of Led Zeppelin songs: simple riffs like "Whole Lotta Love" or "Living Loving Maid (She's Just a Woman)," to the trickier "Good Times Bad Times," "Moby Dick," "The Rover," and the haunting "Tea for One," and then the truly refined acoustic picking of "Bron-Yr-Aur," "Going to California," and, my proudest accomplishment, a note-for-most-notes "Stairway to Heaven." As well as collecting LPs, cassettes, 45s, and CDs of his biggest group, I also followed Page's subsequent career by acquiring copies of his work with the Firm, his first solo album *Outrider*, a rare vinyl issue of his underrated sound track for the film *Death Wish II*, and his *No Quarter* reunion with Robert Plant. At my most imitative I plugged my Gibson RD (forever associated with the Gibson Les Paul, Page did use an RD for one song at Zeppelin's 1979 Knebworth show) through a wah-wah pedal and into my fifty-watt Marshall (not a tube-driven stack like my idol's, but still a Marshall) and stroked it with a cheap violin bow to regale roommates and downstairs neighbors with an extended "Dazed and Confused," a showcase of pick scrapes, flashy bends, and piercing harmonics. In my teenage bedroom a poster of Jimmy Page triumphantly hoisting his double-neck gave witness to my less triumphant practicing on a single-neck, and once in a great while I still don attire with a shrunken and faded white-on-black picture of the guitarist in his white scarf, aviator shades, and SS officer's *Totenkopf* (death's head) cap, an avatar of rock depravity. When it comes to Jimmy Page, I've been there, done that, and got the T-shirt.

I did take care not to become just his mimic. There were other guitarists (and bassists and drummers) I appreciated, and I strived to absorb their methodologies into mine. Besides learning well-known rock anthems, I wrote and played and recorded songs of my own, and Jimmy Page has had to share space in my pantheon with everyone from Angus Young to Chet Baker, from Jimi Hendrix to Merle Haggard, and from Randy Rhoads and the Temptations to Billie Holliday and the Vaughans, Sarah and Stevie Ray. But Page always loomed large for me. Chording a second-position minor with a root on the D string was copped from the intro to "Stairway," and any crying bends or fast lead runs around the sad steps of the Aeolian scale paid homage to "Tea for One," "Since I've Been Loving You," or *Outrider's* "Hummingbird." Retuning my acoustic guitars to the modal resonances of drop-D or even open C were indirect gifts from "Black Mountain Side" and "Bron-Yr-Aur," while solo experiments with microphones and a four-track mixing board always had me observing Page's studio counsel, "Distance makes depth." I have branched out musically, but I know my roots.

In the beginning I held little hope of seeing him perform; my home town of Sault Ste. Marie in northern Ontario was well off the tour circuit for acts of Jimmy Page's rank. At nineteen I was blown away by Presence, a Led Zeppelin tribute act that passed through some local bars a few times to bring hard rock to the hinterland. In attendance at one of their shows, I got into it (and the pitchers of beer) so much that at closing time the singer noted his personal appreciation, "Thanks for rockin' with us, man!" in a Plantish tone; I was very pleased. At another Presence gig the guitar player was introduced as Larry something, who indeed looked, dressed, and performed his part quite well. Between songs the enthusiastic crowd of Saultites called "Jimmy Page! Jimmy Page!" while I took pains to respect him for who he was: standing on my chair, I yelled, "All right, Larry!" Larry was a good guitarist, no doubt, but he was no Jimmy Page. Despite my possession of perhaps one-sixteenth of Page's musical talent, the Presence cheer became a running joke between my friends and me, when I knocked at their apartment doors, guitar in hand, and responded to "Who is it?" with a martial cry of "Jimmy Page!" Among four or five jamming buddies, at any rate, I was willing to stand for all the Jimmy Page we could get.

Years passed and I contented myself with occasionally seeing other Zeppelin cover acts (besides the authentic Rolling Stones, AC/DC, Rush, Neil Young, ZZ Top, and other titans) until, on Friday, May 26, 1995, I got my first and only glimpse of the grail, when Jimmy Page and Robert Plant performed a sold-out show at Vancouver's Pacific Coliseum. In a suitably altered frame of mind, I watched the reunited duo resuscitate Led Zeppelin with "Thank You," "Kashmir," and a literally hair-raising "Since I've Been Loving You"; they also their did new Arabic-tinged songs from *No Quarter*, and even an out-of-nowhere blast of the Doors' "Break On Through." Though seated up near the rafters and off to stage left, I had a clear view of Page deploying his trusty theremin—all swept arms, slapped air, and psychedelic screech—and even from that distance I could see that he smoked very long, king-sized cigarettes. The TV monitors above the band featured close-ups of Page's guitar in the split-screen effect recognizable from *The Song Remains the Same*, and Robert Plant concluded one number with an inimitably regal "Vancouvah—*talk* to me," drawing a tsunami of applause. After the show I could safely say a private circle had closed, and I went to sleep resuming my adulthood, the live music of the flesh-and-blood Jimmy Page ringing in my ears once and for all.

What makes such events so memorable is their rarity. Considering his stature, and contributing to it, Page has kept himself highly inaccessible. Not for him the cathartic, confessional interviews of John Lennon or Pete Townshend, the cheery keep-'em-smiling touring schedules of Paul McCartney or Elton John, the shameless self-promotion of Gene Simmons or David Lee Roth nor (we dearly hope) the "reality" sitcoms of Ozzy Osbourne and Mötley Crüe's Tommy Lee. This reticence has its origins in the initially scant or cool press receptions given to Led Zeppelin in the late '60s, which bitterly annoyed Page, and it has been sustained ever since, partly by design (there is such a thing as too much publicity) but also as a reflection of his own cagey temperament. Talkative enough during Zeppelin's rise, he became more withdrawn as the band hit the gold and platinum marks, then enmeshed himself into a positively Byzantine isolation as he moved from superstar to rock 'n' roll royalty.

Since the '80s, relatively few reporters have sat down to talk freely with Jimmy Page, and in different decades at least a couple of them have met with very raised hackles ("Get on with it, for fuck's sake!"[1] he told one whose tape recorder was being difficult, and to another's question of a Led Zeppelin reunion he shot back, "What do you want to know, for fuck's sake?").[2] As well as drawing a curtain over the personal data of marriage, children, and finances—an understandable privilege of most established celebrities—he usually steers clear of uniquely touchy matters like drugs, death, and the Devil. "You're stuck in that spot with the tape recorder and consequently you can feel a lot of friction coming out," Page has warned. "If [interviewers] start trying to rub you up the wrong way with certain things, you say, 'Well, I don't want to talk about that,' and then he keeps coming back and back and back. There's a variety of things I don't necessarily want to talk about."[3] Even by the standards of his fellow rock legends, Jimmy Page is a daunting specialty.

In preparing this unauthorized biography, I did write to Page in care of his management company in the United Kingdom, informing him of my project, saying I respected his privacy and wouldn't pester him if he didn't want to be pestered, but giving him the particulars of contacting me if he desired any input. I explained that I was not a professional journalist but a writer of critical essays and speculative fiction, as well as a Led Zeppelin fan and an amateur guitarist, and that I was confident I could come up with an accurate and balanced study if he chose not to participate. He chose not to. The lack of response from Jimmy Page or any of his representatives came as little surprise to me, and I consoled myself with the thought that if I had not won his blessing I had not been the object of his curse, either.

The preceding account, therefore, has been pieced together from a wide range of sources on public record: books, newspaper and magazine articles and interviews, and of course music. I have a long familiarity with the Led Zeppelin canon, but in documenting Page's creative output (and his creative stimuli) I acquainted or reacquainted myself with collections of the Yardbirds, Bad Company, the Firm, Deep Purple, Joe Cocker, Van Morrison and Them, Jeff Beck, the Who, the Kinks, Tom Jones, Bert Jansch, John Renbourn, Otis Rush, Muddy Waters, Scotty Moore (with Elvis Presley), James Burton (with Ricky Nelson), and other musicians acknowledged in the body of the story. Stephen Davis's *Hammer of the Gods: The Led Zeppelin Saga* and Howard Mylett's *Jimmy Page: Tangents Within a Framework* served as helpful, though flawed, introductions to the person and chronologies of his achievements. Number-one Zep fan Dave Lewis's *Led Zeppelin: A Celebration* and *Led Zeppelin: The Tight But Loose Files—Celebration II* were treasure troves of daily diaries and completists' info, while Robert Godwin's *Led Zeppelin: The Press Reports* was a mine of raw data. The occasional question-and-answer sessions Jimmy Page has granted proved valuable, but the memoirs of Richard Cole, Angela Bowie, Bebe Buell, Pamela Des Barres, Chris Dreja and Jim McCarty, Willie Dixon, Marianne Faithfull, and Bill Graham were also reviewed, and back issues of periodicals like *Crawdaddy, Creem, Guitar Player, Guitar World, Mojo, Musician, Record Collector,* and *Rolling Stone* stored key details. Life stories of Peter Grant, Kenneth Anger, Leon Theremin and Aleister Crowley merited consideration, as did cultural histories of World War II–era London, postwar Britain, and recreational drugs. Regional maps and architectural descriptions of Page's past and present homes were uncovered, as well as wire-service citations of his latter-day activities. Most cautiously, I checked out Internet sites of varying legitimacy, finding *led-zeppelin.com* and *tightbutloose.co.uk* to be the best maintained and most corroborated. Following this afterword, a complete bibliography of materials referenced is provided, but the rest of its emphases, opinions, omissions, inclusions, and conclusions on the deep and sometimes dark subject of Jimmy Page are, as they say, nobody's fault but mine.

Endnotes

Bring It on Home

1. Young, July 1988.
2. Yorke, 1993.
3. Yorke, 1993.
4. Mylett, 1983.
5. Yorke, 1993.
6. Mylett, 1983.
7. Murray, July 2004.
8. MacDonald, 1995.
9. Mylett, 1983.
10. Mylett, 1983.
11. Murray, July 2004.
12. Murray, July 2004.
13. Murray, July 2004.
14. Neer, June 1991.
15. Crowe, in Fong-Torres, 1976.
16. Murray, July 2004
17. Crowe, in Fong-Torres, 1976.
18. Schulps, in Brackett, 2005.
19. Murray, July 2004.
20. Schulps, in Brackett, 2005.
21. Tolinski, April 2004.
22. Tolinski, April 2004.
23. Tolinski, April 2004.
24. Murray, July 2004.
25. *All Your Own* interview featured in *Rock and Roll* video.
26. Mylett, 1983.
27. Tolinski, winter 2004.
28. Godwin, 2003.
29. Carson, 2001.
30. Murray, July 2004.
31. Mylett, 1983.
32. Schulps, in Brackett, 2005.
33. Murray, July 2004.
34. Murray, July 2004.
35. Murray, July 2004.
36. Mylett, 1983.
37. Murray, July 2004.
38. Yorke, 1993.
39. Mylett, 1983.
40. Welch, 1985.

That's the Way

1. Rosen, July 1977.
2. Godwin, 2003.
3. Mylett, 1983.
4. Tyler, May 2001.
5. Welch, 1985.
6. Welch, 1985.
7. Welch, 1985.
8. Tyler, May 2001.
9. Tyler, May 2001.
10. Rosen, July 1977.
11. Mylett, 1983.
12. Tyler, May 2001.
13. Marten, December 2003.
14. Yorke, 1993.
15. Godwin, 2003.
16. Tyler, May 2001.
17. Yorke, 1993.
18. Yorke, 1993.

19. Carson, 2001.
20. Tyler, May 2001.
21. Murray, July 2004.
22. Tyler, May 2001.
23. Kent, May 1974.
24. Tyler, May 2001.
25. Godwin, 2003.
26. Tyler, May 2001.
27. Resnicoff, November 1990.
28. Kent, May 1974.
29. Mylett, 1983.
30. Welch, 1985.
31. Tolinski, July 2003.
32. Melly, 1972.
33. Tyler, May 2001.
34. Yorke, 1993.
35. Yorke, 1993.
36. Tolinski, April 2004.
37. Marten, December 2003.
38. Murray, July 2004.
39. Burroughs, June 1975.
40. Rosen, July 1977.
41. Welch, 1985.
42. Tyler, May 2001.
43. Mylett, 1983.
44. Tolinski, April 2004.
45. Mylett, 1983.
46. Marten, December 2003.
47. Yorke, 1993.
48. Welch, 1985.
49. Tyler, May 2001.
50. Marten, December 2003.
51. Murray, July 2004.
52. Welch, 1985.
53. Tyler, May 2001.
54. Tyler, May 2001.
55. Yorke, 1993.
56. Rosen, July 1977.
57. Welch, February 1982.
58. Yorke, 1993.
59. Mann, January 1995.
60. Murray, July 2004.
61. Rosen, July 1977.
62. Mylett, 1983.
63. Mylett, 1983.
64. Godwin, 2003.
65. Tolinski, "Light and Shade," winter 2004.
66. Godwin, 2003.
67. Rogan, 1984.
68. Welch, 1985.
69. Marsh, 1983.
70. Di Perna, May 1995.
71. Godwin, 2003
72. Murray, July 2004
73. Rosen, July 1977.
74. Resnicoff, November 1990.
75. Harper, 2000.
76. Rosen, July 1977.
77. Harper, 2000.
78. Murray, July 2004.
79. Thompson, 2005.
80. Carson, 2001.
81. Mylett, 1983.
82. Mylett, 1983.
83. Rosen, July 1977.
84. Mylett, 1983.
85. Mylett, 1983.
86. Thompson, 2005.
87. Marten, December 2003.
88. Marten, December 2003.
89. Godwin, 2003.
90. *www.jackiedeshannon.com*
91. Faithfull, 1994.
92. Marten, December 2003.
93. Marten, December 2003.
94. Welch, 1985.
95. Godwin, 2003.
96. Kent, May 1974
97. Rosen, July 1977.
98. Godwin, 2003.
99. "Dear Guitar Hero," February 2005.
100. Tolinski, April 2004.

101. Rosen, July 1977.
102. Rosen, July 1977.
103. Rosen, July 1977.
104. Rosen, July 1977.
105. Murray, July 2004.
106. Tyler, May 2001.
107. Carson, 2001.
108. Platt, 1983.
109. Tyler, May 2001.
110. Tyler, May 2001.
111. Yorke, 1993.
112. Welch, 2001.
113. Carson, 2001.
114. Rosen, July 1977.
115. Murray, July 2004.
116. Murray, July 2004.
117. Clayson, 2002.
118. Tolinski, January 1998.
119. Leonard, April 1998.
120. Welch, 2001.
121. Murray, July 2004.
122. Kent, May 1974.
123. Godwin, 2003.
124. Welch, 2001.
125. Welch, 2001.
126. Murray, July 2004.
127. Godwin, 2003.
128. Tolinski, July 2003.
129. Welch, 2001.
130. Marten, December 2003.
131. Murray, July 2004.
132. Neer, June 1991.
133. Tolinski, January 1998.
134. Tolinski, winter 2004.
135. Murray, July 2004.
136. Welch, 2001.
137. *Super Lungs* liner notes.
138. Yorke, 1993.
139. Godwin, 2003.
140. Considine, September 20, 1990.
141. Yorke, 1993.

142. Neer, June 1991.
143. Godwin, 2003.
144. Wall, October 2005.
145. Wall, October 2005.
146. "Welch, 2001.
147. Welch, 2001.
148. Wall, October 2005.
149. Yorke, 1993.
150. Godwin, 2003.

When the Levee Breaks

1. Wall, October 2005.
2. Yorke, 1993.
3. Welch and Nicholls, 2001.
4. Dellar, October 2005.
5. Tyler, May 2001.
6. Godwin, 2003.
7. Welch, 2001.
8. Fast, 2001.
9. Godwin, 2003.
10. Godwin, 2003.
11. Lewis, *Celebration*, 2003.
12. Schulps, in Brackett, 2005.
13. Godwin, 2003.
14. Welch and Nicholls, 2001.
15. Tolinski, June 1999.
16. Welch and Nicholls, 2001.
17. Marten, December 2003.
18. Tolinski and DiBenedetto, May 1995.
19. Rosen, July 1990.
20. Tolinski and DiBenedetto, May 1995.
21. Davis, 1986.
22. Carson, 2001.
23. Murray, July 2004.
24. Welch, 2001.
25. Welch, 2001.
26. Welch, 2001.
27. Godwin, 2003.
28. Welch, 2001.
29. DeCurtis, 1995.

30. Cole, 1992.
31. Godwin, 2003.
32. Neely, 1993.
33. Cole, 1992.
34. Godwin, 2003.
35. Godwin, 2003.
36. Godwin, 2003.
37. Godwin, 2003.
38. Tolinski, January 1998.
39. Thompson, July 2004.
40. Rotondi, April 2004.
41. Rosen, July 1977.
42. Godwin, 2003.
43. Herman, 1994.
44. Des Barres, 2005.
45. Herman, 1994.
46. Cole, 1992.
47. Des Barres, 2005.
48. Des Barres, 2005.
49. Tolinski and Di Benedetto, winter 2004.
50. Lewis, *Celebration*, 2003.
51. Tolinski and DiBenedetto, winter 2004.
52. Resnicoff, November 1990.
53. Godwin, 2003.
54. Robinson, November 2003.
55. Yorke, 1993.
56. Godwin, 2003.
57. Tolinski and DiBenedetto, winter 2004
58. Tolinski, July 2003.
59. Tolinski, July 2003.
60. Cole, 1992.
61. Godwin, 2003.
62. Welch, 2001.
63. Welch, 2001.
64. Fast, 2001.
65. Welch and Nicholls, 2001.
66. Des Barres, 2005.
67. Tolinski, July 2003.
68. Godwin, 2003.
69. Godwin, 2003.
70. Hoskyns, June 2003.
71. Resnicoff, November 1990.

Over the Hills and Far Away

1. Welch, 2001.
2. Godwin, 2003
3. Godwin, 2003.
4. Hoskyns, June 2003.
5. Godwin, 2003.
6. Crowe, in Fong-Torres, 1976.
7. Blake, May 2005.
8. Tolinski, April 2004.
9. Crowe, in Fong-Torres, 1976.
10. Mylett, 1983.
11. Tolinski, July 2003.
12. Mylett, 1983.
13. Crowe, in Fong-Torres, 1976.
14. Mylett, 1983.
15. Wall, October 2005.
16. Considine, September 20, 1990.
17. Blake, May 2005.
18. Godwin, 2003.
19. Godwin, 2003.
20. Godwin, 2003.
21. Tolinski and DiBenedetto, winter 2004.
22. Godwin, 2003.
23. Tolinski, January 2002.
24. Aledort, January 2002.
25. Resnicoff, November 1990.
26. Tolinski, January 2002.
27. Lewis, *Tight but Loose*, 2003.
28. Lewis, *Tight but Loose*, 2003.
29. Rosen, July 1977.
30. Tolinski, January 2002.
31. Tolinski, January 2002.
32. Godwin, 2003.
33. Tolinski, January 2002.
34. Tolinski, January 2002.
35. Palmer, *Led Zeppelin* box set notes, 1990.

36. Tolinski, January 2002.
37. Tolinski, January 2002.
38. Mylett, 1983.
39. Mylett, 1983.
40. Kay, May 1985.
41. Godwin, 2003.
42. Burroughs, June 1975.
43. Des Barres, 2005.
44. Considine, September 20, 1990.
45. Tolinski, July 2003.
46. Cole, 1992.
47. Tolinski, January 2002.
48. Lewis, *Tight but Loose*, 2003.
49. Tolinski, January 2002.
50. Godwin, 2003.
51. Tolinski, January 2002.
52. Tolinski, January 2002.
53. Lewis, *Tight but Loose*, 2003.
54. Lewis, *Tight but Loose*, 2003.
55. Lewis, *Tight but Loose*, 2003.
56. Godwin, January 2002.
57. Welch, 2001.
58. Tolinski, July 2003.
59. Fast, 2001.
60. Tolinski, July 2003.
61. Des Barres, 2005.
62. *A to Zeppelin* video
63. Godwin, 2003.
64. Kent, May 1974.
65. Godwin, 2003.
66. Godwin, 2003.
67. Godwin, 2003.
68. Godwin, 2003.
69. Mylett, 1983.
70. Mylett, 1983.

The Rover

1. Tolinski, January 1998.
2. Godwin, 2003.
3. Godwin, 2003.
4. Tolinski, January 1998.
5. Godwin, 2003.
6. Tolinski, January 2002.
7. Godwin, 2003.
8. Welch and Nicholls, 2001.
9. Mylett, 1983.
10. Kent, May 1974.
11. Kent, May 1974.
12. Monty Python, 2003.
13. Des Barres, 2005.
14. Godwin, 2003.
15. Blake, May 2005.
16. Tolinski, July 2003.
17. Kent, May 1974.
18. Godwin, 2003.
19. Godwin, 2003.
20. Tolinski, July 2003.
21. Kent, May 1974.
22. Mylett, 1983.
23. Mylett, 1983.
24. Godwin, 2003.
25. Welch, 2001.
26. Welch, 2001.
27. Mylett, 1983.
28. Welch, 2001
29. Godwin, 2003.
30. Godwin, 2003.
31. Tolinski, July 2003.
32. Lewis, *Tight but Loose*, 2003.
33. Tolinski, July 2003.
34. Buell, 2001.
35. Godwin, 2003.
36. Buell, 2001.
37. Welch, 2001.
38. Welch, 2001.
39. Buell, 2001.
40. Buell, 2001.
41. Buell, 2001.
42. Crowe, 2000.
43. Godwin, 2003.
44. Crowe, in Fong-Torres, 1976.
45. Scaggs, December 26, 2002.
46. Robinson, November 2003.

47. Burroughs, June 1975.
48. Burroughs, June 1975.
49. Lewis, *Tight but Loose*, 2003.
50. Godwin, 2003.
51. Blake, May 2005.
52. Tolinski, July 2003.
53. Tolinski, July 2003.
54. Considine, September 20, 1990.
55. Godwin, 2003.
56. Mylett, 1983.
57. Tolinski, July 2003.
58. Young, July 1988.
59. Des Barres, 1992.
60. Des Barres, 2005.
61. Lewis, *Tight but Loose*, 2003
62. Tolinski and DiBenedetto, winter 2004.
63. Lewis, *Tight but Loose*, 2003.
64. Godwin, 2003.
65. Cole, 1992.
66. Godwin, 2003.
67. Herman, 1994.
68. Godwin, 2003.
69. Mylett, 1983.
70. Godwin, 2003.
71. Godwin, 2003.
72. Landis, 1995.
73. Godwin, 2003.
74. Mylett, 1983.
75. Yorke, 1993.
76. Mylett, 1983.
77. Lewis, *Tight but Loose*, 2003.
78. Lewis, *Tight but Loose*, 2003.
79. Welch, 2001.
80. Welch, 2001.
81. Godwin, 2003.
82. Lewis, *Tight but Loose*, 2003.
83. Des Barres, 1996.
84. Lewis, *Tight but Loose*, 2003.
85. Bowie, 1993.
86. Robinson, November 2003.
87. Tolinski, July 2003.
88. Tolinski, July 2003.
89. Graham, 1992.
90. Graham, 1992.
91. Graham, 1992.
92. Graham, 1992.
93. Graham, 1992.
94. Godwin, 2003.
95. Young, July 1988.
96. Crowe, in Fong-Torres, 1976.
97. Crowe, in Fong-Torres, 1976.
98. Godwin, 2003.
99. Welch, 2001.
100. Wall, October 2005.
101. Hoskyns, June 2003.
102. Lewis, *Tight but Loose*, 2003.
103. Lewis, *Tight but Loose*, 2003.
104. Hoskyns, June 2003.
105. Godwin, 2003.
106. Godwin, 2003.
107. Mylett, 1983.
108. Lewis, *Tight but Loose*, 2003.
109. Robinson, November 2003.
110. Lewis, *Tight but Loose*, 2003.
111. Vaziri, March 12, 2000.
112. Tolinski and DiBenedetto, winter 2004.
113. Wall, October 2005.
114. Lewis, *Tight but Loose*, 2003.
115. Lewis, *Tight but Loose*, 2003.
116. Wall, October 2005.
117. Tolinski, January 1998.
118. Lewis, *Tight but Loose*, 2003.
119. Wall, October 2005.

Tea for One

1. Hilburn, March 21, 1993.
2. Cooper, August 27, 2004.
3. Welch, April 1985.
4. Welch, 1985.
5. Mylett, 1983.
6. Resnicoff, November 1990.

7. Wild, November 25, 1993.
8. Loder and Goldberg, January 19, 1984.
9. Welch, April 1985.
10. Kay, April 1985.
11. Fyfe, August 2005.
12. Wolmuth, April 8, 1985.
13. Welch, May 1985.
14. Welch, April 1985.
15. Lewis, *Celebration*, 2003.
16. Welch, April 1985.
17. Vancouver *Sun*, November 6, 1984.
18. Wolmuth, April 8, 1985.
19. Welch, April 1985.
20. Milkowski, 1995.
21. DeCurtis, February 23, 1995.
22. Yorke, 1993.
23. Lewis, *Tight but Loose*, 2003.
24. Rosen, 2001.
25. Young, July 1988.
26. Resnicoff, November 1990.
27. Young, July 1988.
28. Young, July 1988.
29. Yorke, 1993.
30. Young, July 1998.
31. Yorke, 1993.
32. Lewis, *Tight but Loose*, 2003.
33. Yorke, 1993.
34. DeCurtis, February 23, 1995.
35. DeCurtis, February 23, 1995.
36. Resnicoff, November 1990.
37. Des Barres, 1992.
38. Young, July 1988.
39. Neer, June 1991.
40. Watrous, November 16, 1988.
41. Palmer, November 17, 1988.
42. Cooper, August 27, 2004.
43. Considine, September 20, 1990.
44. Young, July 1988.
45. Yorke, 1993.

46. Yorke, 1993.
47. Tolinski, July 2003.
48. DeCurtis, February 23, 1995.
49. Considine, September 20, 1990.
50. Blush and Petros, 2005.
51. Mylett, 1983.
52. Godwin, 2003.
53. Godwin, 2003.
54. Godwin, 2003.
55. Considine, September 20, 1990.
56. Walser, 1993.
57. Godwin, 2003.
58. Tolinski, April 2004.
59. Murray, July 2004.
60. Kitts, Winter 1994.
61. Di Perna, May 1995.
62. Telleria, 2002.
63. Kay, April 1985.
64. Blackett, March 2006.
65. Rosen, July 1990.
66. Rosen, July 1990.
67. Tolinski, "Heavy Friends," winter 2004.
68. Eddie Van Halen interview selections, July 1990.
69. Eddie Van Halen interview selections, July 1990.
70. Stix, July 1992.
71. Lewis, *Celebration*, 2003.
72. Yorke, 1993.
73. Aerosmith, 1997.
74. Lewis, *Celebration*, 2003.
75. Lewis, *Celebration*, 2003.
76. Young, July 1988.
77. Resnicoff, November 1990.
78. Neer, June 1991.
79. Resnicoff, November 1990.
80. Resnicoff, November 1990.
81. Neer, June 1991.
82. Neer, June 1991.

83. Resnicoff, November 1990.
84. Neer, June 1991.
85. Wild, November 25, 1993.
86. Considine, September 20, 1990.
87. Neer, June 1991.

All My Love

1. Lewis, *Celebration*, 2003.
2. Resnicoff, November 1990.
3. Hilburn, March 21, 1993.
4. Dunn, December 1, 1994.
5. Hilburn, March 21, 1993.
6. Hilburn, March 21, 1993.
7. Lewis, *Tight but Loose*, 2003.
8. Hilburn, March 21, 1993.
9. Young, July 1988.
10. Yorke, 1993.
11. Neely, July 8, 1993.
12. Wild, November 25, 1993.
13. Wild, November 25, 1993.
14. Murray, July 2004.
15. DeCurtis, February 23, 1995.
16. DeCurtis, February 23, 1995.
17. Godwin, 2003.
18. Harrington, September 2, 1998.
19. Fast, 2001.
20. Lewis, *Celebration*, 2003.
21. Lewis, *Tight but Loose*, 2003.
22. Camilli, May 30, 1995.
23. Harper, 2000.
24. Welch, 2001.
25. Tolinski, January 1998.
26. Tolinski, January 1998.
27. Dixon, 1989.
28. Tolinski, January 1998.
29. Tolinski and Di Benedetto, winter 2004.
30. Newquist, August 1998.
31. Harrington, September 2, 1998.
32. Leonard, April 1998.
33. Newquist, August 1998.
34. Newquist, August 1998.
35. Leonard, April 1998.
36. Goddard, April 7, 1998.
37. Leonard, April 1998.
38. Goddard, April 7, 1998.
39. Cooper, August 27, 2004.
40. Cooper, August 27, 2004.
41. Tolinski, "Heavy Friends," winter 2004.
42. Harrington, September 2, 1998.
43. Tolinski, "Heavy Friends," winter 2004.
44. Lewis, *Tight but Loose*, 2003.
45. Lewis, *Tight but Loose*, 2003.
46. Lewis, *Tight but Loose*, 2003.
47. Vaziri, March 12, 2000.
48. Di Perna, July 2000.
49. Vaziri, March 12, 2000.
50. Di Perna, July 2000.
51. Di Perna, July 2000.
52. Vaziri, March 12, 2000.
53. Di Perna, July 2000.
54. Lewis, *Tight but Loose*, 2003.
55. Lewis, *Tight but Loose*, 2003.
56. Tolinski, July 2003.
57. Tolinski, July 2003.
58. Marten, December 2003.
59. Lewis, *Tight but Loose*, 2003.
60. Marten, December 2003.
61. "Dear Guitar Hero," February 2005.
62. "Page Against the Machine," April 1998.
63. "Zeppelin's Page Honored," August 24, 2004.
64. *www.tightbutloose.co.uk*
65. *www.abctrust.org.uk*
66. *www.led-zeppelin.com*
67. Newquist, August 1998.
68. Goddard, April 7, 1998.
69. Leonard, April 1998.
70. Cooper, August 27, 2004.

71. Cooper, August 27, 2004.
72. *www.tightbutloose.co.uk*
73. *www.tightbutloose.co.uk*
74. "Page Wins Damages...,"
    March 29, 2000.
75. "Dear Guitar Hero," February
    2005.
76. Hoskyns, June 2003.
77. "Her Party Draws Guitar
    Gods...," March 2, 2005.
78. Tolinski, "Heavy Friends,"
    winter 2004.
79. Rooksby, 2002.
80. Miller, 1976.
81. Tolinski and Di Benedetto,
    winter 2004.
82. Tolinski, January 1998.
83. Leonard, April 1998.
84. Newquist, August 1998.
85. "Random Notes," February 10,
    1994.
86. Kay, May 1985.
87. Resnicoff, November 1990.
88. Fast, 2001.
89. Newquist, August 1998.
90. Tolinski and Di Benedetto,
    winter 2004.
91. Tolinski, February 2006.

Outrider: Interpreting the Rune of Zoso

1. Kay, April 1985.
2. Rosen, July 1990.
3. Resnicoff, November 1990.

Beyond Zeppelin:
A Selected Discography

Various semi-official anthologies of Page's '60s studio work exist, documenting a variety of efforts with British or British-based one- or no-hit artists. A comprehensive collection would be difficult to assemble due to the guitarist's extensive work between 1963 and 1966 with so many obscure performers and bands—much of which Page himself has forgotten or dismissed. But the best of them, if you can find them, are *Jimmy Page: Session Man, Vol. 1* (Voxx), *Jimmy Page: Session Man Vol. 2* (Archive), and *Hip Young Guitar Slinger* (Castle).

The Who
Page lent his talents to several of the Who's works, including "I Can't Explain." A rare B-side, "Bald-Headed Woman," has Page playing the lead solo.

The Kinks
Page contributes to the Kinks' "You Really Got Me." As with "I Can't Explain," his presence on this classic track may be exaggerated—he has always downplayed it. He was more involved with some Kink album tracks from the same period, e.g. "Revenge."

Them

Page plays on "Baby Please Don't Go," "Gloria," "Here Comes the Night," and most likely the raucous "Mystic Eyes." Though not appreciated by band members replaced or augmented for the sessions, Page's playing propelled these tracks to enduring classic rock status. *The Story of Them Featuring Van Morrison* (Polydor) is the authoritative compilation.

Tom Jones

Page backs up "It's Not Unusual." Impress your friends by telling them what this frothy '60s Brit-pop has in common with "Black Dog" and "Kashmir." Available on *The Best of Tom Jones* (Polydor).

Jimmy Page, Eric Clapton, and Jeff Beck—*Blue Eyed Blues: Charly Blues Masterworks, Vol. 20* (Charly)

One of numerous not-exactly-legitimate reissues of '60s U.K. blues busts featuring Page's home jams with Eric Clapton, as well as takes with the irascible Sonny Boy Williamson.

Various artists—*Hoochie Coochie Men: A History of UK Blues and R&B, 1955–2001* (Indigo)

Good cross-section of cuts from the '50s, '60s, and '70s, including more of Page's Miles Road jams and some live sounds from his stint with Cyril Davies's R&B All-Stars. None of those are truly "official," but worthwhile listening nonetheless.

Burt Bacharach—*Hit Maker!* (Universal Japan)

Rare import disc recorded in 1964–65, featuring Page and other session musicians (including John Paul Jones) backing up the composer on instrumental cuts of his best-known songs. Warning: Do not under any circumstances attempt to play backward.

John Mayall—*Blues Breakers with Eric Clapton (Universal)*
Page produced (but did not play on) "I'm Your Witchdoctor" and "Telephone Blues," "Sitting on Top of the World," and "Double Crossing Time." Early exercises in the recording of hard rock guitar, starring Messrs. Clapton, Gibson, and Marshall.

The Yardbirds—*Ultimate!* (Rhino)
Superlative overview of the Yardbirds' entire history, including the Clapton and Beck tenures. Highly recommended.

Donovan—*Greatest Hits* (Legacy)
Though the singer-songwriter has often claimed Page, John Paul Jones, and John Bonham backed him on "Hurdy Gurdy Man," this assertion has pretty much been discredited (Bonham was never a session player). However, Donovan most likely enlisted the services of Page and Jones at one point or another, so this representative disc is included here.

Jeff Beck—*Truth* (Epic)
Includes "Beck's Bolero," with John Paul Jones and Keith Moon, which Page produced, cowrote, and played electric twelve-string on.

Joe Cocker
Page's standout playing was featured on "With a Little Help from My Friends."

Screaming Lord Sutch—*Lord Sutch and Heavy Friends*
    (Wounded Bird Records)
Recorded in 1969 with performances by Page and John Bonham—but largely disowned by both.

Roy Harper
On 1971's *Stormcock* (Science Friction), Page plays on "Same Old Rock." Highly praised by both Page and Harper buffs. 1985's *Jug-*

ula (Science Friction), another folkish gem, is credited to "Roy Harper and Jimmy Page," and is also highly recommended—it certainly helped bring Page out of his post-Zeppelin slump. Hats off to Harper!

Maggie Bell—*Suicide Sal* (Repertoire)
Originally from 1975, this disc of Swan Song's blues mistress features Page on "If You Don't Know." Noncompletists can skip this one, or buy for the underrated voice of Bell herself.

Stephen Stills—*Right by You* (Atlantic)
Page is on "50/50" and the title song, recorded during his (and Stills's) low-lying days of the early '80s.

The Honeydrippers—*Volume 1* (Es Paranza)
The hit "Sea of Love" and "I Get a Thrill" are both with Page on guitar. It boosted Robert Plant's '80s comeback more than Page's, but sports some tasty R&B and rockabilly licks nonetheless.

Box of Frogs
An '80s reunion of ex-Yardbirds Chris Dreja, Jim McCarty, and Paul Samwell-Smith. Page appears on "Asylum" on their second effort, *Strange Land* (Renaissance). Dreja and McCarty continue to perform occasionally as the Yardbirds.

The Firm—*The Firm* (Atlantic); *Mean Business* (Atlantic)
Page's Firm efforts disappointed many fans when they appeared in 1985 and 1986, but they are worth a revisit. No heavy riffs or classic solos herein, but certainly some smooth rhythm chops in evidence on "Radioactive" and others.

Outrider (Geffen)
Hampered by an erratic choice of guest singers and lyricists, Page's 1988 solo effort still laid down some quality guitar after his muted playing in the Firm. Instrumentals like "Emerald Eyes"

and "Writes of Winter," screaming Les Paul leads on "Prison Blues," and an emotional "Hummingbird," all deserve a listen.

The Rolling Stones—*Dirty Work* (Virgin)
Page's guest-star spot—a solo on "One Hit (To the Body)"—came during the depths of Mick and Keith's feud of the mid-'80s. One of the Stones' more disjointed works.

Willie and the Poorboys—*Willie and the Poorboys* (Castle
Records)
Willie and the Poorboys was originally put together to play shows to benefit Ronnie Lane after he was diagnosed with multiple sclerosis. Page contributes to this studio album, backed by Bill Wyman and Charlie Watts.

Robert Plant—*Now and Zen* (Rhino)
Page joins his former singer for "Tall Cool One" and "Heaven Knows." Also features the original Zeppelin—digitally sampled.

David Coverdale/Jimmy Page—*Coverdale-Page* (Geffen)
Get past Coverdale's vocal clichés and listen for some very strong guitar lines on "Feeling Hot," "Take Me for a Little While," and other tracks. Not a great career move for Page, but proved he still had some shredding left in him.

Jimmy Page/Robert Plant—*No Quarter* (Atlantic); *Walking
Into Clarksdale* (Atlantic)
The maturity of 1994's *No Quarter*—rife with thoughtful and dignified explorations of Zeppelin's Celtic and Arabic leanings— was a pleasant surprise to punters used to overhyped "reunion" albums of classic rockers trying to duplicate their past glories.

Walking Into Clarksdale was a less successful collection of all-new material lacking the indigenous supporting ensembles of *No Quarter*, but still admirable excursions into African and

Middle Eastern modalities. Where the Zeppelin of *Houses of the Holy* and *Presence* may have eventually landed.

The Jimmy Rogers All-Stars—*Blues, Blues, Blues* (Atlantic)
A 1999 tribute to Muddy Water's guitar player. Robert Plant and Jimmy Page were featured on the song "Gonna Shoot You Right Down (Boom Boom)." Album also features Mick Jagger, Eric Clapton, and Taj Mahal.

Jimmy Page and the Black Crowes—*Live at the Greek* (TVT)
Triple-guitar outings of LZ faves from the Crowes 1999 tour with Page (note that it is billed as Jimmy Page *and* the Black Crowes). Two-disc set includes "Heartbreaker," "Ten Years Gone," "Out on the Tiles," and more, plus Page playing the Crowes' "Shake Your Money Maker," hard blues like "Oh Well" and "Mellow Down Easy," and even the Yardbirds' "Shapes of Things." Rock solid.

Various artists—*Good Rockin' Tonight: The Legacy of Sun Records* (Sire)
Robert Plant and Page do their take on Sonny Burgess's rockabilly version of "My Bucket's Got a Hole in It."

Jerry Lee Lewis—*Last Man Standing* (Artist First)
The Sorcerer duets with the Killer on Zep's "Rock and Roll," paying homage to one of his early heroes.

SOUND TRACKS

Death Wish II (Swan Song)
Look for this one. Though Page has never followed up on it, these atmospheric mood pieces, chase sequences, and rockers like "Who's to Blame" demonstrate he has the ability to become another Ry Cooder, Mark Knopfler, or Andy Summers in crossing over from rock 'n' roll to inventive film scores.

John Paul Jones—*Scream for Help* (Atlantic)
"Spaghetti Junction" and "Crackback" feature Page; his only post-Zeppelin outing with the bassist.

Lucifer Rising (Arcanum)
Rare but bootlegged, this brief sound track for Kenneth Anger's film echoes the evocative intro to "In the Evening" and *Death Wish II*. The film itself is available on video and DVD and contains a quick shot of a bearded young Page posing with Aleister Crowley's portrait in the background.

Godzilla (Epic/Sony)
Jimmy Page plays on Puff Daddy's "Come with Me," based on "Kashmir." A groove that heavy was bound to be sampled sooner or later—at least Page was there to play along.

Bibliography

As indicated, this biography is unauthorized and I have had no contact with Jimmy Page in its preparation. I have taken care, therefore, to consider as wide a variety of secondary sources as possible—including material only peripherally on Page—which turned out to hold much valuable and impartial information. I did hear directly from Dave Lewis of the original Led Zeppelin fanzine *Tight but Loose,* and also Lis Butcher of Epsom's Danetree school, and I thank them both for their assistance.

With so much to go over, there were inevitably contradictions and confusions between all the books, articles, and interviews I consulted (e.g., whether the 1958 or 1959 Les Paul was the guitarist's preferred instrument, or the age at which he met Jeff Beck). One piece claimed that Page and Les Paul shared a birthday (they don't), while a Web site suggested Page still owns the Boleskine House (he doesn't). Episodes of Page's life highlighted in one place were barely mentioned in another, and in some cases I had to reconstruct details based on three or four accounts, adding my own interpretation, independent research, and, sometimes, educated guesswork. For numerous musical fine points, I turned to the original recordings, or my own guitars. In general, the less confirmation of a given observation or incident I could obtain, the less space it was granted in the text. I have made nothing up.

All quotations attributed to Jimmy Page and others are taken directly from published or republished interviews. In some I have italicized a word or phrase for emphasis, and in others I have strung together two or more complementary observations taken from separate conversations (separated by ellipses) to better illustrate the speaker's position. Again, no statements have been invented.

Books

Aerosmith, with Stephen Davis. *Walk This Way: The Autobiography of Aerosmith*. New York: Avon, 1997.

Babiuk, Andy. *Beatles Gear: All the Fab Four's Instruments, from Stage to Studio*. San Francisco: Backbeat, 2001.

Baddeley, Gavin. *Lucifer Rising: Sin, Devil Worship, and Rock 'n' Roll*. London: Plexus, 2006.

Barnes, David. *The Companion Guide to Wales*. Woodbridge: Companion Guides, 2005.

Bashe, Philip. *Teenage Idol, Travelin' Man: The Complete Biography of Rick Nelson*. New York: Hyperion, 1992.

Bream, Jon. *Whole Lotta Led Zeppelin: The Illustrated History of the Heaviest Band of All Time*. Minneapolis, MN: Voyageur Press, 2008.

Blush, Steven, and George Petros, eds. *.45 Dangerous Minds: The Most Intense Interviews from Seconds*. New York: Creation Books, 2005.

Bockris, Victor. *Keith Richards: The Biography*. New York: Poseidon Press, 1992.

Booth, Martin. *A Magick Life: The Biography of Aleister Crowley*. London: Hodder & Stoughton, 2000.

Bowie, Angela, with Patrick Carr. *Backstage Passes: Life on the Wild Side with David Bowie*. New York: G. P. Putnam's Sons, 1993.

Brackett, David. *The Pop, Rock, and Soul Reader: Histories and Debates*. New York: Oxford University Press, 2005.

Brett-James, Norman George. *Middlesex*. London: Hale, 1951.

Buell, Bebe, with Victor Bockris. *Rebel Heart: An American Rock 'n' Roll Journey*. New York: St. Martin's Press, 2001.

Carson, Annette. *Jeff Beck: Crazy Fingers*. San Francisco: Backbeat, 2001.

Carter, Walter. *Gibson Guitars: 100 Years of an American Icon*. Los Angeles: General Publishing Group, 1994.

Clayson, Alan. *Led Zeppelin: The Origin of the Species: How, Why and Where It All Began*. New Malden: Chrome Dreams, 2006.

Clayson, Alan. *The Yardbirds: The Band that Launched Eric Clapton, Jeff Beck, Jimmy Page*. San Francisco: Backbeat, 2002.

Cole, Richard, with Richard Trubo. *Stairway to Heaven: Led Zeppelin Uncensored*. New York: Harper Collins, 1992.

Crook, J. Mordaunt. *William Burges and the High Victorian Dream*. London: J. Murray, 1981.

Crowe, Cameron. *Almost Famous* (Screenplay). London: Faber and Faber, 2000.

Crowley, Aleister. *The Book of the Law*. York Beach, ME: Samuel Weiser, Inc., 1976.

Crowley, Aleister. *The Confessions of Aleister Crowley: An Autohagiography*. London: Penguin, 1989.

Dalton, David, ed. *The Rolling Stones: The First Twenty Years*. New York: Alfred A. Knopf, 1981.

Davis, Stephen. *Hammer of the Gods: The Led Zeppelin Saga*. New York: Ballantine, 1986.

Denyer, Ralph. *The Guitar Handbook*. New York: Alfred A. Knopf, 1996.

Des Barres, Pamela. *I'm with the Band: Confessions of a Groupie* (updated edition). Chicago: Chicago Review Press, 2005.

Des Barres, Pamela. *Rock Bottom: Dark Moments in Music Babylon*. New York: St. Martin's Press, 1996.

Des Barres, Pamela. *Take Another Little Piece of My Heart: A Groupie Grows Up*. New York: William Morrow, 1992.

Dixon, Willie, with Don Snowden. *I Am the Blues: The Willie Dixon Story*. New York: Da Capo, 1989.

Drewett, John. *Surrey*. Aylesbury, Buckinghamshire: Shire Publications, 1985.

Faithfull, Marianne, with David Dalton. *Faithfull: An Autobiography*. Boston: Little Brown, 1994.

Fast, Susan. *In the Houses of the Holy: Led Zeppelin and the Power of Rock Music*. New York: Oxford University Press, 2001.

Fong-Torres, Ben, ed. *What's That Sound? The Contemporary Music Scene from the Pages of Rolling Stone*. Garden City, NJ: Anchor Press, 1976.

Frame, Pete. *Pete Frame's Complete Rock Family Trees*. London: Omnibus, 1993.

Gardiner, Juliet. *From the Bomb to the Beatles: The Changing Face of Post-War Britain, 1945–1965*. London: Collins & Brown, 1999.

Gettings, Fred. *Dictionary of Occult, Hermetic and Alchemical Sigils*. London: Routledge & Kegan Paul, 1981.

Glatt, John. *Rage & Roll: Bill Graham and the Selling of Rock*. Secaucus, NJ: Carol Publishing Group, 1993.

Glinsky, Albert. *Theremin: Ether Music and Espionage*. Urbana: University of Illinois Press, 2000.

Godwin, Robert. *Led Zeppelin: The Press Reports*. Burlington, Ontario: Collector's Guide, 2003.

Graham, Bill, with Robert Greenfield. *Bill Graham Presents: My Life Inside Rock and Out*. New York: Delta Trade Paperbacks, 1992.

Halliday, Hugh A. *The Little Blitz*. Ottawa: Canadian War Museum, 1986.

Harper, Colin. *Dazzling Stranger: Bert Jansch and the British Folk and Blues Revival*. London: Bloomsbury, 2000.

Heitland, John. *The Man from U.N.C.L.E. Book: The Behind-the-Scenes Story of a Television Classic*. New York: St. Martin's Press, 1987.

Herman, Gary. *Rock 'n' Roll Babylon*. London: Plexus, 1994.

Iwanade, Yasuhiko. *The Beauty of the 'Burst: Gibson Sunburst Les Pauls from '58 to '60*. Milwaukee, WI: Hal Leonard, 1998.

Jones, Edward, and Christopher Woodward. *A Guide to the Architecture of London*. London: Seven Dials, 2000.

King, Francis X. *Witchcraft and Demonology*. London: Hamlyn, 1987.

Landis, Bill. *Anger: The Unauthorized Biography of Kenneth Anger*. New York: Harper Collins, 1995.

Larkin, Colin, ed. *The Virgin Encyclopedia of Sixties Music*. London: Virgin, in association with MUZE UK, 2002.

Lewis, Dave. *Led Zeppelin: A Celebration*. London: Omnibus, 2003.

Lewis, Dave. *Led Zeppelin: The Tight but Loose Files—Celebration II*. London: Omnibus, 2003.

MacDonald, Ian. *Revolution in the Head: The Beatles' Records and the Sixties*. London: Pimlico, 1995.

Marsh, Dave: *Before I Get Old: The Story of the Who*. London: Plexus, 1983.

Marsh, Dave, and Kevin Stein. *The Book of Rock Lists*. New York: Dell, 1984.

McStravick, Summer, and John Roos, eds. *Blues-Rock Explosion*. Mission Viejo, CA: Old Goat Publishing, 1998.

Melly, George. *Revolt Into Style: The Pop Arts in Britain*. Hammondsworth, England: Penguin, 1972.

Milkowski, Bill. *Jaco: The Extraordinary and Tragic Life of Jaco Pastorius, the World's Greatest Bass Player*. San Francisco: Miller Freeman, 1995.

Miller, Jim, ed. *The Rolling Stone Illustrated History of Rock & Roll*. New York: Random House, 1976.

Monty Python. *Pythons: The Biography*. New York: St. Martin's Press, 2003.

Murray, Charles Shaar. *Crosstown Traffic: Jimi Hendrix and Post-War Pop*. London: Faber and Faber, 1989.

Mylett, Howard. *Jimmy Page: Tangents Within a Framework*. London: Omnibus, 1983.

Neer, Richard. *FM: The Rise and Fall of Rock Radio*. New York: Villard, 2001.

Norman, Philip. *Symphony for the Devil: The Rolling Stones Story*. New York: Dell, 1984.

Ochs, Michael. *1,000 Record Covers*. Cologne: Taschen, 1995.

O'Neill, Daniel. *Sir Edwin Lutyens Country Houses*. London: Lund Humphries, 1980.

Palmer, Robert. *Led Zeppelin: The Music* (Led Zeppelin Box Set notes). New York: Atlantic Records, 1990.

Palmer, Robert. *The Rolling Stones*. Garden City, NJ: Doubleday, 1983.

Paulsen, Kathryn. *The Complete Book of Magic and Witchcraft*. New York: Signet, 1980.

Perry, John. *Meaty, Beaty, Big & Bouncy: The Who*. New York: Schirmer, 1998.

Platt, John A., Chris Dreja, and Jim McCarty. *Yardbirds*. London: Sidgwick & Jackson, 1983.

Platts, Robin. *Burt Bacharach & Hal David: What the World Needs Now*. Burlington, Ontario: Collector's Guide, 2003.

Prown, Pete, and H. P. Newquist. *Legends of Rock Guitar: The Essential Reference of Rock's Greatest Guitarists*. Milwaukee, WI: Hal Leonard, 1997.

Quisling, Erik, and Austin Williams. *Straight Whisky: A Living History of Sex, Drugs, and Rock 'n' Roll on the Sunset Strip*. Chicago: Bonus Books, 2003.

Randolph, Mike. *The Rolling Stones' Rock and Roll Circus*. San Francisco: Chronicle, 1991.

Roberts, Chris. *Tom Jones: A Biography*. London: Virgin, 1999.

Robson, Peter. *The Devil's Own*. New York: Ace, 1969.

Rogan, Johnny. *Van Morrison: A Portrait of the Artist*. London: Elm Tree, 1984.

Rooksby, Rikki. *Riffs: How to Create and Play Great Guitar Riffs*. San Francisco: Backbeat, 2002.

Rosen, Steven. *Free at Last: The Story of Free and Bad Company*. London: SAF, 2001.

Saito, Setsuo. *Jimmy Page: Super Rock Guitarist* (2 volumes). London: Warner Chappell Music, 1989.

Savage, Jon. *The Kinks: The Official Biography*. London: Faber and Faber, 1984.

Telleria, Robert. *Rush Tribute: Merely Players*. Kingston, Ontario: Quarry Press, 2002.

Thompson, Dave. *Cream: The World's First Supergroup*. London: Virgin Books, 2005.

Thompson, Dave. *Smoke on the Water: The Deep Purple Story*. Toronto: ECW Press, 2004.

Thorgerson, Storm, and Aubrey Powell. *100 Best Album Covers*. Willowdale, Ontario: Firefly, 1999.

Unterberger, Richie. *Unknown Legends of Rock 'n' Roll: Psychedelic Unknowns, Mad Geniuses, Punk Pioneers, Lo-Fi Mavericks & More*. San Francisco: Miller Freeman, 1998.

Walser, Robert. *Running with the Devil: Power, Gender, and Madness in Heavy Metal Music*. Hanover: Wesleyan University Press, 1993.

Welch, Chris. *Peter Grant: The Man Who Led Zeppelin*. London: Omnibus, 2001.

Welch, Chris. *Power & Glory: Jimmy Page & Robert Plant.* Port Chester, NY: Cherry Lane, 1985.

Welch, Chris, and Geoff Nicholls. *John Bonham: A Thunder of Drums. The Powerhouse Behind Led Zeppelin and the Godfather of Heavy Rock Drumming.* San Francisco: Backbeat, 2001.

Wyman, Bill, with Richard Havers. *Rolling with the Stones.* New York: Dorling Kindersley, 2002.

Yorke, Ritchie. *Led Zeppelin: The Definitive Biography.* Novato, CA: Underwood-Miller, 1993.

Ziegler, Philip. *London at War, 1939–1945.* Toronto: Alfred. A. Knopf Canada, 1995.

Magazine and Journal Articles

"Dear Guitar Hero." *Guitar World,* February 2005: 44.

"Edward Van Halen" (interview selections). *Guitar World,* July 1990: 48–51.

"Franco Sends Troops to Rio." *Latin American Weekly Report,* November 10, 1994: 507.

"Page Against the Machine." *Guitar,* April 1998: 38–42.

"Random Notes." *Rolling Stone,* February 10, 1994: 23.

"Still Ramblin' On?" *Mojo,* August 2008: 18.

Aledort, Andy. "IV Licks." *Guitar World,* January 2002: 66–102.

Aledort, Andy. "Physical Riffiti." *Guitar World,* May 2005: 60–167.

Ashton, Adrian. "John Paul Jones Zooms Ahead." *Bass Player,* September 1999: 40–81.

Blackett, Matt. "Today's Tom Sawyer." *Guitar Player,* March 2006: 74.

Blake, Mark. "Graffiti Art." *Guitar World,* May 2005: 54–166.

Bosso, Joe, with Greg Di Benedetto. "Physical Riffiti." *Guitar World Presents Guitar Legends,* winter 2004.

Burroughs, William S. "Rock Magic." *Crawdaddy,* June 1975: 34–40.

Considine, J. D. "Led Zeppelin." *Rolling Stone,* September 20, 1990.

Crowe, Cameron. "Secrets of the Object Revealed." *Rolling Stone,* June 3, 1976.

Dann, Geoff. "Since I've Been Strummin' You." *Guitar,* January 1995: 36–39.

DeCurtis, Anthony. "Refueled and Reborn." *Rolling Stone,* February 23, 1995.

Dellar, Fred. "Led Zep Were My Backing Band." *Mojo,* October 2005: 83.

Di Perna, Alan. "Angus Young" (interview). *Guitar World,* May 1995.

Di Perna, Alan. "Birds of a Feather." *Guitar World,* July 2000: 47–205.

Di Perna, Alan. "Pete Townshend" (interview). *Guitar World,* May 1995.

Dunn, Jancee. "Getting the Led Out." *Rolling Stone,* December 1, 1994.

Fyfe, Andy. "The Mojo Hero Award." *Mojo,* August 2005: 55.

Gill, Chris. "Double Fantasy." *Guitar World,* May 2007: 61–118.

Godwin, Robert. "Code Led." *Guitar World,* January 2002: 63–175.

Gress, Jesse. "The Top Ten Jimmy Page Riffs of All Time." *Guitar Player,* November 2005: 88–92.

Gress, Jesse. "Zepplineage: The Roots of Jimmy Page." *Guitar Player,* August 1993: 75–83.

Hoskyns, Barney. "Led Zeppelin" (interviews). *Mojo,* June 2003: 72–85.

Huzinec, Mary. "Passages." *People,* January 30, 1995: 63.

Jeffrey, Don. "Plant, Page Oust Song from Film." *Billboard,* March 5, 1994.

"JR." "Highbrow, Lo-Fi: The Many Sides of Page." *Guitar Player,* February 1998: 107–108

Kane, Joseph. "Alcohol Blamed in Bonham's Death." *Rolling Stone,* November 15, 1980.

Kay, Max. "Jimmy Page" (interview). *Musician,* May 1985.

Kay, Max. "Jimmy Page and Paul Rodgers Stand Firm." *Musician,* April 1985.

Kent, Nick. "The Page Memoirs." *Creem,* May 1974: 40–76.

Kitts, Jeff. "The Man Who Fell to Earth." *Guitar World Presents Guitar Legends,* winter 1994.

Kurutz, Steve. "Flying High." *New York Times Magazine,* September 21, 2003: 56–58.

Leonard, Michael. "Ramble On." *Guitar,* April 1998.

Lewis, Dave. "Led Zeppelin: Physical Graffiti." *Record Collector,* July 2000: 16–23.

Loder, Kurt, and Michael Goldberg. "Rock of Ages: Ronnie Lane & Co." *Rolling Stone,* January 19, 1984: 21–65.

Mann, Richard. "Rough Diamond: The Apprenticeship of Jimmy Page." *Guitar,* January 1995: 26–34.

Marten, Neville. "Jimmy Page" (interview). *Guitarist,* December 2003.

McCourt, Tom. "A Man of Wealth and Taste: Ahmet Ertegun." *Popular Music and Society,* October 2007: 549–51.

Murray, Charles Shaar. "The Guv'nors." *Mojo,* July 2004.

Neely, Kim. "Misty Mountain Memories." *Rolling Stone,* July 8, 1993.

Neer, Dan. "Jimmy Page: Past Perfect." *Guitar,* June 1991.

Newquist, H. P. "Bring It on Home." *Guitar,* August 1998: 28–32.

Palmer, Robert. "Jimmy Page" (concert review). *Rolling Stone,* November 17, 1988.

Prior, Clive. "How Was It for You: Led Zeppelin." *Mojo,* August 2008: 70.

Resnicoff, Matt. "In Through the Out Door." *Musician,* November 1990: 48–72.

Robinson, Lisa. "Stairway to Excess." *Vanity Fair,* November 2003: 358–407.

Rosen, Steven. "Jimmy Page" (interview). *Guitar Player,* July 1977: 32–58.

Rosen, Steven. "Jimmy Page" (interview). *Guitar World,* July 1990: 27–28.

Rotondi, James. "Son of No. 1." *Guitar World,* April 2004: 70.

Sandall, Robert. "Band of the Year: The Q Interview." Q, January 2008.

Scaggs, Austin. "Backstage with Zeppelin." Rolling Stone, December 26, 2002: 25.

Stix, John. "Randy Rhoads" (interview). Guitar for the Practicing Musician, July 1992: 104–149.

Thompson, Art. "Cloning a Masterpiece." Guitar Player, July 2004: 58–62.

Tolinski, Brad. "Black Beauty Rides Again." Guitar World, January 2008: 76.

Tolinski, Brad. "Black Magic." Guitar World, April 2004: 64–162.

Tolinski, Brad. "The Fab IV." Guitar World, January 2002: 60–100.

Tolinski, Brad. "Get Beside Me Satan." Guitar World, February 2006: 52–159.

Tolinski, Brad. "Going Mobile." Guitar World, May 2005: 58–84.

Tolinski, Brad. "The Greatest Show on Earth." Guitar World, July 2003: 80–165.

Tolinski, Brad. "Heavy Friends." Guitar World Presents Guitar Legends, winter 2004.

Tolinski, Brad. "Led Zeppelin." Guitar World, June 1999: 44–46.

Tolinski, Brad. "Radio Daze." Guitar, January 1998.

Tolinski, Brad, with Greg Di Benedetto. "Light and Shade." Guitar World Presents Guitar Legends, winter 2004.

Tyler, Kieron. "Educating Jimmy." Mojo, May 2001: 70–75.

Wall, Mick. "No Way Out." Mojo, October 2005: 76–92.

Welch, Chris. "Page Onstage '85" (two-part article). Creem, April–May 1985.

Welch, Chris, and Dave Green. "Back Pages, New Pages." International Musician and Recording World, February 1982: 22–43.

Wild, David. "Led Zep: The Boxed Life." Rolling Stone, November 25, 1993.

Wolmuth, Roger. "Back from the Led." People, April 8, 1985: 84–86.

Young, Charles M. "Jimmy Page's True Will." Musician, July 1988: 74–84.

Newspaper Articles

"Ex-Led Zeppelin lead guitarist Jimmy Page was fined . . ." Vancouver Sun, November 6, 1984: C-2.

"Ex-Zep's Legal Fees Leave Veteran Broke." Vancouver Sun, October 19, 1999: C-6.

"Guitar God Blesses Warner Music IPO." Vancouver Sun, May 12, 2005: D-1.

"Her Party Draws Guitar Gods, Then Queen Draws a Blank." Toronto Star, March 2, 2005: F-3.

"Led Zeppelin Manager Peter Grant" (obituary). Montreal Gazette, November 23, 1995.

"Page Wins Damages for Story on Bonham's Death." Vancouver Sun, March 29, 2000: E-8.

"Queen Honors Led Zeppelin's Jimmy Page." Associated Press, December 14, 2005.

"Rock Kings Sing for Cadillac." Vancouver *Sun*, January 23, 2002: A-13.

"Zeppelin's Page Honored." Vancouver *Sun*, August 24, 2004: C-2.

Blount, Jeb. "Led Zeppelin's Page Made an Honorary Citizen of Rio de Janeiro." Bloomberg News Service, September 22, 2005.

Camilli, Doug. "Guitar Great Jimmy Page Gets Caught Smokin' in the Boys' Room." Montreal *Gazette*, May 30, 1995: C-8.

Cooper, Tim. "Jimmy Page: Godfather of Rock." *The Independent*, August 27, 2004.

Goddard, John. "Guitar Hero Jimmy Page Tells What Led . . ." CanWest News Service, April 7, 1998.

Harrington, Richard. "Page Is No Led Balloon . . ." Vancouver *Sun*, September 2, 1998: E-4.

Hilburn, Robert. "The Return of Jimmy Page; 'I Feel I Have It in My Heart Again.'" Montreal *Gazette*, March 21, 1993: F-6.

Masterson, Kathryn. "Stairway to Scholarships." *The Chronicle of Higher Education*, July 11, 2008: 54.

Maxwell, Dominic. "Do the Songs Remain the Same?" *The Times* (London), November 16, 2007: 12.

Mulvey, John. "Mothership" (review). *The Times* (London), November 17, 2007: 24.

Vaziri, Aidin. "Q & A with Jimmy Page." San Francisco *Chronicle*, March 12, 2000: 37.

Watrous, Peter. "Jimmy Page at the Ritz." *The New York Times*, November 16, 1988.

Internet

www.abctrust.org.uk

www.ancestry.com

www.jackiedeshannon.com

www.jimmypageonline.com

www.lashtal.com

www.led-zeppelin.com

www.led-zeppelin.org

www.rosshalfin.co.uk

www.scarletpage.com

www.taskbrazil.org.uk

www.tightbutloose.co.uk

www.zoso.jp

Videos / DVDs

A to Zeppelin: The Unauthorized Story of Led Zeppelin. Passport Video, 2004.

Blow-Up. MGM/UA Home Video, 1991.

Invocation of My Demon Brother / Lucifer Rising. Mystic Fire Home Video, 1990.

Led Zeppelin. Atlantic, 2003.

Led Zeppelin: The Song Remains the Same. Warner Home Video, 1999.

Rock & Roll: An Unruly History, v. 3—Crossroads. WGBH/BBC, 1995.

Music

Jeff Beck. *Truth.* Epic EK 66085.

Jeff Buckley. *Grace.* Columbia CK 57528.

Willie Dixon. *The Chess Box.* Chess.

The Firm. *The Firm.* Atlantic 81239.

———. *Mean Business.* Atlantic 81628.

Roy Harper. *Whatever Happened to Jugula?* Science Friction.

Howlin' Wolf. *The Chess Box.* Chess.

Bert Jansch. *The Best of Bert Jansch.* Shanachie.

Robert Johnson. *King of the Delta Blues.* Columbia CK 65211.

Tom Jones. *The Best of Tom Jones.* Polydor.

B. B. King. *The Best of B. B. King.* MCAC-27074.

Freddie King. *Getting Ready.* Shelter 7243.

The Kinks. *The Singles Collection.* Sanctuary CMRCD212.

Led Zeppelin. *Led Zeppelin.* Atlantic 19126.

———. *Led Zeppelin II.* Atlantic 19127.

———. *Led Zeppelin III.* Atlantic 19128.

———. *Led Zeppelin IV.* Atlantic 19129.

———. *Houses of the Holy.* Atlantic 19130.

———. *Physical Graffiti.* Swan Song 2-200.

———. *Presence.* Swan Song 8416.

———. *The Song Remains the Same* (sound track). Swan Song 2-201.

———. *In Through the Out Door.* Swan Song 16002.

———. *Coda,* Swan Song 90051.

———. *Led Zeppelin Box Set.* Atlantic 82144.

———. *Led Zeppelin Box Set 2.* Atlantic 82477.

———. *BBC Sessions.* Atlantic 83061.

———. *How the West Was Won.* Atlantic 7567-8-3587-2.

Van Morrison and Them. *The Best of Van Morrison.* Exile/Polydor.

Ricky Nelson. *Greatest Hits.* Capitol 72435.

Jimmy Page. *Death Wish II* (sound track). Swan Song 8511.

———. *Outrider.* Geffen 23888.

Jimmy Page. *Session Man, Vol. 1.* Voxx.

Jimmy Page and the Black Crowes. *Live at the Greek.* TVT 2140.

Jimmy Page, Jeff Beck, Eric Clapton. *Blue-Eyed Blues.* Charly Blues Masterworks.

Jimmy Page and David Coverdale. *Coverdale-Page*. Geffen 24487.

Jimmy Page and Robert Plant. *No Quarter*. Atlantic 82706.

———. *Walking Into Clarksdale*. Atlantic 83092.

Elvis Presley. *Elvis at Sun*. BMG.

Terry Reid. *Super Lungs*. EMI.

Various. *The Acoustic Folk Box: Four Decades of the Very Best Acoustic Folk Music from the British Isles*. Topic Records.

Various. *Godzilla—The Album* (soundtrack). Sony 69338.

Various. *Hoochie Koochie Men: A History of UK Blues and R&B 1955–2001*. Indigo IGOBX 2501.

Various. *Mojo Presents the Roots of Led Zeppelin*. Mojo.

Muddy Waters. *Electric Mud*. Chess 9364.

The Who. *Meaty Beaty Big and Bouncy*. MCA-37001.

The Yardbirds. *Ultimate!* Rhino.

Index